365 Days of Faith

by James Riddle

Harrison House
Tulsa, Oklahoma

15 14 13 12 11 10   10 9 8 7 6 5 4 3 2 1

365 Days of Faith
ISBN: 978-160683-019-2
Copyright © 2010 by James R. Riddle
El Paso, TX 79915

Published by Harrison House Publishers
P.O. Box 35035
Tulsa, OK 74153
www.harrisonhouse.com

Acknowledgments

Thank You, Father, for opening the eyes of my understanding so that I can know and teach the processes of faith. Thank you, Jinny, for your unconditional love and support. Thank you, Jerome, Jermaine, and Caleb for making me the proudest dad in the whole world. Thank you, Pastor Charles, for providing me with a solid foundation for this book. And thank you, Pastor Charlie, for encouraging me to pursue my calling.

For Kip Hall and the firefighters, policemen, and soldiers in El Paso and all over the world who give their very lives to serve us—you are true heroes of faith.

Introduction

You are about to embark on a faith journey that will change your life forever. As a student of faith for decades, I have studied its processes, followed the contemporary science of it, practiced the precepts, and have been astounded at its absolute significance in all that we think and do. Understanding and practicing the processes of faith can have a greater impact on your life than any endeavor you choose to undertake. That impact is significant, so you must know what faith is.

The average dictionary would give us a relatively simple answer to describe faith, but the way the Bible defines it is quite different. Look at what Hebrews 11:1 says:

Now faith is the substance of things hoped for, the evidence of things not seen.

If you quote that to a true seeker of knowledge, or a deep-thinking critic, they might respond with something like, "Okay, so it is a substance, and an evidence, but what is it made of?" That's all we know from this verse—faith is substance and evidence—but, we still don't know what faith's ingredients are.

A dictionary definition might say that faith is basically belief, but is that truly what Bible faith is? The apostle James warns us that even the devil believes. (James 2:19.) Does that mean that the devil has faith? If belief and faith are synonymous, then is it the same thing to believe in God and to have faith in God? Consider this: if someone came to you and said, "I believe in God," would they think differently if you replied with, "Yes, but do you have faith in God?" The fact is, if we tell someone that faith is belief, or even trust, we are only expressing a half-truth.

It is written: "I believed; therefore I have spoken." Since we have that same spirit of faith, we also believe and therefore speak.

2 Corinthians 4:13 NIV

The apostle Paul says here that Bible faith is speaking what you believe. That is true, but the Word also says that to establish something, two or three credible witnesses are needed. (2 Corinthians 13:1.) In this case, there are two questions that must be answered to establish our definition and institute a biblical concept: Can it be supported with other scripture and does it line up with the Bible's overall message? Let's look at two more verses on faith that will help us find the answer.

By faith we understand that the worlds were framed by the word of God, so that things which are seen were not made of things which are visible.

Hebrews 11:3

God created the worlds through faith—He said it, and it was so. (Genesis 1.) Technically speaking, He created the worlds through perlocution: creation by the spoken word. God believed, and therefore He spoke. That certainly supports our definition. So does His Son Jesus' description of faith:

Whoever says to this mountain, 'Be removed and be cast into the sea,' and does not doubt in his heart, but believes that those things he says will be done, he will have whatever he says.

Mark 11:23

In a nutshell, Jesus is saying that faith is the declaration of an unwavering belief. If you believe, and do not doubt, you shall have what you say. Through these verses it appears our definition of Bible faith, "believing and speaking," has stood the test. However, does it fit the overall message of the Bible? In other words, are there other scriptures that contradict, or further define, our definition?

Since believing and speaking are the two foundations of the definition, what if someone didn't have a tongue? Could they still exercise faith? That raises a new question. Actually, there is a scripture passage in the Bible where a person exercised faith without speaking aloud.

> Suddenly, a woman who had a flow of blood for twelve years came from behind and touched the hem of [Jesus'] garment. For she said to herself, "If only I may touch His garment, I will be made well." But Jesus turned around, and when He saw her He said, "Be of good cheer, daughter; your faith has made you well."
>
> Matthew 9:20-22

Jesus just acknowledged that this woman exercised her faith. She believed and spoke, again confirming our hypothesis that faith is believing and speaking—but she didn't speak out loud. Literally translated, this verse says that she spoke within herself. In other words, she projected her faith through her thoughts. (See v. 21 MSG, NLT.) So faith is much more than just a physiological act of believing and speaking.

Notice that Paul in 2 Corinthians 4:13, "refers to the same spirit of faith." To truly understand faith, then, we must transcend the barriers of this physical world and turn our attention to the realm of the spirit.

> The Spirit searches all things, even the deep things of God. For who among men knows the thoughts of a man except the man's spirit within him? In the same way no one knows the thoughts of God except the Spirit of God. We have not received the spirit of the world, but the Spirit who is from God, that we may understand what God has freely given us. This is what we speak, not in words taught us by human wisdom but in words taught by the Spirit, expressing spiritual truths in spiritual words.
>
> 1 Corinthians 2:10-13 NIV

We alone have the God-given authority to express spiritual truths in spiritual words. Spiritual words do not begin on your physical tongue, but from your spirit within you. By the Spirit of God we know that all things begin in the spirit. As triune beings we are spirit, soul, and body. (Hebrews 4:12.) So the process of faith begins in the spirit, is projected to our thoughts, and is expressed with our tongue. However, the words do not originate on our tongue, but in our spirit. This is such a vital truth.

Faith Is Spiritual

The common denominator that underlies our entire study is words. We believe, and therefore we speak. Our ability to use words absolutely sets us apart from any other being in all of God's creation. We alone are created to be His children. We are created in His image and likeness. (Genesis 1:26.) We are designed to live like He lives and do the things that He does. We are built to be creators through faith. As God speaks the end from the beginning, so do we. (Isaiah 46:10.) As He calls those things that be not as though they were, so do we. (Romans 4:17.)

When we speak in faith, we do not look to what is seen, but what is unseen, just like God. (Hebrews 11:3.) We don't need to be convinced by natural evidence. We know that the force of our faith is spiritual. We know that as soon as our words of faith are spoken, our objective has been birthed in the spirit. So, it is done. In the spirit realm, we immediately have the things that we say. We're not *going* to have them; we *already* have them. From that point on we simply prepare for arrival in this natural world.

So here's my suggested definition for faith: Faith is a spiritual force that is activated when one declares an unwavering belief; it is evidenced by one's actions and is not complete until its intended purpose is manifested. This definition works for nearly every faith verse in the

Bible. (See Romans 10:8-10; James 1:2-8; 2:14-6; Matthew 10:32; 17:20.) There are other ways that the word *faith* is used in scripture, but as for the act of faith, this definition serves us well.

It is important to remember that biblical faith is a process and is not complete until its goal is manifested. (Hebrews 6:12; 10:35-39; 1 Peter 1:9.) Just believing and speaking will not get you what you want. Your words are like seeds. (Mark 4:14-20.) When you plant them, there is a gestation period where they must be allowed to grow. The time required from planting to harvesting varies according to the type of seed and the environment it is given. Every farmer knows that seeds need to be tended to. It is the same with faith—without works it is dead. (James 2:26.) Yet throughout the whole process, in the spirit, it is already done. (Mark 11:23; Hebrews 6:12; Daniel 10:12-13.)

When we realize that faith is a spiritual force within us that brings what we desire into this natural world, we can begin to fathom its awesome power. Faith is truly the substance of a healthy and prosperous life. It is literally the creative power of God, entrusted to mankind. It is the essential fabric of creation. Whether we like it or not, it is the governing force of life, and the first cause of all experience. By faith, we can have literally anything we want that is within the boundaries of God's will.

True faith, then, is not for the shallow heart. It is deeply rooted—it is never moved by circumstances. Circumstances are physical and temporal. Faith is spiritual and eternal. It is the single most powerful thing that God ever gave us. It is the avenue of our dominion in this earth. However, our foundation must be pure and unwavering. Simply put, if we waver in the sea of doubt, we will not receive. (James 1:2-8.)

You may think that living by faith is too hard and that it's impossible to live a doubt-free life. Understand that thoughts of doubt may come to you in battalions, but you don't have to accept a single one. You can train yourself to live a successful faith walk, and ultimately have an absolutely extraordinary life.

It is my desire to help you reach that goal through this book. I'm going to start by briefly outlining what I call "The Ten Essential Elements of a Successful Faith Walk." If you incorporate these principles into your day to day living, never forgetting that the Holy Spirit is in you to assist you every step of the way, your life will never be the same.

The Ten Essential Elements of a Successful Faith Walk

1) Belief

• Belief is the foundation of faith. Actually, it's the most important factor of faith, because faith cannot exist without it. (2 Corinthians 4:13.)

• All beliefs are based on references. Learn to train your mind to focus on references that are in line with God's promises. (Matthew 12:35; Romans 12:2.)

• Learn how to program your reticular activating system. God designed your brain to be trained.

• Doubt and belief cannot co-exist. For faith to work, belief must be absolutely unwavering. (James 1:6-7.)

2) Vision

• You must have a goal. Goals are the key to success in every life venture.

• Know what you want and be able to see it accomplished in your mind's eye. (Habakkuk 2:2.)

• Don't let your vision be blurry. Give your faith focus—know specifically what you want and believe that you presently have it. (Mark 10:51; 11:23.)

3) Affirmation

• This is what gives life to your faith goal. (Proverbs 18:21.)

• When you speak in faith, be thankful. An attitude of gratitude is an essential element of receiving. (Psalm 95:2; Philippians 4:6.) Note: Don't just be thankful for the answer to your prayer. Thank your heavenly Father for all of the blessings you enjoy every single day, no matter how small or seemingly insignificant. In this way you will develop a thankfulness habit.

• Speak in the present tense. Hope says you'll have it sometime in the future. Faith says you have it right now. (Hebrews 11:1; Mark 11:23.)

4) Preparation

• Faith without works is dead. The evidence of your faith is in the actions you perform as you prepare for your harvest. (James 2:14-18.)

• If your faith didn't produce an instant miracle, then you must submit to a faith plan. Create a workable strategy for the achievement of what you desire, and work that strategy with unshakeable confidence. (Habakkuk 2:1-4.)

• Break down long-term faith plans into short-term faith steps. No faith plan is effective if you don't know what needs to be done at the present moment.

5) Association

• Associate with believers who are strong in faith. You will become like those with whom you associate. So, choose your peers wisely. (Hebrews 10:24-25; 2 Corinthians 6:14.)

• Choose a church that is both faith oriented and friendly to your faith goals. (Hebrews 10:24-25.)

- Choose the right kind of peer group for non-church related activities (business/career, pleasure, school, and so on). Your peers should help you achieve your faith goals, not hinder you. (1 Corinthians 15:33; Proverbs 2:24-25.)

- Love mediocre people, but keep them at a distance as much as possible. If you are around them too much, they will adversely affect your faith.

6) Emotion

- If you truly believe, then the answer is as good as done. So rejoice! (Philippians 4:4-6.)

- Be fervent. Emotional content is like the gas pedal of your faith. This is probably the most overlooked power force in our faith arsenal. (James 5:15-17.)

- Emotion is what brings meaning to what you desire. The more it means to you, the more powerful the result.

7) Resilience

- Be known as a person who can take a punch. Troubles are a part of life. Yet, no matter how many you face, you can overcome every one! (John 16:33.)

- Learn to wade through adversity in order to get to the blessing.

- Don't allow yourself to be a whipping boy. Be a tough-as-nails scrapper who gets back up and fights no matter how many times you get knocked down! (Proverbs 24:16.)

8) Patience

- Allow time for gestation. You do not become a doctor by attending one anatomy class, or an Olympic runner by jogging for a week. If you do not receive an instant miracle, you must condition yourself to wait and to work while you wait. (Hebrews 6:12; Isaiah 40:28-31.)

• Creation works in harmony with what you believe. This takes time. (Mark 9:23; Romans 8:25.)

• An athlete may see themselves winning, believe it with all of their heart, speak it daily, and have a plan to accomplish it. Yet without patience, they may do too much at one time, cause too much stress on their muscles, and end up getting injured.

• A business person may have a brilliant idea, believe in their ability to accomplish it, constantly affirm their belief, and act upon that belief with unwavering diligence; but they still have to work in harmony with the rest of the world. Too much too soon could result in major financial disaster. You may be ready, but you need to make sure others are ready as well.

9) Perseverance

• Never quit. (1 Corinthians 4:12; 2 Timothy 2:3.)

• Remember, God created you to be a scrapper, not to be fainthearted. It is spiritually illegal for you to be overcome. So dig in your heels, narrow your eyes, and have bulldog tenacity.

• See setbacks as opportunities to display the glory of God. (1 Peter 2:20.)

10) Harvest

• You will reap if you faint not. (Galatians 6:7-9.)

• The purpose of all faith is to get something. This can be for you or for others, but the harvest is always the ultimate objective. So you must remain unwavering. Never let go of your vision. Never stop believing. Never stop speaking what you believe. Stick to the plan and work it relentlessly. You will receive! (James 1:2-8.)

Living by these principles has changed my life immensely. I know that no matter what I face, faith is my victory. Instead of getting up and worrying about my day, I now make my declaration, "Get ready world. I'm about to show you something extraordinary!" That's the attitude I want this book to birth in you. Know that you are a believer, a faith warrior, a partner with God, and the devil's worst nightmare. You are built for faith. Honor God by being the person you are created to be. It is your greatest testimony to a lost and dying world.

By Faith, God's Righteousness Is Now Your Righteousness

My Prayer for Today

For in it the righteousness of God is revealed from faith to faith; as it is written, "The just shall live by faith."
–Romans 1:17

Father, what a glorious truth it is that I have become the righteousness of God in Christ Jesus my Lord. (Romans 3:22.) My day-to-day living is no longer dependent on my own meager ability to gain Your favor. I know that I am welcome at Your throne in spite of myself. Because of Your free gift to me, I am now made clean. Lord, right now I make my commitment to You to act on what I believe. I thank You that I no longer stand in my own ability, but in Your ability. I am now one with You in spirit and Your Word is a mighty weapon on my lips.

My Confession for Today

I am the righteousness of God in Christ Jesus and my life is lived by faith. This righteousness is not my own; it is God's gift to me. My right standing with God is not based on my own goodness, but the goodness of Jesus. His righteousness is now my righteousness. In Him, I now have all the justification I need to receive any and every promise in God's Word. It is written, "The righteous shall live by faith." Therefore, by faith I claim every promise as mine in Jesus' name.

January 2

You Are Built for Endurance

Therefore do not cast away your confidence, which has great reward. For you have need of endurance, so that after you have done the will of God, you may receive the promise.
–Hebrews 10:35-36

My Prayer for Today

Father, I know that You are faithful and I have total confidence in Your Word. I will not allow circumstances to sway me from what I know to be true. Your Word has never failed. It is tested, tried and true. Through it, I have a strength and determination that overcomes all obstacles and laughs in the face of every trying circumstance. I see Your reward in front of me and I am determined to stand fast until it is manifested in my life. No matter what I face, I will endure to the end and receive what You have promised.

My Confession for Today

Eternity shall not remember me as a shallow person who doubted the Lord. No, I am resolved to persevere through any and every difficulty, not looking at the circumstance, but with my eyes fixed on God's promise. I will not throw down my faith, because I know in due time I will reap and be richly rewarded. I remain confident that once I have fulfilled the requirements of the promise, I will receive it in its full measure. Therefore, my present condition shall not make me waver and the events that surround me cannot make me afraid.

Make God Your Unwavering Confidence

My Prayer for Today

Now the just shall live by faith; but if anyone draws back, My soul has no pleasure in him.
—Hebrews 10:38

Father, I know that Your Word is truth. It has authority over and above every circumstance and situation that I face. To not have confidence in Your Word is like declaring that my situation is more powerful than You are. I won't do that. I will not shrink back from what You have promised. I stand fast in the integrity of my God. With You, all things are possible. My heart's desire is to put a smile on Your face by believing and receiving in spite of what my eyes can see or what the circumstances are showing.

My Confession for Today

If I look to the circumstance and give up on my faith in the promise, there is no obligation for it to be fulfilled in my life. Faith is the avenue that God has chosen to bring forth His blessings into the earth. I know that if I refuse to walk by faith, the promise will remain dormant no matter how much I believe in it. Therefore, today I make my commitment to speak God's Word with power, patience and unwavering persistence. I hold forth His Word as the final authority and dispel every doubtful thought that would turn me from the truth.

January 4

Your Deeply Rooted Faith Shall Deliver You

Therefore do not cast away your confidence, which has great reward. For you have need of endurance, so that after you have done the will of God, you may receive the promise.
–Hebrews 10:35-36

My Prayer for Today

Father, I know that shallow belief is inadequate in Your sight. Just knowing that Your Word is true will not bring Your promises to pass in my life. You have asked me to believe without wavering, and to trust You without hesitation. Therefore, I purpose in my heart to be steadfast. I know I will see Your goodness in the land of the living. Your promises are just as "right now" as my faith. I choose to make Your Word the absolute final authority. No matter what I see, or what anyone else says, I will not draw back, but will continue to believe to the saving of my soul.

My Confession for Today

What a perfect day it is to be a pain in the devil's neck. Today, I stand strong against fear and temptation. I am strong in the Lord and the power of His might. God's own love, power and consistency are flowing through me at this very moment. This is a faith day! I do not shrink back and cringe in view of the circumstances. I do not falter at the sound of an evil report. To the contrary, I am one who continues to believe and receive promise after promise, and I enjoy God's round-the-clock deliverance in my life.

Your Faith Is the Proof that You Have What You Desire

My Prayer for Today

Now the just shall live by faith; but if anyone draws back, My soul has no pleasure in him.
–Hebrews 10:38

Father, I know that what things so ever I desire when I pray, if I believe I receive them, I shall have them. It is Your Word to me and Your Word is unfailing truth. This gives me great confidence, Lord. I am fully confident that my expectations will be realized. Though I may not see the end of my faith at this present moment, I know that I shall have the things that I say. My faith in Your Word is all the evidence I need. It is the very substance that manifests Your glory in my life. Thank You, Father, for bringing to pass my deepest desires, in Jesus' name.

My Confession for Today

My faith is the very substance of the things that I hope for. It is the certainty that what I do not see will soon be manifested in my life. I am not moved by what I see in this natural world. My environment is subject to the power of the Word. Therefore, I will stand in the utter certainty that my situation can and will be changed. I place the entirety of my confidence in the promise of God. I declare that the Word is my final authority. I will not steer from it, even a little to the right or left. I am steadfast, unwavering and immovable. My foundation remains secure and by faith, all that I do prospers.

January 6

Faith Sets in Motion the Things of the Spirit

By faith we understand that the worlds were framed by the word of God, so that the things which are seen were not made of things which are visible.

–Hebrews 11:3

My Prayer for Today

Father, Your precepts and laws are thoroughly wonderful. By the law of faith, You framed the worlds with Your words. You called those things that be not as though they were and thus they became. It's so amazing that You would call me to live the same way—to speak Your Word and believe that I shall have the things that I say. Since this is what You ask of me and what is pleasing in Your sight, I commit myself to a life of it. From this day unto eternity I will believe Your Word and speak it into my life with unyielding trust in its absolute integrity.

My Confession for Today

I have a thorough understanding of the processes of faith. I understand that through faith, God created the worlds with His Word. All that I see now was made out of what cannot be seen by the physical eye. God has called me to live by the same process. When I believe and speak in perfect alignment with the will of God, the things that I say are manifested. My faith is a spiritual force that overcomes physical circumstances. It is more real than what my eyes can see or what my body may feel. It is more powerful than any problem, hindrance, or setback. It is the spiritual force that brings God's glory into my life experience.

God Wants You to Act like He Does

My Prayer for Today

Father, help me to live a life that pleases You in every way. I know that to please You I must first believe You. I must set aside all human logic and trust You with my whole heart. Let me be perfect in this, Father. Assist me. Train me. Enlighten the eyes of my understanding that I may clearly see Your direction for my life. Let me not be wise in my own eyes, but always maintain a sharp focus on Your Word. By this alone, I find favor and high esteem in Your sight.

Without faith it is impossible to please Him, for he who comes to God must believe that He is, and that He is a rewarder of those who diligently seek Him.
–Hebrews 11:6

My Confession for Today

I know that without faith it is impossible for me to please God. In order for me to draw near to Him, I must first believe that He exists, and then that He will reward me as I diligently seek Him. I believe both. I have assurance in my heart that His Word rings true in my life. Therefore, I fix all of my will on pleasing Him in every way. To do this, I must make demands on the power that He has given me and call those things that be not as though they were. (Romans 4:17.)

January 8

God's Word Kindles the Fire of Faith

So then faith comes by hearing, and hearing by the word of God.
—Romans 10:17

My Prayer for Today

Father, only by Your Word can I live the life of faith that You desire for me to live. Through Your Word I have partaken of Your divine nature, a faith nature that brings forth miracles from the unseen world. (2 Peter 1:4.) By Your Word I obtain all things that pertain unto life and godliness. (2 Peter 1:3.) It is only by Your Word that I can ask and receive so that my joy is made full. (John 16:24.) So fill me with understanding of Your precepts. Teach me to know Your wisdom and instruction. Bring me revelation knowledge of every promise so that I can live my life with a strength of faith that overcomes all evil and sets every captive free.

My Confession for Today

I am committed to live a life that is pleasing to God in every way. Therefore, I will do whatever it takes to be strong in Him and in the power of His might. I do not live by bread alone, but by the ever living Word of God. His Word to me is my spiritual sustenance. (Matthew 4:4.) It strengthens and nourishes my spirit, and keeps my life on a clear path toward my divine destiny. I will not play the fool and live my life as a spiritual weakling because I refuse to feed on His promises. The more I feed on the Word, the more I experience God's power and presence in my life.

Be Self-Aware!

My Prayer for Today

Father, I thank You so much for Your grace and mercy toward me. Thank You for the divine enabling that I have to live my life with honor and integrity. I thank You that You have not given me a spirit of fear, but of power and love and a sound, sober mind. (2 Timothy 1:7.) In You, I have all that I need and more. With You, nothing is impossible for me. You have dealt to me the measure of faith. Feed me with revelation and I will go forward to do Your will.

For I say, through the grace given to me, to everyone who is among you, not to think of himself more highly than he ought to think, but to think soberly, as God has dealt to each one a measure of faith.

–Romans 12:3

My Confession for Today

I stand by God's grace alone. I do not esteem myself more highly than I should, for I know that in and of myself I am nothing. Rather, I think of myself with sober judgment. I know that my value in the sight of God is inestimable and that He has given me the measure of faith to put me over in this life. However, I do not forget that all that I have, I have been given. I am totally, completely and joyfully dependent upon my God. He alone is my strength and the security by which I live. I trust Him completely and I am not afraid.

Create a Plan to Fulfill Your Vision

Then the LORD answered me and said: "Write the vision and make it plain on tablets, That he may run who reads it. For the vision is yet for an appointed time; but at the end it will speak, and it will not lie. Though it tarries, wait for it; because it will surely come, it will not tarry."
—Habakkuk 2:2–3

My Prayer for Today

Father, with all of my heart I want Your will to be done for my life. I don't want to live a fantasy life with lofty goals that I will never achieve, nor do I want to gain fame and fortune in ventures that are outside of Your perfect will. Therefore, right now I ask You to give me a vision and a goal. Reveal to me Your perfect plan for my life. Show me what it is that You want me to do and how You want me to do it. Lay before me the steps that I must take, and I will write the vision down and run with it.

My Confession for Today

When I receive my clear-cut vision, a divine faith plan unthwartable in the hands of the diligent, I write it down and make it a clear, understandable, and unmistakable declaration in my life. I place this plan where I will regularly see it so that I will have a continuous reminder and a source of focus toward my inevitable goal. I speak of the end from the beginning and stand in full confidence that the Lord and I will see it through to its fulfillment.

Let Love Guide All that You Do

My Prayer for Today

Father, I always want my priorities to be in line with the character that You portray. Help me not to be selfish or religious as I walk this life of faith. Keep me focused in a single-minded pursuit of Your will. I know that Your nature is love and when I walk in love, I show that I am born of You and know You. Help me to love others as You have loved me. Help me to be the son/daughter that You have created me to be.

Though I have the gift of prophecy, and understand all mysteries and all knowledge, and though I have all faith, so that I could remove mountains, but have not love, I am nothing.
–1 Corinthians 13:2

My Confession for Today

The mysteries and knowledge of God dwell within me. I have faith that can move mountains and my faith operates within the boundaries of love. (Matthew 17:20.) I am committed to love others as God has loved me. The Holy Spirit, who is love, dwells within my heart and His love is perfected in me. As I go about my business this day, I seek the good of others. I am patient, kind, and forgiving. I focus on that which is good instead of seeking to expose what is bad. My first thought in all things is to honor God by walking in love.

January 12

Love Makes Your Faith Worthwhile

And now abide faith, hope, love, these three; but the greatest of these is love.

—1 Corinthians 13:13

My Prayer for Today

Father, I know that this day will afford me the opportunity to be offended. I know that if I look for a reason to get upset, I will find it. Help me not to do that, Lord. Help me to mimic Your ways as a true disciple. As the child of Your loins, I purpose in my heart to show Your character in all that I do. May it be said of me that I take after my Father— that in all that I do, I show myself to be just like You. May my faith be strong, my hope be confident, and my love be genuine. But of these three, Father, make my love shine the brightest.

My Confession for Today

I understand the processes of godly faith. First, I set a goal. This is my hope and the expectation of what I desire to receive. Then I put my faith into operation, believing that I have received what I hope for, confessing with my mouth my specific desires, and preparing for when they come into this natural world. Through it all, my central focus is love. It is the very springboard of all of my faith and hope. My hope does not live without it and my faith does not work, but within it.

Honor the Word

My Prayer for Today

Father, I know that the entirety of Your Word is truth. If You say that all of Your promises are mine in Christ Jesus, then that is what I choose to believe. This is Your righteous judgment and it endures forever. It is You, Father, who have caused me to be in Christ Jesus. It is You who initiated this covenant, and it is You who have given me the Holy Spirit as a guarantee. I am Abraham's seed and a joint heir with Jesus. (Galatians 3:29; Romans 8:17.) All that is His, is now mine as well. I thank You for this, Father. I can now dig through Your Word knowing that any promise I find is one that I can claim as my own.

The entirety of Your word is truth, and every one of Your righteous judgments endures forever. Princes persecute me without a cause, but my heart stands in awe of Your word. I rejoice at Your word as one who finds great treasure.
—Psalm 119:160–162

My Confession for Today

I recognize that all of my Father's promises are eternally faithful. I tremble in knowing that they have been given to me on a personal level. When I find one, I rejoice as one who has found buried treasure and is made rich beyond his wildest dreams. No matter what I face, the Word will see me through. Though I am persecuted without cause and suffer troubles on every side, I can hold up the Word in faith and find deliverance every single time.

January 14

Believe First, Then Pray

Then Jesus said to the centurion, "Go your way; and as you have believed, so let it be done for you." And his servant was healed that same hour.
—Matthew 8:13

My Prayer for Today

Father, Jesus once said, "If you've seen Me, you've seen the Father." (John 14:9.) He also said that He did not come to do His will, but Your will. Every place He went, He was willing to meet the needs of all who would just believe. I know that belief is not a feeling; it is an unwavering choice. Therefore, Father, in spite of how I feel, I choose to believe. I know that You are faithful and that Your Word is true. In You I have confident hope. I fully expect that this day Your Word will be fulfilled in my life.

My Confession for Today

As I believe, so it shall be done for me. When I speak to mountains, they are removed. I have the things that I say. (Mark 11:23.) The action of my faith is to believe and speak, and what I believe I have presently received, that is what I shall have. Therefore, I declare this day to be a day of reckoning. I speak to every evil thing that Satan has attacked me with and command it to be removed from my life. I say that poverty, sickness, and despair are removed, and that prosperity, health, and joy are mine. This is what I say, this is what I believe, and this is what I have.

Jesus Is Your Steadfast Support

My Prayer for Today

Father, help me to always recognize my oneness with Jesus. Help me to understand that in Your eyes I died with Him, was buried with Him, and was raised to new life in Him. Help me to know that even at this very moment I am seated together with Him in heavenly places. (Ephesians 2:6 KJV.) Help me to understand that as long as I am in Him, I shall endure and reign with Him. I confess, Father, that He alone is the Source of my salvation. I will never deny Him and go about trying to establish my own righteousness. I know that even if I falter or fail, He never will.

This is a faithful saying: For if we died with Him, we shall also live with Him. If we endure, we shall also reign with Him. If we deny Him, He also will deny us. If we are faithless, He remains faithful; He cannot deny Himself.
—2 Timothy 2:11–13

My Confession for Today

I am a faith warrior who maintains unwavering belief. I died with Jesus; therefore, my life is now hidden in Him and only through Him am I able to receive any of God's promises. I endure and persevere. I never give up. I never contradict or refuse Him, so that He will never have to refuse and hold back His promise from me. I know that His Word is faithful. Even if I were faithless and failed to believe and receive His promise, He would remain faithful and His Word would remain true. God cannot lie, for to do so would be to deny His very self.

January 16

God Knows Your Heart and Hears Your Prayer

Whatever prayer, whatever supplication is made by anyone, or by all Your people Israel, when each one knows his own burden and his own grief, and spreads out his hands to this temple: then hear from heaven Your dwelling place, and forgive, and give to everyone according to all his ways, whose heart You know (for You alone know the hearts of the sons of men).
–2 Chronicles 6:29-30

My Prayer for Today

Father, I thank You that in Christ Jesus I am made new. I am born from above and my heart is made perfect in Your sight. I am now the temple in which You dwell. You hear my every prayer, forgive my every sin, and give me every desire of my heart. I commit myself to You, Father. Lead me on the path of righteousness and teach me to live according to Your precepts. (Psalm 23:3.)

My Confession for Today

All of my supplications, the prayers that I pray with a sense of need, are important in God's sight. He hears every one. And yet, I realize that He responds to each person according to their ways and not their needs. Therefore, I make my ways the ways of God. My supplications are answered because I respond to His promises in the spirit of faith. I believe them with all of my heart and declare their reality in my life regardless of the circumstances. This is His way of receiving, and I make it my own.

Count Your Blessings and Be Thankful

My Prayer for Today

Father, I thank You for every good thing which is in me in Christ Jesus my Lord. In Him, I have unconditional access to Your very throne. (Hebrews 4:16.) In Him, I have every good promise of prosperity, peace, healing, and fulfillment. I have eternal life. I have an address in heaven. All of my needs are met with Your abundance. My heart is the very home of the Holy Spirit. I have Your anointing that removes every burden and destroys every yoke. (Isaiah 10:27.) Knowing all of this, how can I not be effective?

That the sharing of your faith may become effective by the acknowledgment of every good thing which is in you in Christ Jesus.
—Philemon 1:6

My Confession for Today

I acknowledge that God has given me the ability to have a full and complete understanding of everything that belongs to me in Christ Jesus. I have the mind of Christ. (1 Corinthians 2:16.) When I give, the same is given back to me good measure, pressed down, shaken together, and running over. (Luke 6:38.) Jesus bore my sicknesses and carried my pains, the chastisement to justify my peace was laid upon Him, and with the stripes that wounded Him, I am healed. (Isaiah 53:4-5.) I am delivered from the power of darkness and translated into the kingdom of God's dear Son. (Colossians 1:13.) Nothing is impossible for me, because the omnipotent God, my very Savior, dwells within me. (Matthew 17:20.)

January 18

Rest Secure in the Finished Work of Christ Jesus

For he who has entered His rest has himself also ceased from his works as God did from His.
—Hebrews 4:10

My Prayer for Today

Father, I thank You that it is by grace that I am saved through faith. (Ephesians 2:8-9.) I did not earn this, nor do I deserve it. There are no works of righteousness that I can perform to clean myself up in order to be acceptable in Your sight. All You ask is that I receive Your free gift to me so that I may enter into Your rest. Jesus said it so plainly when He said his yoke is easy and His burden is light. (Matthew 11:30.) I am fully in Your hands, Lord, and I rest in Your finished work.

My Confession for Today

I am very eager to enter into God's rest through the avenue of faith. I do not forget that the only way I can enjoy this rest is through the Apostle and High Priest of my confession: Christ Jesus my Lord. (Hebrews 3:1.) He alone is my justification and my right to receive from the Father. Therefore, if I wish to enter His rest, I must simply believe in His promise and speak it into my life. When I do this, my High Priest takes my confession before the throne of God and sees to it that I have what I say.

God's Word Is Alive!

My Prayer for Today

Father, Your Word is living and powerful. It is sharper than any two-edged sword, piercing even to the division of my soul and spirit. It cuts through to my joints and marrow. It discerns the very thoughts and intents of my heart. It is pure, like silver tried in the furnace of the earth. (Psalm 12.) By Your Word, You formed the heavens, and the host of them by the breath of Your mouth. (Psalm 33:6.) Lord, give me an intimate understanding of Your Word. Help me to know the power of Your Word on my lips. I incline my ear to Your wisdom and I apply my heart to Your understanding. Teach me, Father, that I may honor You with the life of faith You have called me to live.

For the word of God is living and powerful, and sharper than any two-edged sword, piercing even to the division of soul and spirit, and of joints and marrow, and is a discerner of the thoughts and intents of the heart.
—Hebrews 4:12

My Confession for Today

I consider the promise of God to be true in my life no matter what the circumstance may be. I rest in full assurance of faith that God is well able to do what He has promised; for the Word of God is living and active within me. It is sharper than any two-edged sword and is able to even penetrate the boundaries of my spirit, soul and body— it judges the thoughts and intents of my heart.

Your Faith Has Backup

Seeing then that we have a great High Priest who has passed through the heavens, Jesus the Son of God, let us hold fast our confession.
—Hebrews 4:14

My Prayer for Today

Father, the perfection of Your salvation is astounding. It is almost unfathomable to think that Jesus knows my every temptation and sympathizes with my weaknesses. He was tempted in every way that I am tempted, yet He remained sinless. (Hebrews 4:15.) I have given in to temptation many times, but He never did. He knows everything that I go through, and holds nothing against me. He never judges me or finds reason not to take my prayers before Your throne. Every prayer that I pray in faith, He gladly presents to You, and because He is my High Priest, You grant my every request. I will forever stand in awe and wonder at such unconditional love and acceptance.

My Confession for Today

I have a High Priest (Jesus, the Son of God, my elder Brother and my Lord) who has entered the heavenly temple on my behalf. I hold firmly to my confession of faith without wavering or giving in to the circumstances; for I do not have a High Priest who is unable to sympathize with my weaknesses, but one who was tempted in every way that I am and yet remained victorious. It is He who takes my request before God's throne, and it is He who makes sure that I have the things that I say.

You Have an Open Invitation to the Throne of God

My Prayer for Today

> *Let us therefore come boldly to the throne of grace, that we may obtain mercy and find grace to help in time of need.*
> *—Hebrews 4:16*

Father, there is no greater privilege in my life than to be welcome at Your throne. Jesus paved the way ahead of me and removed every obstacle that could keep me from You. (Hebrews 9:12.) I come boldly and joyfully take my place as a prince/princess in the court of Your palace. My rights as Your son/daughter have been purchased and secured by the blood of Jesus. You have seated me at Your right hand in the place of highest honor. (Ephesians 2:6.) Honor me now with Your fellowship, instruction, and assistance, Father. I come in faith knowing that my every need and desire is now met, in Jesus' name.

My Confession for Today

Through Jesus, I can now approach the very throne of God, the throne of grace, with boldness and confidence, without the slightest sense of inadequacy whatsoever. I am the recipient of God's mercy. His supernatural ability is now within me. In Jesus, the way has been opened for me to freely receive God's help in any and every circumstance. It doesn't matter if it is my fault or not, for by His grace (unmerited, undeserved favor) He has given me His Word that He will help me and put me back on my feet.

January 22

In Christ Jesus, Every Promise Is Yours

For all the promises of God in Him are Yes, and in Him Amen, to the glory of God through us.
—2 Corinthians 1:20

My Prayer for Today

Father, I thank You that in Christ Jesus I no longer have to worry about whether or not You will answer my prayers. You have given me Your Word that all of Your promises are mine in Him. I now have the opportunity to be an avenue of Your glory in this earth. I am in Christ Jesus, and through Your Word, He is now glorified in me. Teach me to know Your truth, Father. Bring to my remembrance every good promise of Your Word that I may bear much fruit and bring glory to Your name.

My Confession for Today

All of God's promises are mine to receive. Every time that I pray in line with the precepts of His Word, the answer is guaranteed. As I am in Christ Jesus, and His Word abides in me, I can ask what I will and it will be done for me. (John 15:7.) In this is my Father glorified: when I speak His Word in faith and bear much fruit in honor of His name.

Be Fearless

My Prayer for Today

> God has not given us a spirit of fear, but of power and of love and of a sound mind.
> —2 Timothy 1:7

Father, I thank You for showing me the immensity of Your love for me. Your perfect love casts all fear from my life. (1 John 4:18.) The judgment of Your wrath was poured out on Jesus, freeing me from all fear and condemnation. I know that for me to allow fear to enter my mind would be contrary to the life of faith that You have called me to live. Therefore, I cast fear out and declare in agreement with Your Word that I now have a spirit of power, and love, and a sound mind. Nothing can make me afraid, for I am in Christ Jesus and He has set me free! (Romans 8:2.)

My Confession for Today

The love of God has been shed abroad in my heart by the Holy Spirit and this love declares that there is no longer any reason to be afraid. (Romans 5:5.) God has not given me a spirit of fear and cowardice, but of power (miraculous ability), love, and self-control. By this truth, I remain fully confident in my spiritual walk. I choose faith over fear, and love over cowardice. Through love and the God-given power within me, I am changing this world for the glory of God.

January 24

Cast Your Cares Upon the Lord

You younger people, submit yourselves to your elders. Yes, all of you be submissive to one another, and be clothed with humility, for "God resists the proud, but gives grace to the humble." Therefore humble yourselves under the mighty hand of God, that He may exalt you in due time, casting all your care upon Him, for He cares for you.
—1 Peter 5:5-7

My Prayer for Today

Father, thank You for teaching me to be humble and submissive to others. Without Your guidance I could easily fall into selfish pride. So I humble myself under Your mighty hand that You may exalt me in due time. I cast all of my cares upon You, for You care for me. Far be it from me to think so highly of myself that You are forced to resist me. All that I am and have come from You alone. Without You I can do nothing, but with You I can do all things. (John 15:5; Philippians 4:13.) In light of this truth, I submit to Your perfect timing. Promote me according to Your will and purpose and not my own. (Ephesians 1:11.)

My Confession for Today

I am clothed with humility and covered in God's grace. I refuse to allow selfish arrogance to become a part of my character. I see others as just as important as myself. I keep all of my ambitions free of greed and egotism. I do not seek to exalt myself, but give place to the will of God. I humble myself under His mighty hand, knowing that He will exalt me in His perfect timing. I cast all of my fears, worries and anxieties upon Him, for He cares for me deeply and will not allow me to be overcome by troubles and sorrow.

Know What You Want

My Prayer for Today

Father, I'm not about to let religious tradition or false humility keep me from all that You have to give. I know that by faith I can receive all that I need to live a happy, healthy and productive life. I could care less what anyone thinks of me, or says about me. I am a faith man/woman first to last and I am completely unashamed to call upon You to meet my needs. You are the ultimate giver, Father, and I am more than willing to receive what You want me to have.

When he had come near, He asked him, saying, "What do you want Me to do for you?" He said, "Lord, that I may receive my sight." Then Jesus said to him, "Receive your sight; your faith has made you well."
–Luke 18:40–42

My Confession for Today

I know where the Source of life's power is and I recognize my total and complete dependency upon Him in every way. Without His mercy and grace, I am nothing. Therefore, I will call upon the Lord in total dependence and confidence in His mercy. I draw near to Him in respect, calling on His name and receiving by faith those specific things that are provided for me in our covenant.

January 26

Your Faith Is a Spiritual Force Within You

Since we have the same spirit of faith, according to what is written, "I believed and therefore I spoke," we also believe and therefore speak.
—2 Corinthians 4:13

My Prayer for Today

Father, I thank You that I have the spirit of faith in my life. I speak what I believe and the things that I say come to pass. I stand by Your grace and receive all that You have for me. All things are mine, through Jesus. My heart abounds with thanksgiving as I receive every good blessing of Your Word. Help me to maintain my focus, Father. Help me to persevere through every obstacle and trial I must face. My light afflictions, which are for a moment, are working for me a more exceeding and eternal weight of glory, for I do not look at what my eyes can see, but what they cannot see. I know that what I see is temporary, but what I cannot see (the world of the spirit) is eternal. (2 Corinthians 4:17-18.)

My Confession for Today

Faith is a spiritual power and the tool that God has given me to bring forth an abundance of good fruit in my life. It is written of the spirit of faith, "I believed; therefore, I have spoken." This is my faith in operation. I take the promise into my heart, believe it with all of my soul, and speak it forth until it is manifested in my life.

You Will Only Receive According to Your Faith

My Prayer for Today

Father, I know that in order to receive from You, I must first believe in You, and know that You will reward me as I diligently seek You. (Hebrews 11:6.) You do not answer my prayers outside of the realm of faith. Therefore, I say to You right now, let it be unto me according to Your Word. I believe that You are well able to perform all that You have promised and since You said that all of Your promises are mine in Christ Jesus, I receive every single one of them right now by faith. (Romans 4:21; 2 Corinthians 1:20.) According to my faith, let it be unto me.

When He had come into the house, the blind men came to Him. And Jesus said to them, "Do you believe that I am able to do this?" They said to Him, "Yes, Lord." Then He touched their eyes, saying, "According to your faith let it be to you."
–Matthew 9:28-29

My Confession for Today

I firmly believe in the power and ability of God that is within me. According to my faith (my believing and speaking the answer) all of my needs and godly desires become a reality in my life. I do not need to earn the right to them, nor do I have to beg for them. They are presently mine, in Christ Jesus. The treasure of God's promises is mine for the asking. Every spiritual blessing is mine. Every promise of joy, peace, health, and prosperity is mine. I believe I have received them, and therefore I have them.

January 28

Faith Is Faith, No Matter How Small

So the Lord said, "If you have faith as a mustard seed, you can say to this mulberry tree, 'Be pulled up by the roots and be planted in the sea,' and it would obey you."
—Luke 17:6

My Prayer for Today

Father, I thank You for revelation knowledge of Your promises. Thank You for revealing to me that faith is faith, whether it be large or small. As long as I believe, I can speak to whatever problem I face, command it to leave, and it absolutely must obey me. Thank You for this faith authority, Father. I know that You will back what I say and see to it that what I believe is not in vain. I trust You with all of my heart, Lord. I do not lean to my own understanding, but rest secure in Your Word. (Proverbs 3:5.)

My Confession for Today

I use my faith as if it were a seed. When I speak to a problem and believe that those things that I say have to come to pass, I shall have the things that I say. It may not look like anything is happening, but the seed of my faith has entered in and is doing its job well. When I align my words in agreement with the Word of God, whatever I am speaking to must obey my commands. My faith is a servant to me and it is my duty to use it to bring forth the blessings of the Kingdom into the earth.

Speak to the Mountain!

My Prayer for Today

Father, I thank You for instructing me in the ways of faith. By faith, You created the worlds by Your Word, bringing forth the visible from that which is invisible. (John 1:1-3; Colossians 1:16.) You are a faith God and continually call those things that be not as though they were. (Romans 4:17.) You even see me as a finished product. Your relationship with me is not based on what You presently see of me, but what You are calling me forth to be. I choose to be a good son/daughter and live by the same process. When I speak to a problem, and do not doubt in my heart, but believe the things that I say have come to pass, I shall have the things that I say.

My Confession for Today

I am constantly functioning in God-like faith. I AM created me as a faith being. (Exodus 3:14.) Through the expression of my focused belief, I receive everything that I desire. When I command a mountain (a formidable circumstance or barrier) to be removed and cast into the sea, and have no doubt that it will happen, it will happen. Everything that I believe with my heart and speak from my mouth, within the boundaries of God's will, becomes reality for me.

"Have faith in God," Jesus answered. "I tell you the truth, if anyone says to this mountain, 'Go, throw yourself into the sea,' and does not doubt in his heart but believes that what he says will happen, it will be done for him. Therefore I tell you, whatever you ask for in prayer, believe that you have received it, and it will be yours.
—Mark 11:22-24 (NIV)

January 30

Believe in the Lord

He [Abram] believed in the LORD, and He accounted it to him for righteousness.
—Genesis 15:6

My Prayer for Today

Father, I am humbled by the knowledge that I have been freely acquitted of all charges that You could lay against me. Every sin, from the beginning to the end of my life, has been eradicated from my record. Jesus paid my full price, and now all that You ask of me is to believe that I have received it. (1 Corinthians 6:20.) I know that what I believe I have received, that is what I shall have. (Mark 11:24.) Father, I believe Your Word that a righteousness apart from the law of Moses has become my own. My righteousness is by faith in Christ Jesus and I am justified freely by Your grace through the redemption that He wrought for me. (Romans 3:21-24.)

My Confession for Today

I believe in God. I have steadfast confidence in His complete integrity. He has given me the right to stand fearlessly in His presence. Because I have believed His promise and spoken it into my life, I am now fully acquitted and made righteous. Through faith, Jesus is now the propitiation for my sins and His righteousness has become my own. (1 John 4:10; Romans 3:22.) I do not establish myself based on my own goodness or penance. In Christ, I am already established as righteous before God for all of eternity.

Have No Fear of the Giants in the Land

My Prayer for Today

Father, it's my confidence in Your love for me that causes me not to fear. You did not spare Your own Son, but delivered Him up for me. How shall You not now freely give me all things? (Romans 8:32.) You never leave me nor forsake me. (Hebrews 13:5.) You live within my heart. What is there then to be afraid of? You are my light and my salvation. You are the very strength of my life. (Psalm 27:1.) You build Your hedge of protection around me. (Psalm 139:5.) You cover me with Your feathers and under Your wings I take refuge. (Psalm 91:4.) You're my loving Father, and my dwelling place is between Your shoulders. (Deuteronomy 33:12.) Though a host may rise against me and I find myself against overwhelming odds, I shall not be afraid, but rest in the comfort of Your embrace. (Psalm 27:3-5.)

If the LORD delights in us, then He will bring us into this land and give it to us, 'a land which flows with milk and honey.' Only do not rebel against the LORD, nor fear the people of the land, for they are our bread; their protection has departed from them, and the LORD is with us. Do not fear them.
–Numbers 14:8-9

My Confession for Today

My Father delights in me. He has brought me into a spacious and fertile land and has bid me to claim it as my own. I have no fear of those who set themselves up as my enemies. The giants in the land are bread for me. They have no defense that can stand against the Lord. He has removed all protection from them and has bid me to take the land. Therefore, I will take it. The Lord is with me and I am well able.

February 1

Be Patient

We desire that each one of you show the same diligence to the full assurance of hope until the end, that you do not become sluggish, but imitate those who through faith and patience inherit the promises.
—Hebrews 6:11-12

My Prayer for Today

Father, I claim the harvest that You have promised. You do not forget or ignore the work and labor of love that I have shown toward your name. (Hebrews 6:10.) You see all that I have done and all that I have given. I have Your Word that You will give me an abundant return and a fruitful harvest. I stand in confident hope that I shall reap if I faint not. (Galatians 6:9.) I know that You have made all grace abound toward me so that I have all sufficiency in all things and can abound to every good work. (2 Corinthians 9:8.)

My Confession for Today

God sees the work that I have done and rewards me accordingly. When I give, it is with full assurance of His faithfulness to the very end. I refuse to become indifferent, faithless and stagnant, believing that the circumstance reigns over the Word and thus giving up on my faith. Instead, I am an imitator of those who through faith and patience (endurance; persistence) continually inherit God's promises.

Run with Endurance

Therefore we also, since we are surrounded by so great a cloud of witnesses, let us lay aside every weight, and the sin which so easily ensnares us, and let us run with endurance the race that is set before us,
—Hebrews 12:1

My Prayer for Today

Father, You know the sin that most easily ensnares me. You know my every struggle and my every weakness. Yet through faith my weakness turns to strength so that I can be valiant and set to flight the armies of the enemy. Your grace is sufficient for me. When I am weak, the power of Christ rests upon me to make me strong. Therefore, I make my boast in You and You alone. (2 Corinthians 12:9.) I am strong in You and in the power of Your might. (Ephesians 6:10.) I lay aside every weight and the sin that so easily besets me and I run this race with endurance and perseverance to the end.

My Confession for Today

I am resolved to run my race with patient endurance and unwavering persistence. I look away from all distractions that would keep me from those things that Jesus has provided. I reject the image of the world and take hold of an image in my mind of what cannot be seen with my natural eyes. It is my mind's image, in accordance with what God has promised, that is the true reality. I purpose in my heart to see things through the eyes of God.

February 3

Look to Jesus as Your Greatest Example

Looking unto Jesus, the author and finisher of our faith, who for the joy that was set before Him endured the cross, despising the shame, and has sat down at the right hand of the throne of God.
—Hebrews 12:2

My Prayer for Today

Father, there is nothing more precious in my life than the gift of Jesus. He is my ultimate faith hero. He saw the end from the beginning and it filled Him with joy. To think that I was why He suffered and that I was what brought Him joy is beyond my comprehension. He did not give in to even the worst of circumstances because He knew that His reward was on the other end. The reward, Father, is me. You have identified me with Him in every way so that all that He accomplished is set to my account. All that is left for me to do is praise You and give You thanks.

My Confession for Today

Jesus is the model on which I build my faith. In Him, I am now a recreated born-again son/daughter of God. (John 3:7,15.) I am the joy of the Father, Jesus, and the Holy Spirit. (Zephaniah 3:17.) All that Jesus suffered was for me and now I am fully justified and acquitted of all charges laid against me. (Colossians 2:13-14.) I am identified with all that Jesus is and all that He did. (John 17:23.) I have His own anointing within me at this very moment. (Ephesians 1:23 NLT.) Through Jesus, I am now one with God in spirit and in purpose. (Ephesians 2:10.)

Find Strength and Encouragement in the Lord

My Prayer for Today

For consider Him who endured such hostility from sinners against Himself, lest you become weary and discouraged in your souls.
–Hebrews 12:3

Father, I thank You for the example that Jesus gave me. His demonstration of patient, enduring faith is a standard for us all. He did not become discouraged and give up, but pressed on and endured more pain and agony than anyone ever has. He did it all because He knew that a promise was to be kept. It was a promise of salvation for me. He placed His Spirit into Your hands knowing that Your Word would be fulfilled. (Luke 23:46.) He could have stopped it all, but He chose to believe. He trusted You with all of His heart despite what He was going through. Above all else, Father, teach me to be just like Jesus.

My Confession for Today

I follow Jesus' example, considering it carefully so that I will not grow weary and lose heart. I remain a man/woman of faith despite any situation I may find myself in. I do not look to the circumstances as the final authority, but believe in God (in His Word and in His promises) and speak words of faith to those circumstances until the manifestation of what I say, in line with the Word, comes to pass.

February 5

Have the Kind of Faith that Shelters Many

Another parable He put forth to them, saying: "The kingdom of heaven is like a mustard seed, which a man took and sowed in his field, which indeed is the least of all the seeds; but when it is grown it is greater than the herbs and becomes a tree, so that the birds of the air come and nest in its branches."
–Matthew 13:31-32

My Prayer for Today

Father, I do not pray for great faith or to have my faith increased. I just pray for a revelation of the purity of faith that You have already given me. I know that the tiniest seed of pure faith, planted at the root of a problem, will bring forth my deliverance. Your kingdom is seed…time… and harvest. (Genesis 8:22.) I am wise enough to know that there is time between the planting of a seed and the reaping of a harvest. Therefore, Father, I commit myself to patient endurance. I will plant my seeds of faith in full assurance that in time I will harvest all of the benefits of Your promise.

My Confession for Today

I operate the principles of the Kingdom in the spirit of faith that has been given to me. I understand that when I sow Kingdom principles, they are like grains of mustard seed. Though they are small in the midst of all other seeds that have been sown into my life, through faith and patience, I can water them until their roots have choked out all that does not bring glory to God. In this manner, I receive such an abundance of blessings that I have all that I need and plenty left over. My life is a refuge to everyone in my circle of influence.

Let Nothing Steal Your Joy

My Prayer for Today

Father, I am determined that no matter what I face I will maintain a joyful attitude. Nothing is impossible for my faith to overcome. Therefore, I will remain patient through trials, all the while joyfully proclaiming the end from the beginning. (Isaiah 46:9-10.) There is not a single circumstance that can nullify what You have promised. You have declared that all things are possible for me. (Mark 9:23.) Nothing but my own lack of persistence can keep Your promises from being fulfilled in my life.

My brethren, count it all joy when you fall into various trials, knowing that the testing of your faith produces patience. But let patience have its perfect work, that you may be perfect and complete, lacking nothing.
–James 1:2–4

My Confession for Today

I maintain my joy despite the trials that I face. I know that my faith overcomes all adversity, and the testing of my faith produces in me an enduring patience. Patience is now an unfailing part of my character. I am mature and complete in it. I am confident, persistent, optimistic, and filled with hope. Through faith and patience, I lack no good thing in my life. (Hebrews 6:12.)

February 7

Be Single-Minded with Your Faith

But let him ask in faith, with no doubting, for he who doubts is like a wave of the sea driven and tossed by the wind. For let not that man suppose that he will receive anything from the Lord; he is a double-minded man, unstable in all his ways.
—James 1:6-8

My Prayer for Today

Father, Jesus taught us to ask what we will and it will be done for us. (John 15:7.) The expression of my desire is the first step toward receiving it. So I will make my desire clear. I will not dishonor You by being double-minded, flaky, or fickle. Help me to be decisive, consistent, and resolute. Help me to see the end plainly so that I may call it forth from the beginning. (John 16:13; Isaiah 46:10; Romans 4:19.) Keep my vision clear, my path straight, and my purpose unwavering. (Ephesians 1:11.)

My Confession for Today

I am single-minded in my faith. I ask and receive based upon my unwavering belief. Circumstances do not guide my thinking. God has placed within me the ability to change circumstances. He has bid me to ask what I will so that my joy may be full. (John 16:24.) Anything that I want, within the boundaries of God's will, is mine for the asking. God gives to me liberally and without reproach. (James 1:5.) I trust that He is faithful and will fulfill His promises to me.

Faith Without Works Is Dead

My Prayer for Today

Thus also faith by itself, if it does not have works, is dead.
—James 2:17

Father, help me to keep my faith alive by the works that I produce. I know that a goal without a workable plan is little more than a fantasy. Therefore I ask You for wisdom to build my faith plan. (James 1:5.) Open my understanding so that I know every detail of the steps I must take. (Ephesians 1:18.) Break it down for me in such detail that I know exactly what to do at each moment. Be my unfailing partner, Father, so that I can achieve my goals and live the life of my dreams.

My Confession for Today

I maintain a working faith. I do not just give mental assent to the truth of the Word, but act upon it, bearing an abundance of righteous fruit in my life. I am a person of purpose. (Ephesians 1:11.) My position in Christ Jesus is God's gift to me, but He did not create me to live as one who is lazy and unproductive. (Romans 8:1-2.) To the contrary, I am industrious, diligent, creative, and affluent. My faith only has value in the fruit that it produces and in Christ Jesus, I produce fruit in abundance. (Luke 6:44-45.)

February 9

Do Not Give in to Terror

He shall say to them, Hear, O Israel: Today you are on the verge of battle with your enemies. Do not let your heart faint, do not be afraid, and do not tremble or be terrified because of them; for the LORD your God is He who goes with you, to fight for you against your enemies, to save you.
–Deuteronomy 20:3–4

My Prayer for Today

Father, I thank You for the ability that I have within me to be a world overcomer. I know that every day I am on the verge of battle with those who seek my demise. But, I won't give in to terror, Father. You are within me with all of Your power and authority. No enemy can withstand the strength of Your mighty arm. (Jeremiah 32:17.) No strategy can thwart Your wise counsel. (1 Timothy 1:17.) Therefore, I will never give in and never be afraid.

My Confession for Today

I am a fearless faith warrior willing to face off with any enemy on any ground. I boldly take the offensive, for I know the One in whom I believe and I am fully aware of His capabilities within me. It is the Lord who goes before me. (Deuteronomy 31:8.) He is the first to confront the enemy on my behalf. I have nothing to fear. I refuse to give in to terror, trembling, or panic. The Lord fights for me, and I stand in His victory!

Walk by Faith, Not by Sight

My Prayer for Today

Father, thank You for giving me certainty in all that I do. Your very Spirit is within me to ensure my harvest. I have no need to be moved by circumstances, for You have given me the ability to create circumstances. Everything that I face can change. Therefore, I am always confident. I trust in the ability You have given me. My faith makes me the master of every situation. Regardless of what my eyes see, I will move forward and advance Your kingdom with power, certainty, and unfailing commitment.

My Confession for Today

Now He who has prepared us for this very thing is God, who also has given us the Spirit as a guarantee. So we are always confident, knowing that while we are at home in the body we are absent from the Lord. For we walk by faith, not by sight.
—2 Corinthians 5:5-7

I am created with a unique purpose for a vital mission. (Ephesians 1:11.) By the power of the Holy Spirit within me, I live above failure. Defeat is not even possible for me. As long as I maintain my faith, my life is as the days of heaven even on this earth. (Deuteronomy 11:21.) I am not moved by what I see, feel or experience. (Psalm 62:6.) Those are natural circumstances. I am moved only by what I choose to believe. My faith transcends all and brings God's abundant blessings into my life to the praise of His glory.

February 11

Be Strong and Courageous, for the Lord Is Always with You

No man shall be able to stand before you all the days of your life; as I was with Moses, so I will be with you. I will not leave you nor forsake you. Be strong and of good courage, for to this people you shall divide as an inheritance the land which I swore to their fathers to give them. Only be strong and very courageous, that you may observe to do according to all the law which Moses My servant commanded you; do not turn from it to the right hand or to the left, that you may prosper wherever you go.
–Joshua 1:5–7

My Prayer for Today

Father, I know that as You were with Moses, so are You with me. However, knowledge without action is no more powerful than ignorance. Therefore, in all my actions this day I will recognize that You are within me. I will be strong and courageous no matter what I face. With Your principles as my guide, nothing can stop my prosperity.

My Confession for Today

I am a son/daughter of God and He is with me wherever I go. He never leaves me nor forsakes me. By His power within me, not one of my enemies can succeed against me. I am strong and courageous. I encounter danger and difficulties with firmness and without fear. I'm bold, brave, and resolute. I'm always triumphant. I fulfill my calling in a spirit of valor and determination that overcomes all obstacles, hindrances, or setbacks.

Speak the Word

My Prayer for Today

Father, thank You for Your Word that guides me through the many paths of this life. Your unfailing Law shall not depart from my mouth. I know that its purpose is for my good, and its precepts are for my success. In it I find all that I need to live a happy and prosperous life.

My Confession for Today

I speak the Word continually. I meditate upon it day and night so that I may do all that is written therein. By this, I make my way prosperous, have good success, and deal wisely in all of the affairs of my life. I do not shrink back from God's Word. I am faithful, strong, vigorous, bold, and courageous. Fear has no place in my life, for the Lord is with me wherever I go!

This Book of the Law shall not depart from your mouth, but you shall meditate in it day and night, that you may observe to do according to all that is written in it. For then you will make your way prosperous, and then you will have good success. Have I not commanded you? Be strong and of good courage; do not be afraid, nor be dismayed, for the LORD your God is with you wherever you go.
—Joshua 1:8–9

February 13

Nothing Is Impossible for You

"Why could we not cast it out [of the epileptic boy]?" So Jesus said to them, "Because of your unbelief; for assuredly, I say to you, if you have faith as a mustard seed, you will say to this mountain, 'Move from here to there,' and it will move; and nothing will be impossible for you."
—Matthew 17:19–20

My Prayer for Today

Father, thank You for revealing to me the power of faith. I know that if I can believe, anything is possible for me. The moment I declare my unwavering belief, You cause what I desire to be birthed in the Spirit. Therefore, I commit myself to focus on the goal rather than the circumstance, for You are faithful to change the circumstance through the projection of my belief.

My Confession for Today

My faith is a spiritual force that is alive within me. When I use it, it is like a seed planted at the root of the problem. As I cultivate it [continually believing and speaking the answer], it overtakes and uproots whatever is standing in my way. Even a mountain poses no difficulty for me. When I tell it to move, it moves. With the faith that God has given me, nothing is impossible for me. (Romans 12:3.)

Every Problem Has a Faith Solution

My Prayer for Today

Father, I make my commitment to You not to complain or look for reasons not to believe. I know that the resilient and persistent always achieve success. Therefore, I will remain constant, knowing that there is a faith solution to every problem. When adversity arises, You are the guide who will see me through it. (Isaiah 49:10,13 NIV.) Let me know what to do, Father, and I will obey Your instruction. (Isaiah 30:21.)

My Confession for Today

I am steadfast in adverse circumstances. I choose to believe that there is always a solution to every problem. God, the perfect Counselor, is dwelling within me with all of His wisdom and power. (Isaiah 9:6; John 17:23.) Therefore, I cannot be driven to fear. My faith is the source of change. So in whatever state I am in, I know that with God's guidance I can produce the miracle that I need to see me through.

But as one [of the sons of the prophets] was cutting down a tree, the iron ax head fell into the water; and he cried out and said, "Alas, master! For it was borrowed." So the man of God said, "Where did it fall?" And he showed him the place. So he cut off a stick, and threw it in there; and he made the iron float.
–2 Kings 6:5-6

February 15

There Is Always More on Your Side!

*So he answered,
"Do not fear, for
those who are with
us are more than
those who are
with them."*
–2 Kings 6:16

My Prayer for Today

Father, thank You for all of the extras You've provided for me in this life. I always have the edge on my enemies. In You, I have a vision of the truth that transcends every circumstance. Your power within me guarantees my victory. When I walk into a room, You walk into a room. When the devil rises with a horde of soldiers, I need only to call upon You and You send such a force of angels that the demons disperse like cockroaches scurrying into the darkness.

My Confession for Today

I am not afraid when the enemy comes in like a flood. (Isaiah 59:19.) Though they come in by night and surround me with a great army, I am not stirred to terror. (2 Kings 6:14-17.) When others panic and cry out in fear, I remain steadfast. I know the One in whom I have put my trust. I also know that there are more on my side than any army the enemy can muster. I do not trust in what I see, for I know that what I do not see is where the real power is. The Lord's angels have surrounded me to do battle on my behalf. Therefore, I cannot be shaken and I will not be afraid!

The Greatest Partner in the World Dwells Within You

My Prayer for Today

Father, thank You for making me a world overcomer. No matter what I face, You are within me to ensure my success. It doesn't matter what position I find myself in, whether in the lead or trailing the pack, I always have the edge. If I'm in dead last, it is nothing more than an opportunity to relish the come-from-behind victory. It is really good to be Your son/daughter, Lord. Praise be to Your holy name.

> *You are of God, little children, and have overcome them, because He who is in you is greater than he who is in the world.*
> *–1 John 4:4*

My Confession for Today

I am a born-again child of the living God. (John 3:7,15.) I am of a different breed from the rest of the world. (John 17:11,14-16.) Satan, devils, and all spirits of anti-Christ are subject to my authority. (Luke 10:19.) God Himself is my partner. I am one with Him in spirit and all that I do is based upon His counsel. I am created to be a creator. (Genesis 1:1, 26.) Through strength of faith, I am changing this world for the glory of God.

Unchain Your Faith

So Jesus answered and said to them, "Assuredly, I say to you, if you have faith and do not doubt, you will not only do what was done to the fig tree, but also if you say to this mountain, 'Be removed and be cast into the sea,' it will be done. And whatever things you ask in prayer, believing, you will receive."
–Matthew 21:21-22

My Prayer for Today

Father, thank You for revealing to me that whatever things I ask in prayer, believing, I will receive. This is my revelation of faith without limits. I do not have to be concerned with religious restrictions, or worldly thinking. I am not bound by what others think I should be, nor am I a product of my environment. I am a product of the decisions I make while in my environment, and I have decided to live the life of my dreams by faith.

My Confession for Today

I engage my faith by believing the Word and speaking it to the problem. My faith is pure and focused with a deep-seated belief free of all doubt. I know that when I believe in God's power within me I can speak to any problem and it must obey my command. Whatever I ask for in faith, if I believe I have received it, regardless of the circumstances, I shall have it.

Be Close to the Lord

My Prayer for Today

Father, my greatest priority is to be close to You. Without Your fellowship, nothing is worthwhile. Teach me to hear Your voice and do those things that glorify Your name. (Psalm 27:11; John 10:27.) Teach me to be like You in every possible way. (2 Corinthians 3:18.) Build within me a strength of character that overcomes all ungodly influence. Show me how to love the unlovely, ignore religious ignorance, and to be the person You have created me to be.

> Draw near to God and He will draw near to you. Cleanse your hands, you sinners; and purify your hearts, you double-minded.
> *–James 4:8*

My Confession for Today

As I draw near to God, He draws near to me. I purify my heart from all double-mindedness, and remain fixed and immovable in my faith. (1 Corinthians 15:58.) I am in Christ Jesus and have been exalted to a life full of joy and endless victory. The desires of my heart are fully manifested to the praise of God's glory. With God inside of me, I am way too strong to be overcome by heavy burdens.

February 19

Don't Worry About How It Will Happen, Just Know that It Will Happen

And He said, "The kingdom of God is as if a man should scatter seed on the ground, and should sleep by night and rise by day, and the seed should sprout and grow, he himself does not know how."
—Mark 4:26-27

My Prayer for Today

Father, I may not understand how You cause faith to work, but I can trust that You have everything under control. All I have to do is trust the process and I can live such an amazing life that the world will look on with awe. Help me to apply my faith wisely, Father. Help me to understand and reject all of the religious ideas that hinder the advancement of Your kingdom. Make me strong in your anointing so that I may influence this world for Your glory. Isaiah 10:27; Ephesians 6:10.)

My Confession for Today

My heavenly Father has placed the seed of His Word in my hands and I am faithful to sow it into my life. Whatever need I have, whether for healing, peace, prosperity, joy or anything else that is promised to me in the Word, I receive as if it were a grain of mustard seed. (Mark 4:31-32.) Though my circumstances do not show a harvest, once I have planted my seed, no power on earth can stop it from coming to me.

Submit to the Process

My Prayer for Today

For the earth yields crops by itself: first the blade, then the head, after that the full grain in the head.
—Mark 4:28

Father, I know that the processes of faith take time. Therefore, I submit to patience. (James 1:4.) No matter what I see with my natural eyes, I know that I have what I believe. (1 Corinthians 5:7.) Harvest is in my future because I have presently received. Constantly remind me of Your Word, Lord. Fill my mind with references that strengthen my resolve so that I may receive in increased measure to the praise of Your glory.

My Confession for Today

All of my godly desires are manifested for me on a regular basis. When I speak in faith, the seed of my words are planted at the root of the problem. As I continue to affirm my faith, the seed is watered. I remove the weeds that choke my seed by rejecting thoughts of doubt and unbelief. (Mark 4:19.) I am a magnet for God's abundance. My harvest is a constantly flowing blessing in my life.

February 21

The Harvest Is the Goal

But when the grain ripens, immediately he puts in the sickle, because the harvest has come.
–Mark 4:29

My Prayer for Today

Father, I thank You for teaching me how life works. Through Your instruction I have come to know what it means to believe and receive. (Mark 11:24.) I am now attentive to the processes of faith and remain fully aware of the ripening harvest all around me. Give me wisdom and keen understanding to know the perfect timing to put in my sickle and reap the blessings You have given me.

My Confession for Today

I remain faithful and diligent, believing and speaking the Word into my life, and never allowing thoughts of doubt to progress in my mind. The Word within me grows and grows until I have such an abundant harvest that there is plenty left over to share with others in need and provide them with a place of refuge and rest. I welcome all of God's abundant blessings into my life. I am built for increase and fashioned for plenty. I draw prosperity to myself easily and joyfully every day of my life.

Don't Fear the Words of Others

My Prayer for Today

Father, I am intimately familiar with the criticisms of the faithless, and I thank You for shielding me against their many attacks. Their disapproval of my faith has no bearing on my commitment to do Your will. You are not the God of mediocrity and You get no glory from poverty. In You, I increase from faith to faith. (Romans 1:17.) I enjoy my life thoroughly and abound in Your provision.

My Confession for Today

I have no fear of the words of the enemy and his underlings. My Father has delivered me with a sure and certain deliverance. When the enemy comes against me, he will fall by a sword from his own kingdom. As for me, I flourish within the hedge of God's protection. (Job 1:10; Psalm 139:5.) I am healthy, wealthy, and wise. Love is the central principle that guides my purpose. (1 Corinthians 13:13; Ephesians 1:11.) Like my Father, I am a blessing to the world.

Isaiah said to them, "Thus you shall say to your master, 'Thus says the LORD: "Do not be afraid of the words which you have heard, with which the servants of the king of Assyria have blasphemed Me. Surely I will send a spirit upon him, and he shall hear a rumor and return to his own land; and I will cause him to fall by the sword in his own land."'"
–2 Kings 19:6-7

February 23

You Are Blessed Forever

For You, O my God, have revealed to Your servant that You will build him a house. Therefore Your servant has found it in his heart to pray before You. And now, LORD, You are God, and have promised this goodness to Your servant. Now You have been pleased to bless the house of Your servant, that it may continue before You forever; for You have blessed it, O LORD, and it shall be blessed forever.
−1 Chronicles 17:25-27

My Prayer for Today

Father, I thank You that as I build Your house, You in turn build mine. You have promised me this goodness and are pleased to perform it on my behalf. In You, I am blessed beyond measure, and what You have blessed is blessed forever!

My Confession for Today

I have confidence in my heavenly Father. He is on my side and I have no reason to fear. (Psalm 118:6.) I have His Word that He will build my house in safety. My family — all of my posterity — is blessed. I rejoice in God's blessings upon my family, for I have this confidence: what the Lord blesses is blessed forever!

Doubt Will Render You Powerless

My Prayer for Today

Father, teach me to reject false testimonies and bad reports. Teach me to focus solely on possibilities. I am called a believer, and I intend to be just that. Far be it from me to limit You in this world. You have chosen to pour Your power into the avenue of faith; therefore, I shall live by faith, receiving blessings in abundance and being an abundant blessing to all. (Habakkuk 2:4; Romans 1:17; Galatians 3:11; Hebrews 10:38; Proverbs 28:20.)

Now He could do no mighty work there, except that He laid His hands on a few sick people and healed them. And He marveled because of their unbelief. Then He went about the villages in a circuit, teaching.
—Mark 6:5–6

My Confession for Today

I am God's own faith warrior. I advance His kingdom with an effortlessness that awes my peers. I draw to myself all of the Lord's good and perfect gifts. (James 1:17.) I clearly understand my mission, and I thoroughly enjoy fulfilling it. I am powerful, joyful, industrious, creative, intelligent, faithful, and loving. With God as my ever-present and indwelling partner, I am a blessing to this world. (Hebrews 13:5.)

The Father's Presence Within You Produces Fruit

> *Do you not believe that I am in the Father, and the Father in Me? The words that I speak to you I do not speak on My own authority; but the Father who dwells in Me does the works. Believe Me that I am in the Father and the Father in Me, or else believe Me for the sake of the works themselves.*
> *—John 14:10-11*

My Prayer for Today

Lord, You are my Father and You dwell within me. You did not take up residence here for no purpose. There is a mission that You desire for me to accomplish in this life. (Ephesians 1:11.) You designed me to be the only one who can fulfill such a mission in the way You intend for it to be performed. The evidence of Your presence in my life is in the fruit that I produce. (Matthew 7:16.) You have given me words to speak and a Word to believe. Therefore, I choose to have faith in Your ability within me and faithfully do what You have called me to do.

My Confession for Today

I believe wholeheartedly that Jesus is in the Father and that the Father is in Jesus. Since I am in Christ Jesus, I am also in the Father, and the three of us are one. (John 17:22-23.) I now perform mighty miracles and deeds of power through Jesus' name. (Mark 16:17; John 14:13.) I can easily make money, stay healthy, and be a blessing to others. My employer/business is blessed because of me. I have a winner's spirit and make winners of everyone in my circle of influence. (1 Corinthians 15:57; 2 Corinthians 2:14-15.)

You Can Do What Jesus Did

My Prayer for Today

Father, I purpose in my heart to be disciplined with my words. You have taught me that faith filled words remove unwanted mountains and destroy oppressive yokes. Great works are performed by the fruit of my lips. (Isaiah 57:19) Therefore, I will not allow myself to develop a habit of speaking faithless words, nor will I allow idle words to become the regular pattern of speech in my life. I am wise enough to know that sticks and stones may break bones, but words can cause internal injuries that may never heal. (Proverbs 18:8 KJV.) Therefore, I will speak what is good and right that I may bring healing and prosperity to everyone I know. (Proverbs 15:23; 16:23-24.)

"Most assuredly, I say to you, he who believes in Me, the works that I do he will do also; and greater works than these he will do, because I go to My Father. And whatever you ask in My name, that I will do, that the Father may be glorified in the Son.
–John 14:12-13

My Confession for Today

My union with Jesus has given me abilities far beyond my natural capacity. I am fully capable of doing the very same things that He did in His earth walk. He has even made me able to do greater things than He did, because He has risen and gone on to the Father. (John 14:12.) I express my faith wisely and with purpose. I constantly advance, improve, and find ways to benefit others. Through faith I am a powerforce in this earth. (Hebrews 11.)

February 27

Jesus Is Still Working for You

If you ask anything in My name, I will do it.
—John 14:14

My Prayer for Today

Thank You, Jesus, for being my prayer partner. As I am in You, You are in the Father, and we three are one. (John 17:22-23.) That's a powerful partnership, and I don't take it for granted. I acknowledge that I am every bit a part of You, and You are every bit a part of me. I move forward in life with the confidence that my faith is backed by Your omnipotence and therefore my harvest is guaranteed.

My Confession for Today

Jesus Himself, through His name, brings to pass whatever I command in this natural world. Everything outside of His will must bow to His authority. (Philippians 2:9-10.) Whatever I ask for, in His name, I receive so that the Father may be glorified through the Son. (John 14:13.) Only through Jesus are my prayers answered. He has given me the very power of attorney to use His name. It is like a legal document proclaiming that all of the power that is in His name is now mine to use. I can freely draw upon all that He is and all that He has. Whatever I have asked for in His name, I can confidently claim as done.

Be Strong and Courageous for Those You Love

My Prayer for Today

Father, I know that sometimes in order to get out of problems, I must go through them. In this I have reason to smile, for I know that I am not alone. I am strong and of good courage because I know that You are with me. (Psalm 23:4.) I am strong for my people because I have Your Word that You will honor my faith. (John 12:26.) Therefore, I will do what is good in Your sight, overcome all adversity, and bring glory to Your name in this earth. (2 Corinthians 8:21.)

> Be of good courage, and let us be strong for our people and for the cities of our God. And may the LORD do what is good in His sight.
>
> –1 Chronicles 19:13

My Confession for Today

I am strong and very courageous! My actions are not birthed in fear, but in courage. I am a bold and fearless child of the living God, and I stand up courageously for my people. I am built for endurance. I never give in, and I never quit. Through me, the Lord does what is good and right in this earth.

February 29

Your Faith Makes You Well

Then Jesus said to him, "Go your way; your faith has made you well." And immediately he received his sight and followed Jesus on the road. —Mark 10:52

My Prayer for Today

Father, this is a good day to follow Jesus on the road! His way has become my way. What He does, I do. How he acts, I act. He is my Guide, my mentor, my brother, and my friend. (Psalm 32:8; Romans 8:29 NIV; James 2:23.) Thank You for Your Word, Father, that provides the models of behavior for me to follow. Thank You for the testimonies of Jesus and for revealing to me that I can live by the same anointing. By Jesus' example, I am destined to live a happy and successful life of faith. (Romans 1:17.)

My Confession for Today

I am a follower of Jesus. He is the model for my behavior and the wisdom by which I live. Through Him, I have strength to reach my destination. My personality radiates with His love and confidence. I am powerful, honest, influential, creative, diligent, resourceful, and sincere. My character does not waver when my audience changes. I am a steadfast and faithful servant of the Lord. (1 Corinthians 15:58.)

As Your Faith Increases, so Does Everything Else

My Prayer for Today

Father, I know that my future is found in my present actions. Therein is my hope and the promise of better things. As my faith is increased, so is my sphere of influence. The more I have, the more I can do, and the more I do, the more Your kingdom advances. In all of this, Father, help me to see where I best fit into the plan. Teach me to do exactly what I should do and to avoid being something that I am not meant to be.

> Not boasting of things beyond measure, that is, in other men's labors, but having hope, that as your faith is increased, we shall be greatly enlarged by you in our sphere.
>
> –2 Corinthians 10:15

My Confession for Today

I am created to be a unique individual with gifts and qualities distinct from all others. I am the perfect person to complete my mission in life. What I am called to do suits me to a "T." (Jeremiah 29:11.) It is the most joyfully fulfilling mission that I could possibly imagine. As I exercise my faith and move forward in my calling, the area of ministry around me greatly expands.

March 2

Your Faith Is the Same as Jesus' Faith

For I through the law died to the law that I might live to God. I have been crucified with Christ; it is no longer I who live, but Christ lives in me; and the life which I now live in the flesh I live by faith in the Son of God, who loved me and gave Himself for me.
—Galatians 2:19-20

My Prayer for Today

Father, I thank You for my identification with Christ Jesus. In Him I live and move and have my being. (Acts 17:28.) He is my complete redemption and forgiveness of my sins. (Ephesians 1:7 NIV.) Through His death, I died to the law and can now approach You without fear of rejection. As He is Your Son, I also am Your son/daughter. (Romans 8:29.) I am Yours and You are mine, and all hindrances to our fellowship are removed forever! (Mark 15:37-38; Hebrews 9:12, NLT.) For this I am eternally grateful, Father. All praise be to Your holy name.

My Confession for Today

I, through the Law, died to the Law, so that I may live for God. I am crucified with Christ. It is no longer I who live, but Christ lives in me. And the life that I now live, I live by the faith of the Son of God, who showed His love for me by becoming my sin substitute. All that I am, in righteousness, justification, redemption, and more is in Him. His faith is my faith and His life is my life.

You Have the Power of Grace

My Prayer for Today

I do not set aside the grace of God; for if righteousness comes through the law, then Christ died in vain.
—Galatians 2:21

Father, I thank You that right now I am considered as righteous as Jesus Himself. (2 Corinthians 5:21). I don't have to try to perfect myself in order for You to accept me; I am all that I need to be in Christ Jesus. He alone is my strength and my eternal ability to stand in Your presence without any sense of inadequacy. (Hebrews 4:14-16.) Therefore, I boldly claim my place and nuzzle snuggly between Your shoulders for all of eternity. (Deuteronomy 33:12.)

My Confession for Today

I absolutely refuse to set aside this wonderful grace and turn back to the Law, which produced in me spiritual death. (Romans 7:4-6.) Jesus did not die for me in vain. My righteousness does not come through the good deeds outlined in the Law, but by Jesus alone. (Romans 3:22,26.) Nothing, absolutely nothing can rob me of my place in Christ. From this day unto eternity, I claim my rightful place in the kingdom of almighty God.

March 4

Let It Be Unto You According to the Word

The angel...said to her..."For with God nothing will be impossible." Then Mary said, "Behold the maidservant of the Lord! Let it be to me according to your word." And the angel departed from her.
—Luke 1:35, 37-38

My Prayer for Today

Father, what an amazing faith example You have given me in Mary. Her unwavering belief in Your Word brought forth the greatest miracle of all. May I so honor You with my faith. Let it be unto me according to Your Word. Let every good promise be manifested in my life in all of its fullness, in Jesus' name.

My Confession for Today

With God, the Greater One who is within me, nothing is impossible. (1 John 4:4.) Every promise that He has given me has within it the power of fulfillment. (2 Corinthians 1:20.) Therefore, what He says that I am, that is what I am; and, what He says I can do, that is what I can do. (Philippians 4:13.) All that His Word declares about me is fulfilled as I take hold of it in faith and put it into operation in my life.

Be of Good Cheer, You Are a Child of Faith

My Prayer for Today

Father, I know that wisdom sees the world through other people's eyes. This woman did not ask for a miracle, but took it by faith. Then, when Jesus asked who touched Him, thinking she had violated some standard of ethics, she came trembling and confessing to Him. But Jesus answered, "Be of good cheer." How wonderful it is to know that You are pleased when we take what we need by faith. This day I rejoice with that woman and receive what I need by the power of the faith within me.

My Confession for Today

In Jesus, I have a keen perception of the workings of the power of God in my life. By faith, I am made well. I have entered into the peace that supercedes all worldly understanding. (Philippians 4:7.) My mind is alert and receptive to the truth. Every cell of my body works in the way that God intends for it to work. My focus is always on God's will and not human or religious understanding. (Psalm 40:8.)

Jesus said, "Who touched Me... for I perceived power going out from Me." Now when the woman saw that she was not hidden, she came trembling; and falling down before Him, she declared to Him in the presence of all the people the reason she had touched Him and how she was healed immediately. And He said to her, "Daughter, be of good cheer; your faith has made you well. Go in peace."
–Luke 8:45,46–48

March 6

You Are Perfected by Faith

This only I want to learn from you: Did you receive the Spirit by the works of the law, or by the hearing of faith? Are you so foolish? Having begun in the Spirit, are you now being made perfect by the flesh?
—Galatians 3:2-3

My Prayer for Today

Father, I reject the religious idea that once we are born again we have to perfect ourselves in order to keep our salvation. I began this new life in the Spirit, and I shall rely on the Spirit to preserve and perfect me to the end. Only one act of righteousness is worthy of mention and I didn't perform it, Jesus did. He took my place and all that He requires is that I receive His sacrifice by faith. That alone is my righteousness and justification.

My Confession for Today

I did not receive the Holy Spirit by the works of the Law, but by the hearing of faith. I am not so foolish as to turn to my own efforts to justify myself after I have admitted that I can't and that I need Jesus. I am not the fool who begins a new life in the Spirit, then turns back to works of righteousness to earn his justification. Jesus alone has made me perfect, not works!

The Lord Shall Raise You Up

My Prayer for Today

Father, I thank You that my sins are forgiven in Christ Jesus. You have taken away every barrier that could hinder me from receiving all that You have for me. The only barriers left are those I create myself. Raise me up above all doubt, Father. Bring elders into my midst who are full of faith and the Spirit. Reveal to me all that I must do in order to live a healthy and prosperous life. (3 John 1:2.)

My Confession for Today

All troubles, adversities, and misfortunes are subject to my faith. What I believe about myself and my environment is what lays the foundation for what I will have in my life. God's power is always working for me. (Ephesians 3:20.) When I pray my prayers of faith, the Lord is faithful to raise me up. When others pray for me, their prayers are added to mine, increasing my power to overcome troubles of every kind. (James 5:16.)

Is anyone among you sick? Let him call for the elders of the church, and let them pray over him, anointing him with oil in the name of the Lord. And the prayer of faith will save the sick, and the Lord will raise him up. And if he has committed sins, he will be forgiven.
—James 5:14-15

March 8

Be Fervent

The effective, fervent prayer of a righteous man avails much.
—James 5:16

My Prayer for Today

Father, I stir myself up with fervency. I direct my emotions to praise You with my whole heart. I reject doubt and fear, holding fast to Your Word with the courage of a lion. I declare with fanatical boldness that my God reigns. (Isaiah 52:7.) I know the One in whom I believe and I will not allow foolish vacillations to hinder my prayers. (2 Timothy 1:12.) May the heat of my words brand the devil's head that he may always be reminded of my victory.

My Confession for Today

I rest in full confidence that the Lord loves me and has forgiven all of my sins. (John 16:27; Colossians 1:14.) However, I am wise enough to know that all of my actions have consequences and that sin is a hindrance to my healing. (John 5:14.) Therefore, I live my life with wisdom, feeding my body what it needs and treating it the way that God intends for it to be treated. Through faith, I receive my healing and through wisdom, I keep it.

Be Wise, Strong, and of Good Courage

My Prayer for Today

Father, I take hold of the wisdom and understanding that You have promised me. You have anointed my mind with insight and cunning ability. You open Your Word to me as an unfailing guide. (Psalm 119:105.) In it, I find the strength and courage to face my enemies. I have no need to be afraid, for You are always with me to ensure my success.

My Confession for Today

I am a wise and productive son/daughter of the living God. I move forward in life with a powerful anointing. In all that I do, I achieve extraordinary success. (Joshua 1:7-8.) I laugh in the face of fear and doubt for I know the One in whom I have placed my trust. I am strong and of good courage for the Lord is always with me to shield me and give me the victory. (Matthew 28:20; Psalm 3:3; 1 Corinthians 15:57.)

Only may the LORD give you wisdom and understanding, and give you charge concerning Israel, that you may keep the law of the LORD your God. Then you will prosper, if you take care to fulfill the statutes and judgments with which the LORD charged Moses concerning Israel. Be strong and of good courage; do not fear nor be dismayed.
–1 Chronicles 22:12-13

March 10

Faith Is Your Connection to God's Unlimited Provision

Therefore He who supplies the Spirit to you and works miracles among you, does He do it by the works of the law, or by the hearing of faith?
—Galatians 3:5

My Prayer for Today

Father, I deeply appreciate all that You have provided for me. I know that without Jesus I would be wholly unworthy to claim anything from You. (2 Corinthians 1:20 NIV.) He alone is my claim to spiritual entitlements. I don't have to follow a list of rules to prove my worthiness, for I am already made worthy by His precious blood. (Romans 3:25; Ephesians 1:7.) Because of Him I now have every right to receive all that I desire and more by faith.

My Confession for Today

God does not give me His Spirit and do miracles in and through me because of the good works that I do, or because I am sinless. He does these things because I believe in His Word and speak it in the spirit of faith. (2 Corinthians 4:13.) My belief is the springboard for miracles in my life, not my works of righteousness. (Romans 3:27; 4:6.)

You Are Blessed with Abraham

My Prayer for Today

Father, once again I come before You to make my unwavering declaration that I believe. I believe that You are the one true God and that You bless those who put their trust in You. (John 17:3; Psalm 2:12.) I confess before You that I am a man/woman of faith. I am righteous in Christ Jesus and blessed with believing Abraham. I am a son/daughter of Abraham, not by bloodline or genealogy, but by the faith that has been credited to me for righteousness.

My Confession for Today

I consider Abraham a chief role model for my faith. As it is written, "[He] believed God, and it was credited to him as righteousness" (Romans 4:3 NIV.) I am blessed in every way that Abraham was blessed and more. (Hebrews 8:6 NIV). I never cringe at the promise, but receive it regardless of what my eyes see or what my body feels. (2 Corinthians 5:7.) The anointing of God on my life causes me to prosper more and more until my influence is felt by the world leaders of my day. (Daniel 2:46-48 NIV.)

> *Therefore know that only those who are of faith are sons of Abraham. And the Scripture, foreseeing that God would justify the Gentiles by faith, preached the gospel to Abraham beforehand, saying, "In you all the nations shall be blessed." So then those who are of faith are blessed with believing Abraham.*
> *—Galatians 3:7-9*

March 12

You Are Not Under the Law of Moses

For as many as are of the works of the law are under the curse; for it is written, "Cursed is everyone who does not continue in all things which are written in the book of the law, to do them."

—Galatians 3:10

My Prayer for Today

Father, I thank You that in Christ Jesus I am dead to the Law. (Romans 7:4.) The curse no longer has any legal claim on me. (Galatians 3:23-25.) The Book of the Law is wholly insignificant to my salvation. Jesus fulfilled it and set it aside for me. (Matthew 5:17.) Now all of my righteousness, justification, and redemption are found in Him. (1 Corinthians 1:30.) I do not look to my personal acts of righteousness to prove me worthy to approach You and receive what I desire. I come before You boldly and without hesitation, Father, for Jesus has made me worthy! (Hebrews 4:16.)

My Confession for Today

I will not put myself back under the Law, thereby putting myself under the curse, for it is written, "Cursed is anyone who does not continue to [or without fail] do everything written in the Book of the Law" (Galatians 3:10 NIV). Therefore, it is abundantly clear that I cannot be justified by the Law because I, along with everyone else in this world, have failed to keep it at one time or another. (Romans 3:20; John 7:19.)

In All Things, Live by Faith

That no one is justified by the law in the sight of God is evident, for "the just shall live by faith." Yet the law is not of faith, but "the man who does them [statutes, judgments] shall live by them."
—Galatians 3:11-12

My Prayer for Today

Father, in and of myself I have no defense that can vindicate me of wrongdoing. By myself, I am entirely guilty and worthy of condemnation. I have no excuse that can withstand the court of heaven, nor do I have acts of righteousness that can erase my guilt. I have only one claim and one defense: JESUS. I claim Him as my Lord, my brother, my friend, and my advocate. (Romans 8:29; James 2:23; 1 John 2:1.) I claim identification with all that He is and all that He did for me. (Colossians 1:19-22.) In Him, I now claim my rights as Your own son/daughter and heir to the kingdom. (Romans 8:16-17.) In all that I do, I shall live as a son/daughter of the kingdom is supposed to live: by faith.

My Confession for Today

I am justified by faith alone and not works. In Christ Jesus, I am now fully acquitted of any wrongdoing from the day of my birth to the day of my death. (John 3:16 MSG.) I am now perfect in the eyes of God and considered worthy of all that He has to offer.

March 14

You Are Redeemed by Faith

Christ has redeemed us from the curse of the law, having become a curse for us (for it is written, "Cursed is everyone who hangs on a tree"), that the blessing of Abraham might come upon the Gentiles in Christ Jesus, that we might receive the promise of the Spirit through faith.
—Galatians 3:13-14

My Prayer for Today

Father, I thank You that in Christ Jesus, I have found my redemption. He took my penalty so that through faith I might receive the blessing of Abraham and the promise of the Spirit. Because of Jesus, You are now my Father and I am Your son/daughter. The price has been paid on my behalf and my position has been secured for all of eternity. (1 Corinthians 6:20; Hebrews 10:10, NLT.)

My Confession for Today

Jesus redeemed me from the curse of the Law, being made a curse for me, for it is written, "Cursed is [the one] who is hung on a tree" (Galatians 3:13 NIV). He redeemed me so that, through Him, I could receive the same blessings that were showered upon Abraham, and so that through faith I could receive the promise of the Spirit. I am now a born-again, re-created, sinless child of the living God! (1 John 3:9; Romans 4:7-8; 6:10-12.)

You Are the Seed of Abraham in Christ Jesus

My Prayer for Today

Father, I thank You that in Christ Jesus I am now Abraham's seed. Jesus is now my covenant security and the guarantee of the promises. Through Him I claim every blessing of the covenant. Father, by Your Word I am blessed when I come in and blessed when I go out. (Deuteronomy 28:6.) Command Your blessing on my storehouses and on everything I set my hand to do. (Deuteronomy 28:8.) Let's show the world what it means to be a prince/princess in Your kingdom.

My Confession for Today

My covenant with God has been ratified. The promises were spoken to Abraham and his Seed. Jesus is that Seed and since I am in Him, the benefits belong to me. I am now the recipient of every good promise of the covenant and the blessing of Abraham has been placed upon me. (Galatians 3:14.) The only way it can ever be taken from me is for it to be taken from Jesus. He is the security of my covenant with God and the certainty that I will receive its blessings.

Brethren, I speak in the manner of men: Though it is only a man's covenant, yet if it is confirmed, no one annuls or adds to it. Now to Abraham and his Seed were the promises made. He does not say, "And to seeds," as of many, but as of one, "And to your Seed," who is Christ.
—Galatians 3:15-16

March 16

You Have Work to Do

David said to his son Solomon, "Be strong and of good courage, and do it; do not fear nor be dismayed, for the LORD God—my God—will be with you. He will not leave you nor forsake you, until you have finished all the work for the service of the house of the LORD."
—1 Chronicles 28:20

My Prayer for Today

Father, I am committed to You in every way. My life is Yours to mold into whatever You want it to be. Teach me Your way and reveal the plan and purpose that You have for me. (Psalm 27:11; Ephesians 1:11.) Above all else, help me to be the person You have created me to be. (Psalm 139:15-16.) Help me to see through the smoke screens that the devil lays before me and to ignore the religious ideas that are not Your will. (Isaiah 1:13 MSG.)

My Confession for Today

My Father gives me understanding in all that He has called me to do. I am well able to accomplish every task that is set before me. I have no reason to fear or be dismayed. I am strong and very courageous. I will not forget that my Father God is with me in everything that I do. He will not fail me. He sees to it that I have all that I need and stays with me as an ever-present help until all of the work is finished.

Work Your Faith Within the Confines of Love

My Prayer for Today

Father, help me to make love the fountain spring of all that I do. May every word that I speak and every thought that I think be saturated with love. There is no fear in love, therefore let courage be my mantra. (1 John 4:18.) May my reputation be one that breeds love, hope, and encouragement for all. In other words, Father, help me to be like You in every way.

My Confession for Today

By faith and the Holy Spirit's lead, I patiently wait in eager expectation for the righteousness for which I hope (or the answer to what I am praying for). I understand that it doesn't matter what kind of ritual I perform or what kind of penance I do. All that matters is that I am using my faith (affirming my belief through my actions and words) and expressing it through love.

We through the Spirit eagerly wait for the hope of righteousness by faith. For in Christ Jesus neither circumcision nor uncircumcision avails anything, but faith working through love.
–Galatians 5:5–6

March 18

God Has Taken His Stand with You

And he said, "Listen, all you of Judah and you inhabitants of Jerusalem, and you, King Jehoshaphat! Thus says the LORD to you: 'Do not be afraid nor dismayed because of this great multitude, for the battle is not yours, but God's.'"
—2 Chronicles 20:15

My Prayer for Today

Father, when I look at the vastness of Your creation, the huge stars, the billions of galaxies, and the tininess of earth, I can seem so small and insignificant. But what is size when the God of all creation dwells within me? (Genesis 1:1; 1 Corinthians 3:16.) What is strength when the Greater One has filled me with His own power to succeed? (1 John 4:4; 2 Timothy 1:7.) I know that no matter what I face, no matter what the odds or the enemy, I have the victory. (1 Corinthians 15:57.) Knowing this, I find no cause for fear. Stress and anxiety will have to seek their shelter elsewhere, for they have no place with me.

My Confession for Today

I have set my face like flint to be true to the Lord. (Isaiah 50:7.) I hold fast to His promises and trust in the security of our covenant. I remain confident that when the enemy attacks me with a great horde of allies bent on my destruction, the Lord shall stand to His feet and make His proclamation, "This battle is Mine!" Whom shall I fear? (Psalm 27:1.) Who can defeat my Father in heaven? He is the Lord of hosts. (Isaiah 1:24.) I shall not be afraid. I shall take my position and stand my ground!

Believe God—Honor His Prophets

My Prayer for Today

Father, when You speak a word to Your prophets, giving them wisdom and warning for Your church, I take it as the very breath from Your lips.I believe in You with my whole heart, and so I am established. I believe Your true prophets, and therefore I prosper. Yet guard me, Father, for there are false prophets in the earth. (Matthew 7:15-16.) Guard me against their tyranny and greed so that I may not stumble in this walk of faith.

My Confession for Today

I listen for my Father's commands. I take heed to the voice of His prophets and I prosper in the midst of the turmoil. I praise His name for the victory even in the heat of the battle. I give Him glory, for His mercy and loving-kindness endure forever! (Psalm 106:1.) It is the Lord who fights my battles. (Deuteronomy 20:4.) All of my enemies fall in a great destruction. As for me, I am showered with gifts and an endless supply of blessings. (Ezekiel 34:26 NLT.)

> *So they rose early in the morning and went out into the Wilderness of Tekoa; and as they went out, Jehoshaphat stood and said, "Hear me, O Judah and you inhabitants of Jerusalem: Believe in the LORD your God, and you shall be established; believe His prophets, and you shall prosper."*
> *–2 Chronicles 20:20*

March 20

Watch Your Mouth

For we all stumble in many things. If anyone does not stumble in word, he is a perfect man, able also to bridle the whole body.
–James 3:2

My Prayer for Today

Father, train me in the ways of words. Teach me to speak what is good and right. Teach me to bridle my tongue that I may control my destiny. I know that to change my life, I must change my attitude; to change my attitude, I must change my words; and to change my words, I must change what I believe. Therefore, help me to believe, in line with Your Word, what I cannot see so that I may live a life that glorifies You in every way. (2 Corinthians 5:7.)

My Confession for Today

My words are the bridle that guides my whole body and like the rudder of a ship, they will take me where I want to go (or where I don't want to go if I'm not careful). My tongue, though small in comparison to the other parts of my body, is powerful beyond measure. With it, I am able to make great boasts that can bring either blessings or disaster into my life. (Proverbs 18:21.) Its power is comparable to the way a small spark can set an entire forest on fire. (James 3:3-6.)

Take Heed to Wisdom

My Prayer for Today

> Whoever listens to me will dwell safely, and will be secure, without fear of evil.
> —Proverbs 1:33

Father, make me wise that I may dwell safely and be secure, without the fear of evil. Give me a thorough understanding of the ways of faith. Teach me to program my mind to believe the right things so that the foundations of my words may be sound. Fill the treasury of my heart with good references and remind me of them when I face the troubles of the day. (1 Samuel 30:6.)

My Confession for Today

I heed the ways of wisdom and live my life in safety. I am at peace—free from the fear that comes from an evil report. (Psalm 112:7.) By the guidance of the Spirit, I always make the right decisions. (John 16:13.) I forget past mistakes and only retrieve references that are conducive to powerful living. I am free in Christ to be who I am and to live in the way that brings me the most joy and fulfillment. It is a tremendous pleasure and honor to live within the will of my God.

March 22

Rely on God Before Men

The fear of man brings a snare, but whoever trusts in the LORD shall be safe.
—Proverbs 29:25

My Prayer for Today

Father, You are the chief mentor in my life. All of the advice of men must come second to Your counsel. (Psalm 1:1; 73:24.) When men bring threats and fearful tidings, I do not fear them; in You alone I place my trust. You are the God of all the universe and are well able to protect me. I am safe and secure in the palm of Your hand. (John 10:29.)

My Confession for Today

I am a brave man/woman. I fully understand that my circumstances are subject to my faith. (2 Corinthians 4:18.) I can change anything in my life that does not bring glory to God. I am fully committed to my Father. I do His will in my life without complaining or faultfinding. My faith moves mountains today, making room for all of the blessings God wants me to enjoy. (Mark 11:23; Psalm 84:12.)

Let Not Your Heart Be Troubled

My Prayer for Today

Peace I leave with you, My peace I give to you; not as the world gives do I give to you. Let not your heart be troubled, neither let it be afraid.
—John 14:27

Father, I am not concerned about the troubles that I face. I have You, therefore I have everything. The things that I can lose are nothing when compared with You. (Philippians 3:8.) You create all and hold it together by the word of Your power. (Hebrews 1:3.) If I lost everything but my enthusiasm for You, I know You would return me to victory. I do not have to trust what the world has to offer; I have what my Father has to offer. Everything else pales in comparison.

My Confession for Today

I have, at this moment, the very peace of Jesus within my heart. He has given it to me, not as the world gives, but as He gives. It is mine forever. He will never take it from me. I will not allow my heart to be troubled or afraid. In Jesus, I have a boldness of faith and confidence that puts me over in every situation.

March 24

God Will Strengthen You, Help You, and Uphold You

Fear not, for I am with you; be not dismayed, for I am your God. I will strengthen you, yes, I will help you, I will uphold you with My righteous right hand.
—Isaiah 41:10

My Prayer for Today

Father, I know that the strong edify and encourage, while the weak criticize and discourage. You are the strongest of the strong. You are always with me to build me up when I am feeling down. You strengthen me and assist me when I am feeling overwhelmed. You always uphold me with Your righteous right hand so that I may never be destroyed. To You I give my whole allegiance. You alone are worthy of all praise, honor, and glory.

My Confession for Today

I have no cause to fear, for my God is with me. I will not be dismayed, for God is my Father and He has promised to never leave me, nor forsake me. (Hebrews 13:5.) He strengthens me and assists me in every circumstance. He upholds me with His righteous (His faithful, reliable) right hand so that my victory is made certain.

You Are the Lord's and He Is Always with You

My Prayer for Today

Father, You are my Creator. You took the time and care to mold me into the person I see in the mirror every day. I know that You do nothing without a purpose. (Romans 8:28.) So, my life has a purpose. (Ephesians 1:11.) When I see the care that You put into me, I find no cause to be afraid. (Psalm 139:14.) You call me by my name and claim me as Your own. (Isaiah 43:1.) You are jealous for me and love me with a passion that defies my critics. (Deuteronomy 4:24; 2 Corinthians 12:2.) No matter what I face, You are always with me. Even in the midst of the most disastrous circumstances, You are there to pull me through.

My Confession for Today

I have no cause to fear, for I am redeemed! God called to me personally, speaking my name and calling me His own. I belong to God. I am His own son/daughter and He loves me with all of His heart. (Jeremiah 31:3.) When I pass through the troubles of life, He is with me. The raging rivers cannot sweep over me. I walk through fiery trials with confidence and emerge unharmed. I stand in the midst of Satan's fire, shielded by God's hedge of protection. (Psalm 139:5.) Not even the smell of the smoke can touch me.

But now, thus says the LORD, who created you, O Jacob, and He who formed you, O Israel: "Fear not, for I have redeemed you; I have called you by your name; you are Mine. When you pass through the waters, I will be with you; and through the rivers, they shall not overflow you. When you walk through the fire, you shall not be burned, nor shall the flame scorch you."
–Isaiah 43:1-2

March 26

God Will Not Give You Cause to Be Ashamed

Do not fear, for you will not be ashamed; neither be disgraced, for you will not be put to shame; for you will forget the shame of your youth, and will not remember the reproach of your widowhood anymore. For your Maker is your husband, the LORD of hosts is His name; and your Redeemer is the Holy One of Israel; He is called the God of the whole earth.
–Isaiah 54:4–5

My Prayer for Today

Father, I trust You with all of my heart. Your grace surrounds me like a shield lifting me to heights I never could imagine. (Psalm 5:12.) Shame and disgrace are no longer a part of my life. You are my Maker and my Redeemer. You give me passion and purpose so that I can live my life with absolute fulfillment. (Ephesians 1:11.) Make me self-aware that I may know my calling. Show me my gifts and give me direction to use them. I know You are good to me and that my occupation in life is found in the things I most love to do. You are perfect in all of Your ways and You make my life's mission totally suited to my nature and personality. Give me wisdom, Father, to know what that is.

My Confession for Today

I have no fear of shame, disgrace, or humiliation, for I am united in a perfect covenant partnership with my heavenly Father. (Hebrews 8:6 NLT.) He works both in and through me to make me victorious in every circumstance. (Philippians 2:13; 1 Corinthians 15:57.) I do nothing apart from His counsel, and all that I do prospers without fail. (Psalm 1:1-3.)

Abide in Jesus and Let His Words Abide in You

My Prayer for Today

Father, the walk of faith that You have called me to is a walk that bears fruit. Therefore, teach me the processes of receiving. Show me how to get things done with excellence. Make my life one of superior quality, reflecting Your character in every way. Bring to my remembrance all that You have taught me in Your Word. (John 14:26.) Show me a vision of my future and reveal the plan that I must follow to reach it. (Jeremiah 29:11.)

If you abide in Me, and My words abide in you, you will ask what you desire, and it shall be done for you. By this My Father is glorified, that you bear much fruit; so you will be My disciples.
–John 15:7- 8

My Confession for Today

I am in vital union with Jesus, living and remaining in Him continually. His Word dwells within me, rooted and grounded within the depths of my heart. Through the Word, I have a complete revelation of the will and purpose of my Father. As a result, whatever I ask of the Father in Jesus' name, in line with the Word and in incessantly active faith, I am guaranteed to receive. (John 14:14.) My Father is honored and glorified when I bear an abundance of fruit. By this, I show myself to be a true disciple of Jesus.

March 28

You Are Established in Righteousness

In righteousness you shall be established; you shall be far from oppression, for you shall not fear; and from terror, for it shall not come near you.
—Isaiah 54:14

My Prayer for Today

Father, I thank You that I am an established man/woman. I am the righteousness of God in Christ Jesus my Lord. (2 Corinthians 5:21.) I am far from oppression, for You have shielded me on all sides. (Psalm 5:12.) Fear and terror are far from me as I step forward in the faith plan You have revealed to me. I am committed, devoted, steadfast, and persistent. I turn neither to the right hand nor to the left, but remain fast at Your heels as You guide me on the paths of this life. (Joshua 1:7; Psalm 16:11.)

My Confession for Today

I choose to be a brave and powerful man/woman of God. I have complete authority over all fear, anxiety, stress, and terror, and cast them far from my life. (Luke 10:19.) If I come under attack in any way, I know it is not the Lord's doing. All of His actions toward me are for good and never evil. It is He who gives me strength to conquer the enemy. (Psalm 68:35.) No weapon formed against me can prevail over me. This is part of my inheritance as God's son/daughter and my righteousness and justification come from Him. (Isaiah 54:17.)

Salvation Is God's Gift to You

My Prayer for Today

Father, no matter how much work I do in the Spirit, I always remain aware that none of it earns me points toward salvation. I am saved by grace through faith, and this is not of myself, but is Your gift to me. An eternity of bliss is mine forever, secured by the blood of Jesus and the seal of the Holy Spirit. (John 14:1-3; Revelation 1:5; Ephesians 1:13.) I need not look to myself at all to receive or maintain what You have blessed me with as a free gift. I stand in righteousness, not of myself, but as a recipient of the sacrifice You made for me. (1 Corinthians 1:30 NLT.)

For by grace you have been saved through faith, and that not of yourselves; it is the gift of God, not of works, lest anyone should boast.
—Ephesians 2:8-9

My Confession for Today

It is by grace that I have been saved through faith—and this doesn't come to me through my own striving to obtain or even maintain it, for it is God's gift to me. My salvation does not come to me by works, by penance, or by anything else that I can do other than just receive it. I can in no way boast about what I have done to gain God's favor and love. It has been given to me as a gift by grace alone.

March 30

You Are God's Offspring

"In Him we live and move and have our being. As also some of your own poets have said, 'We are His offspring.'"
—Acts 17:28

My Prayer for Today

Father, I thank You that You have made me Your own son/daughter. I am a new creation in Christ Jesus, born again in the Spirit, recreated in absolute perfection, built to be a child of Your very loins, and patterned to be like You in every way. (2 Corinthians 5:17; Genesis 1:26.) You are first and foremost omniscient and eternal, and infinitely higher than all. (John 8:58; Revelation 1:8.) You are forever above me, forever my superior, and forever my Lord. (Isaiah 45:22, 55:8-9.) Yet, I am born of you. You are my own Father, my love, my friend, my mentor, my Savior, and my God. (Isaiah 38:17; Proverbs 18:24.)Forever I swear allegiance to Your glorious name!

My Confession for Today

I am the offspring of God. When people see me, they see Him in me. (John 17:21,23.) I take after Him in every way. I look like Him, talk like Him, and live like Him. My hands are wrapped within His coattails and my eyes never leave Him. When He moves, I move. What He says, I confirm. He is my greatest hero and I worship Him in every way.

No One Is More Anointed or Powerful than You

My Prayer for Today

Father, I thank You that You created me as one among many equals. No one else is more important, more powerful, or more anointed than me. (Romans 8:11 MSG.) I do not pattern myself after others, trying to mimic their ways in order to be what they are. I know that I am fearfully and wonderfully made, with unique talents and gifts that I alone can share. (Psalm 139:14.) The copycat is always a step behind, so why should I be a step behind when I am created to take the lead? (Deuteronomy 28:13.) No, Father, I will not dishonor You by trying to be anything other than what You have created me to be, and I will not exalt another to receive honors that You have not given. (Romans 12:4-5; Ephesians 4:11-13.)

Elijah was a man with a nature like ours, and he prayed earnestly that it would not rain; and it did not rain on the land for three years and six months. And he prayed again, and the heaven gave rain, and the earth produced its fruit.
–James 5:17-18

My Confession for Today

I am the equal of Moses, Elijah, and every hero of faith. Elijah himself was just a man. He was not a unique creation who was given rare gifts so he could do things better than I can. His spiritual capacity was no greater than mine. He was anointed of God, and so am I. (2 Corinthians 1:21.) If Elijah, then, being just a man, could produce miraculous things by faith, I can do such things as well; for God is no respecter of persons and will hear my prayer just as He heard Elijah's. (Acts 10:34.)

April 1

Don't Be Intimidated

"Do not be afraid of their faces, for I am with you to deliver you," says the LORD. Then the LORD put forth His hand and touched my mouth, and the LORD said to me: "Behold, I have put My words in your mouth."
—Jeremiah 1:8-9

My Prayer for Today

Father, I thank You for the revelation knowledge of Your Word. Open the eyes of my understanding and train me how to use it for Your glory. (Ephesians 1:18.) You gave the Word to me to keep me on track and bring into existence the life for which I am most suited. So, no matter what the circumstance or situation, I won't be intimidated for I know that I have the victory. (1 Corinthians 15:57.)

My Confession for Today

I go everywhere the Lord sends me and do whatever He commands me to do. I do not allow fear or intimidation to hinder me in my calling. I know full well that God's power is within me and nothing can defeat me. (Romans 8:11; 2 Corinthians 12:9.) I have His Word in my heart and in my mouth. (Matthew 12:34.) It is a powerforce that causes what I desire to be manifested in my life. When I speak it in faith for an intended result, I have the things that I say. (Mark 11:23-24.)

Leaven Your Life with Faith

My Prayer for Today

Again He said, "To what shall I liken the kingdom of God? It is like leaven, which a woman took and hid in three measures of meal till it was all leavened."
–Luke 13:20-21

Father, my first priority is to honor You with my life. Therefore, make me wise in the ways of faith. Build within me habits that are essential to a successful walk of faith. Help me to always recognize that there are steps that I must take, seeds that must be planted, and a gestation period for those seeds to grow. (Mark 4:26-28.) Your Word declares that the benefits of Your promises are obtained through faith and patience. (Hebrews 6:12.) So I shall let patience have her perfect work allowing for the growth and development of the goal I intend to achieve. (James 1:4.)

My Confession for Today

I operate the principles of the kingdom faithfully. They are like the tiny bit of yeast that it takes to make the bread rise. When I put them into operation, it does not look like anything is happening. But I know that, in time, the yeast of God's kingdom principles will infiltrate the whole lump (every issue of my life) until each part of it is saturated and controlled by them.

April 3

You Are Held Secure by the Power of God Through Faith

Blessed be the God and Father of our Lord Jesus Christ, who according to His abundant mercy has begotten us again to a living hope through the resurrection of Jesus Christ from the dead, to an inheritance incorruptible and undefiled and that does not fade away, reserved in heaven for you, who are kept by the power of God through faith for salvation ready to be revealed in the last time.
–1 Peter 1:3-5

My Prayer for Today

Father, the resurrection has birthed in me a living hope. I know that there is an inheritance that awaits me that is undefiled and incorruptible, and that through faith I am kept by Your power until that glorious day when I enter the gates of heaven to receive it. It is Your power alone, Father, that provides my present security, and You alone are the key to my eternal inheritance.

My Confession for Today

God, who in His great mercy towards me has given me the New Birth, a living hope through the resurrection of Jesus, is now my own Father. I am a partaker of an inheritance that can never perish, spoil, or fade. Through faith, I am shielded by God's power until the coming of the salvation that is to be revealed in the last time. In that day all aspects of the curse will be removed and I will no longer have to fight to maintain what is mine as a child of God. (1 Timothy 6:12.)

Genuine Faith Is a Priceless Commodity

My Prayer for Today

Father, I choose to live my life like a well from which others can draw faith. With Your perpetual assistance I can overcome any trial, obstacle, or adverse situation. (Romans 8:37.) I will not give in to doubt or waver in the sea of unbelief. I trust in Your Word and the power that You have promised. By faith, and through the power of the living Word, I can receive any desire of my heart. (Proverbs 10:24.) Gold and precious stones will perish, but my faith is spiritual and eternal. It shall never perish.

My Confession for Today

I greatly rejoice that, even though I now must persevere through many griefs and trials, eternity awaits me at the end of the race. Griefs and trials are but an opportunity for me to show that my faith is genuine. My faith is precious to me—a commodity of greater worth than gold. Like gold, it is proved genuine when I am tested by trials and tribulations of every kind. But unlike gold, which perishes even when refined, my faith shall endure in abundant production and will result in praise, glory and honor when Jesus returns.

In this you greatly rejoice, though now for a little while, if need be, you have been grieved by various trials, that the genuineness of your faith, being much more precious than gold that perishes, though it is tested by fire, may be found to praise, honor, and glory at the revelation of Jesus Christ.
–Peter 1:6-7

April 5

Faith Is Your Salvation

[Jesus Christ] whom having not seen you love. Though now you do not see Him, yet believing, you rejoice with joy inexpressible and full of glory, receiving the end of your faith—the salvation of your souls.
–1 Peter 1:8-9

My Prayer for Today

Father, You are the center of all my joy. The one thing that brings me elation above all else is my closeness with You. (Psalm 16:11.) I love You with all of my heart. The greatest benefit of my salvation is the privilege of being with You. To be one with You, to enjoy Your presence and fellowship, to know that You are forever my Father and my friend brings me joy inexpressible and full of glory.

My Confession for Today

Though I have not seen Jesus, I love Him and believe in Him. The joy He brings me is beyond description. All of my deepest hopes and dreams are realized in Him. In Him I have been made new. (2 Corinthians 5:17.) Every good and perfect blessing is now mine to enjoy. Because of Christ's sacrifice, God commands the blessing upon me and sees to it that the words that I speak come to pass. (Galatians 3:13-14; Hebrews 3:1.)

Love Life and See Good Days

My Prayer for Today

Father, I truly desire to love my life. It is only my mistakes that have caused me to reap destruction. But this is a new day. You have revealed to me the ways of faith and the power that it wields. By faith, I shall see good days. (Hebrews 11:1.) Your eyes are always upon me and Your ears are open to my prayers. You cause the things that I believe and speak to come to pass so long as I do not waver. (Romans 4:16-21.) There is no reason why I cannot build a life that is truly worth living.

My Confession for Today

I am a lover of life who continually sees good days. I refrain my tongue from speaking negative things. I speak the truth at all times and never allow lies and deceit to become a part of me. I turn away from evil and only do that which is good. I am a seeker of peace and pursue it with all of my will. The Lord's eyes never leave me and I rest in His embrace. He is my shield of protection in this life. (Psalm 18:2.) His ears are always opened to my prayers so that He can fulfill His Word on my behalf. (Numbers 23:19.)

For "He who would love life and see good days, let him refrain his tongue from evil, and his lips from speaking deceit. Let him turn away from evil and do good; let him seek peace and pursue it. For the eyes of the LORD are on the righteous, and His ears are open to their prayers; but the face of the LORD is against those who do evil."

–1 Peter 3:10-12

April 7

Rebuke the Winds and the Waves

[Jesus] said to them, "Why are you fearful, O you of little faith?" Then He arose and rebuked the winds and the sea, and there was a great calm.
–Matthew 8:26

My Prayer for Today

Father, as fear is the mirror image (or reverse) of faith, it surely must be just as powerful. Yet, decision overpowers them both. I will not allow fear to rain its torment and destruction upon me. Life and good things are my inheritance. I am a child of faith; therefore, adverse circumstances are not a problem for me. They must yield to the sound of my voice as I speak in faith. (Mark 11:23.)

My Confession for Today

Nothing is powerful enough to cancel my faith. So when the winds and the waves roar, I remain confident. I am headed in the direction of my dreams. I have spoken the end from the beginning and therefore it is done. (Isaiah 46:10.) Even when those around me panic because of the circumstances, I remain steady as a rock. My faith is in play and my destiny is sealed. (Ephesians 1:13.)

Be a Hearer, Speaker, and Doer of the Word

My Prayer for Today

> The word is very near you, in your mouth and in your heart, that you may do it.
> —Deuteronomy 30:14

Father, Your Word is the light by which I live. (Psalm 119:105.) Its power sees me through the tribulations of life so that I may reap the benefits of Your blessings. Teach me to be persistent, Father. Open Your Word to me that I may know how to use it to advance Your kingdom and bring Your goodness to every area of my life. (Ezra 7:9-10.)

My Confession for Today

The Word of faith is in my mouth continually. I keep it near to me — in my mouth, in my mind, and in my spirit—so that I may do and have what I say. I do not just hear it and speak it, but I do it. (James 2:18,26.) I am focused, steadfast, single-minded, and action oriented. By this, my faith is made complete and I receive all that I desire and more.

April 9

Choose the Good Things of God

See, I [Moses] have set before you today life and good, death and evil, in that I command you today to love the LORD your God, to walk in His ways, and to keep His commandments, His statutes, and His judgments, that you may live and multiply; and the LORD your God will bless you in the land which you go to possess.
–Deuteronomy 30:15-16

My Prayer for Today

Father, You have placed before me life and good things, and knowledge of how to avoid death and evil things: in Your Word You instruct me in the way that I should go so that I may live my life in happiness and contentment. (Deuteronomy 28.) All of Your commands are for good and not one is burdensome. All of your judgments are pure and right. Your ways bring life, increase, and blessing as opposed to sickness, poverty, and destruction. It's not that hard of a choice, Father. I choose life!

My Confession for Today

The Lord has set before me life and good things, but death and evil things are also available. The choice is mine. I choose to adhere to the statutes of His covenant. I walk in all of His ways so that I may live His abundant life and multiply in this earth. Because I have chosen life, my Father is very pleased to bless me with His divine favor, good fortune, happiness, prosperity, and wonderful things of every kind.

Face Stress with an Attitude of Perseverance

My Prayer for Today

Father, thank You for training me to be a good soldier of the faith. (2 Timothy 2:3-4.) The devil can roar and prowl all he wants; he'll gain no foothold here. It doesn't matter what I face or suffer; I will never give in, and I will never quit. Strengthen me for the battle, Father. Establish me as a steadfast and immovable warrior who endures to the end. (Matthew 10:22.)

My Confession for Today

I remain self-controlled and alert, for I know that my enemy, the devil, prowls around like a roaring lion looking for someone to devour. I am fully aware of his evil schemes and he can never catch me by surprise. I resist him, standing firm in faith. My Father, the God of all grace, who called me to His eternal glory in Christ, will Himself restore and deliver me out of any and every adverse circumstance the devil devises against me. (Psalm 34:10; Proverbs 11:8.) In Christ, I am strong, firm, steadfast, and immovable—a solid rock who gives the devil a perpetual headache.

Be sober, be vigilant; because your adversary the devil walks about like a roaring lion, seeking whom he may devour. Resist him, steadfast in the faith, knowing that the same sufferings are experienced by your brotherhood in the world. But may the God of all grace, who called us to His eternal glory by Christ Jesus, after you have suffered a while, perfect, establish, strengthen, and settle you.

–1 Peter 5:8-10

April 11

Contend Earnestly for the Faith

Beloved, while I was very diligent to write to you concerning our common salvation, I found it necessary to write to you exhorting you to contend earnestly for the faith which was once for all delivered to the saints.
—Jude 1:3

My Prayer for Today

Father, grant me revelation of the truth. Fill me with the knowledge of the true faith, once for all delivered to the saints. Our common salvation comes through believing and speaking: confessing the lordship of Jesus and believing that He is raised from the dead.(Romans 10:9.) Faith is the key, Father. It is the key to receiving all that I need in this life and beyond. (Romans 4:16 NLT.) Train me thoroughly, then, so that I may be abundantly productive.

My Confession for Today

I earnestly contend for the faith that was once for all delivered to the saints. I cannot be duped by critics who try to add to Jesus' finished work. All that I am and all that I have is found in Christ. All that He did is set to my account. (Philippians 4:17.) His righteousness is now my righteousness, and His faith is now my faith. (Romans 3:22; (Galatians 2:20 KJV.) I fully understand faith's nature and its production of true holiness and provision for my life.

Faith Is Your Victory!

My Prayer for Today

Father, I thank You that through faith I have become Your very own son/daughter. I am now Your offspring made to be like You in every way. (Acts 17:28; Genesis 1:26.) Thank You, Father, for the revelation of faith which brings me victory in every circumstance.

> For whatever is born of God overcomes the world. And this is the victory that has overcome the world—our faith.
> *–1 John 5:4*

No matter what I face, I can count on You to partner with me to ensure my success. Teach me to have complete control of my thought life, Father. (2 Corinthians 10:5.) Show me how to focus my attention and powerfully express my unwavering belief.

My Confession for Today

I have been born of God and have overcome the world. My faith is my victory. All circumstance must yield to it. Through my faith, I overcome obstacles, setbacks, and troubles of every kind. The yoke that I have been given is easy and its burden is light. (Matthew 11:30.) There is nothing that I must do that should weigh heavy on me. My faith mission is easy to perform. It is the joy of my life and my everlasting fulfillment.

April 13

God Performs His Word Today

Then the LORD said to me, "You have seen well, for I am ready to perform My word."

–Jeremiah 1:12

My Prayer for Today

Father, I recognize that You are honorable in all things. Your Word is not like the word of men. When You speak, it is accomplished. (Psalm 33:9) Not a single word that passes from Your lips goes unfulfilled. Therein is my confidence, Lord. When I put my trust in Your Word, it is well placed. (Psalm 119:42-47.) All that You have promised is fulfilled in me as I speak Your Word in faith.

My Confession for Today

The Lord watches over His Word to see that it is performed in my life. When I meditate upon it, pour my belief into it, and speak it for an intended result, it goes forth from my lips and begins to change my circumstances. (Romans 10:8; Mark 11:23-24.) This pleases the Lord and He is overjoyed to work together with me to get things done. (Hebrews 11:6.) He does not let any of my words fall to the ground but fulfills every single one. (1 Samuel 3:19.)

This Is a Day of Rejoicing

My Prayer for Today

Father, I thank You for being such a kind, loving, and thoroughly capable mentor. You coax me in the way that I should go. You lead me in a plain path for Your name's sake. (Psalm 23:3.) Every day You give me new reasons to praise You. You are always speaking to me and leading me on a triumphant journey toward Your throne. In You, I have resources beyond measure as well as the ability to receive and enjoy them. (Philippians 4:19.) All praise be to Your holy name.

My Confession for Today

The Holy Spirit leads me with a gentle hand, speaking to me softly and drawing me along a miracle filled path glorifying the name of Jesus. (John 16:13.) He gives me abundance in the midst of the desert and opens a door of hope in a troubled land. I respond to Him as a child, in absolute faith and trust. He is not a taskmaster to me, but my covenant partner and friend.

Therefore, behold, I will allure her, will bring her into the wilderness, and speak comfort to her. I will give her her vineyards from there, and the Valley of Achor as a door of hope; she shall sing there, as in the days of her youth, as in the day when she came up from the land of Egypt.
–Hosea 2:14-15

April 15

The Only Thought that Counts Is the One You Believe

As soon as Jesus heard the word that was spoken, He said to the ruler of the synagogue, "Do not be afraid; only believe."

—Mark 5:36

My Prayer for Today

Father, every day this world furnishes me with an abundance of opportunity for doubt. My faith is attacked regularly by those who have only known fear in their lives. Help me to live above it, Father. (Colossians 3:2.) Your Word commands me to be strong and of good courage. (Joshua 1:9.) I have no reason to fear, for You are always with me and You are on my side. (Psalm 118:6.) You, the very Creator of all, have my best interests at heart. Therefore, I shall not be afraid, but only believe.

My Confession for Today

When I am faced with an evil report in the natural realm, I remain calm and continue to believe. (Psalm 112:7.) I do not allow fear to rob me of what God has done for me. My faith brings to pass what I need regardless of what is seen or known in the natural world. When I speak the convictions of my heart, the words go forth to create new circumstances. (Matthew 12:34; Luke 6:45.) The Spirit works together with my thoughts to make them my experience. (John 14:26; Galatians 5:25.)

Your Spirit Is Empowered with God's Strength

My Prayer for Today

Father, I thank You that the anointed One and His anointing dwells within me. I am a man/woman of power and authority. I am Your child, recreated and born from above, a member of the royal court of heaven. I stand by grace and live by faith. (Romans 5:2; Galatians 2:20.) You take all of my past mistakes and use them as stepping stones on the road of victory. Because of Your commitment to me, Father, I have nothing to fear. Earth is my training ground and heaven is my home. Nothing will ever change that.

That He would grant you, according to the riches of His glory, to be strengthened with might through His Spirit in the inner man, that Christ may dwell in your hearts through faith.
—Ephesians 3:16–17

My Confession for Today

Out of His glorious riches, God strengthens me with unfathomable power, through the Holy Spirit. It is my spirit that receives this strength. I have been made new so that Christ (the anointed One and His anointing) can dwell in my spirit through faith. It is this power within me that brings forth the things that I desire into the earth.

April 17

Be at Peace in the Midst of the Storm

They came to Him and awoke Him, saying, "Master, Master, we are perishing!" Then He arose and rebuked the wind and the raging of the water. And they ceased, and there was a calm. But He said to them, "Where is your faith?"
—Luke 8:24–25

My Prayer for Today

Father, in You I never have reason to fear. No matter what happens, though storms may rage, and the threat of danger lurks from without and from within, You are always with me. I rest in Your embrace, Father. What have I to fear? What can man do to me? (Psalm 118:6.) Is there a single circumstance more powerful than You? Even if death itself were to overwhelm me, You are always there to raise me up. (John 6:40.) Therefore, I will not give in to fear, but continue to believe.

My Confession for Today

I am a man/woman of faith. I reject all fear and anxiety in my life, casting it all on the shoulders of the One who bears my burdens. (1 Peter 5:7.) I am not seized by fear in any circumstance. I have the Word on my lips that covers and protects me in any situation. I use my faith every hour of every day, believing and speaking to the problem, and commanding the circumstance to get in line with the perfect will of God. (Mark 11:23-24.) I am a victor here, not a victim, and I am in command of any given situation.

You Never Have to Fight Alone

My Prayer for Today

Father, there are those who hate me without good cause. Take note of them, Lord, and confront them on my behalf. You are my strength and my refuge. I have no trust in the might of my arm or the weapons of this world. (Psalm 147:10-11 MSG.) My trust is in You, Father, and in the weapons You have provided. (2 Corinthians 10:4; Ephesians 6:10-18.) I take up my spiritual armor and move forward to conquer. By Your power within me I overcome every foe, placing my heel on their necks signifying total and eternal victory.

My Confession for Today

"Come near, put your feet on the necks of these kings." And they drew near and put their feet on their necks. Then Joshua said to them, "Do not be afraid, nor be dismayed; be strong and of good courage, for thus the LORD will do to all your enemies against whom you fight."
–Joshua 10:24–25

I am strong in the Lord and in the power of His might. (Ephesians 6:10.) I remain focused on my goal and never allow Satan's distractions to hinder me. I continually slam the enemy to the ground and place my heel upon his neck! I am a man/woman of aggressive faith. God has given me the power, the right, and the authority to have the kind of life that is a joy to live, and I will not allow Satan or his minions to steal it from me.

April 19

Don't Let Fear Rob You of Your Harvest

When Jesus heard [that Jairus' daughter was dead], He answered [Jairus], saying, "Do not be afraid; only believe, and she will be made well."
–Luke 8:50

My Prayer for Today

Father, I commit myself to believe You without wavering. Others may bring a bad report in order to stop my faith, and even mock my stubborn trust, but my hope is in You. To be wise is to know that You alone are God and there is no other. (Psalm 86:10.) To be honorable is to give Your Word precedence over all things. True honor comes only to the wise, but mockery comes to both the wise and the foolish. (Proverbs 15:33; Matthew 27:41; Proverbs 1:22 NIV.) So, let the mockers mock, I choose to believe.

My Confession for Today

I am never seized with alarm, or struck by fear when a bad report comes. (Psalm 112:7.) I believe in the power and ability of God within me, and I am confident that He will cause me to triumph in any situation. All that I need has already been provided. Therefore, my attention is fixed and my belief is unwavering. I have the things that I say in Jesus' name. (Mark 11:23.)

There Is Harvest Insurance in Good Relationships

My Prayer for Today

Look to yourselves, that we do not lose those things we worked for, but that we may receive a full reward.
–2 John 1:8

Father, I thank You for giving me a balanced perspective. I know that faith is a work in progress right up until harvest time. I must take heed to myself, and continue to believe. I also know, Father, that You do not intend for me to work alone. I am not a loner in this walk of faith. You are my first and most important partner and You lead me to others who are pleased to assist me. May I always remember that two are better than one, and a three stranded cord is not easily broken. (Ecclesiates 4:9,12.) If I turn away help, I'll carry my burdens by myself. (Galatians 6:2.) So, Father, I enlist Your assistance and that of others You bring across my path in all of my work.

My Confession for Today

I am careful not to lose ground in my faith. I refuse to listen to those who try to steer me away from the things of God; I gladly embrace the help of those You send my way. I know that as long as I don't give up on my faith, I will obtain that for which I have believed. The promise for me is secure and I will be fully rewarded.

April 21

The Word Is Presently Working

For I am the LORD. I speak, and the word which I speak will come to pass; it will no more be postponed.
—Ezekiel 12:25

My Prayer for Today

Father, I thank You for the promise You have given me. I am fully confident that You are honorable. The Word You speak comes to pass. Every promise You have given is immediately mine. (2 Corinthians 1:20.) I do not have to wait for it or perform some penance to be worthy of it. It is mine right now in Christ Jesus. Armed with this knowledge, I will express my faith in full confidence that I have received that for which I have believed.

My Confession for Today

God does not delay in keeping His promises to me. In the spiritual realm, I immediately have what I believe I have received. I rejoice in the promise, and I am confident in its fulfillment. I have all that I desire despite what I see in the natural realm. (2 Corinthians 5:7.) It is the Spirit that gives life; the natural counts for nothing. The promises that I speak are Spirit and they are life. (John 6:63.)

Be Faithful when Under Attack

My Prayer for Today

Father, I know that in this world I will suffer tribulation, but I am of good cheer for Jesus overcame the world on my behalf. (John 16:33.) Now, by faith I can overcome anything that I face. No enemy is too strong and no problem is without remedy. I am an overcomer, Lord. I am Your child and by Your strength within me I shall go forward and conquer. (Philippians 4:13; Romans 8:37.)

My Confession for Today

If anyone is to go into captivity, into captivity he will go. If anyone is to be killed with the sword, with the sword he will be killed. This calls for patient endurance and faithfulness on the part of the saints.
—Revelation 13:10 (NIV)

I am conditioned for endurance and strength of faith in the midst of the most trying circumstances. Nothing can thwart my faith plan, for God Himself has provided the power to fulfill it. My outlook is always good, and my attitude is always positive. Courage and tenacity are unfailing parts of my character. I always outlast adversity and fight through the final round.

April 23

Jesus Alone Is Your Justification

Where is boasting then? It is excluded. By what law? Of works? No, but by the law of faith. Therefore we conclude that a man is justified by faith apart from the deeds of the law.
—Romans 3:27–28

My Prayer for Today

Father, I thank You for the revelation that no one is justified by the deeds of the law, but only by faith. Fault finders are out there pointing their fingers and demanding my perfection to prove my worthiness, but I have no worthiness apart from You. My trust is in You and You alone. The works that I produce are the result of my faith. They are not its building blocks, but its fruit. I claim only Your grace and mercy, Father. My works are simply the by-product of a faith-filled life.

My Confession for Today

I no longer boast of myself and the things that I have done. Not one of my good deeds can earn me a place in the family of God. I enter in on the basis of faith alone. (Ephesians 2:8-9.) I am justified and made righteous by faith, not works. The Law has nothing to do with my justification. I am justified solely by the substitutionary sacrifice of Jesus on my behalf. (Romans 3:24; 5:9.)

Do Not Trust in Yourself, but in His Grace

My Prayer for Today

Father, help me to never place my trust in religious ideas. There are wolves in abundance that have infiltrated the church and seek to place Your children in bondage. (Matthew 7:15.) Help me to fight them off, Father. Help me to expose their tyranny and set the captives free! (vv. 16-20.) Your promise has only one source of surety, and that is by faith that it may be received according to grace. Help me turn a deaf ear to the faith blockers, Lord. I am none-the-better when they praise me, and none-the-worse when they criticize me. You alone are the foundation on which I stand and not my own filthy works of righteousness. (Ephesians 2:19-20; Isaiah 64:6.)

Therefore it is of faith that it might be according to grace, so that the promise might be sure to all the seed, not only to those who are of the law, but also to those who are of the faith of Abraham, who is the father of us all.
—Romans 4:16

My Confession for Today

My inheritance of God's promise is the outcome of my faith. (Hebrews 6:12.) By believing in the promise and speaking of it as if it were mine, God has an avenue to give it to me as an act of grace (unmerited, undeserved favor). This overcomes the obstacles that imprison God's giving heart and is the surety that guarantees that I will receive His promise in my life.

April 25

Speak of What You Cannot See as if You Can See It

(As it is written, "I have made you a father of many nations") in the presence of Him whom he believed—God, who gives life to the dead and calls those things which do not exist as though they did; who, contrary to hope, in hope believed, so that he became the father of many nations, according to what was spoken, "So shall your descendants be."
–Romans 4:17-18

My Prayer for Today

Father, teach me to have faith like Yours. You give life to the dead and call those things that be not as though they were. The world calls this foolishness, Father, but You call it faith and demand that I live by it. (1 Corinthians 1:27; Romans 1:17.) So, I set the past behind me and press on. (Philippians 3:13-14.) I believe that I have received what You have promised, and I claim it presently regardless of what my eyes see or what the critics tell me. (Mark 11:24.) I am a man/woman of faith and patience and live in a constantly flowing harvest from Your Word.

My Confession for Today

I walk in the faith of Abraham (the father of my faith). Against all hope, I believe. Despite my circumstances, I have the assurance of my faith. I believe in the promise and speak of it as fulfilled. I do not need any more evidence than the fact that God has promised it to me.

Don't Let Circumstances Guide Your Faith

My Prayer for Today

Father, I am committed in my reliance on Your absolute integrity. You are not a man that You should lie, nor the son of man that you should repent of what you have promised. (Numbers 23:19.) You know all and see all. You knew the very moment that You made the promise that I would be here this day trusting in it. Therefore, I am confident that what You have spoken, You are willing and able to perform.

My Confession for Today

Regardless of the natural circumstances, I call those things that be not as though they are. (Romans 4:17.) I believe and declare God's Word to be true in my life. The things that I have spoken forth in faith I already have. It doesn't matter if I see them or not. They are mine. I will not allow unbelief or mistrust to make me waiver, but shall grow strong, empowered by faith, giving praise and glory to God.

Not being weak in faith, [Abraham] did not consider his own body, already dead (since he was about a hundred years old), and the deadness of Sarah's womb. He did not waver at the promise of God through unbelief, but was strengthened in faith, giving glory to God.
–Romans 4:19-20

April 27

The Lord Backs His Word on Your Behalf

Being fully convinced that what He had promised He was also able to perform.
—Romans 4:21

My Prayer for Today

Father, I trust in the integrity of Your promise. You are God, the very Creator of the universe. (Colossians 1:16.) Your faith brought forth the sun, the moon, the stars and all that dwells within them. (Genesis 1; Acts 4:24.) With You, nothing is impossible. Therefore, I stand confident that I have received the desires of my heart. (Psalm 37:4.) Your willingness to bless me is clear. You have removed every barrier that could make me unworthy. (Ephesians 2:11-16.) So here I am, Father. Bless me with the abundance You desire for me to have.

My Confession for Today

I believe that God is trustworthy and I am fully convinced that He is able to keep His Word and do what He has promised. I understand that all of God's blessings begin in the spirit. Therefore, I must believe and speak before I see them in the natural realm. (Mark 11:24; Hebrews 11:1.)

His Resurrection Is Your Justification

My Prayer for Today

Father, I thoroughly believe in Your Word, and I receive Your righteousness by faith. I believe it in my heart and I confess it with my mouth: "I am the righteousness of God in Christ Jesus my Lord." In Him, I am perfect in every way. In Him, I live and move and have my being. (Acts 17:28.) He is my all in all, Father. (Ephesians 1:23.) He is my sonship, my justification, my acquittal, my right to receive, and the surety of our covenant. (Romans 8:17; 3:24-26; Hebrews 7:22.) He became all that I am that I may become all that He is. (Isaiah 53:5, 11-12.) In this I give You glory, Father. All praise be to Your holy name.

My Confession for Today

Therefore "it was accounted to him for righteousness." Now it was not written for his sake alone that it was imputed to him, but also for us. It shall be imputed to us who believe in Him who raised up Jesus our Lord from the dead, who was delivered up because of our offenses, and was raised because of our justification.
–Romans 4:22-25

I am the righteousness of God in Christ Jesus. (Romans 3:22.) This righteousness is granted to me because I believe in and put my total reliance upon God, who raised Jesus my Lord from the dead. It was Jesus who took my place, was betrayed and put to death because of my sin, but was raised again once my justification was secured.

April 29

Rejoice in the Word

*Your testimonies
I have taken as a
heritage forever,
for they are the
rejoicing of my
heart. I have
inclined my heart
to perform Your
statutes forever, to
the very end.*
—Psalm 119:111-112

My Prayer for Today

Father, I know that You have placed within me excellence of spirit. You Yourself are dwelling within me with all of Your superior qualities and virtues. (1 Corinthians 3:16; 6:16.) I am constantly under Your influence. As I incline my heart to live by Your precepts, You magnify Your anointing that I may fulfill them. (Luke 4:4.) By the anointing that I have in Christ Jesus, I can do all things, fulfill all things, and receive all things. (Philippians 4:13.) Your partnership causes the impossible to become the inevitable in my life. (Mark 10:27.)

My Confession for Today

The Word is my heritage and the proclamation of my rights. It is the joy of my life and my heart is fixed on keeping it to the very end. (Psalm 57:7.) When I speak, my intentions are formed in the spirit. My faith overcomes all adversity and creates for me the circumstances that I am believing for. (Mark 4:23-24.)

Be Single-Minded

My Prayer for Today

I hate the double-minded, but I love Your law.
—Psalm 119:113

Father, there is but one way that leads to life, and that is the way of unwavering faith. (Proverbs 10:16.) Just as responsibility is the prerequisite for independence, so is faith the prerequisite for Your blessings. I cannot receive if I refuse to believe. (James 1:7.) To live like You I must imitate You, and to imitate You I must not be moved by natural circumstances. (Ephesians 5:1; Psalm 62:6.) You are Spirit and as all things begin with You, so do all things begin in the Spirit. (John 4:24.) What is seen is made from what is unseen and is therefore subject to it. (Genesis 1:1-21; Hebrews 11:3.) I understand this, Father, and I commit myself to live by it as long as I have breath within me.

My Confession for Today

I refuse to mingle with, listen to, or debate with double-minded and faithless men. (James 1:5-6; Psalm 1:1.) I will not allow their cancerous ways to pollute my life and draw me away from the joy and prosperity that my Father has provided. I am and ever shall be single-minded, steadfast, patient, and persevering.

May 1

Find Refuge in the Word

You are my hiding place and my shield; I hope in Your word.
—Psalm 119:114

My Prayer for Today

Father, Your Word is sustenance for me to build my strength, a shield to protect me from wavering, a guide for me in the midst of the darkness, provision for me in the day of trouble, and my hope for a better tomorrow. (Psalm 119:105.) You have magnified Your Word above Your name, and thus I magnify it as the final authority in my walk of faith. (Psalm 138:2.) I believe in the integrity of Your promise and receive it in its fullest measure in Jesus' name.

My Confession for Today

I am focused on the Word. It is my shield and my refuge in times of trouble. By it, I am sustained in good health and will live a long and enjoyable life. (Proverbs 4:20-22; 3:13,16.) All of the great and precious promises of God are mine to receive. (2 Corinthians 1:20; 2 Peter 1:4.) By God's Word, blessings crown my head and all of heaven is in my corner. (Romans 8:38-39; Hebrews 12:1.)

Wield Your Shield

My Prayer for Today

Father, thank You for revealing to me that when I speak to a problem and maintain unwavering belief that I have received what I have spoken, I shall have the things that I say. (Mark 11:24.) By this I quench all of the fiery darts of the enemy. When he says I can't, by faith I prove that I can. When he places obstacles in my path, by faith I plow right through them. When he accuses me, points out my faults, and pronounces me guilty, by faith I stand in Your righteousness, Father, a redeemed, sanctified, and justified son/daughter of the living God. (Revelation 5:9; 1 Corinthians 6:11.)

> *Above all, taking the shield of faith with which you will be able to quench all the fiery darts of the wicked one.*
> *—Ephesians 6:16*

My Confession for Today

I have the shield of faith extinguishing all of the fiery darts of the enemy and covering me as I advance. When a fiery dart of disease hits, I believe in and speak the Word over it and it is extinguished. (1 Peter 2:24.) When a fiery dart of financial disaster hits, I believe and speak the Word over it and it is extinguished. (Philippians 4:19.) When any fiery dart comes, I use my faith, believing and speaking the Word over the problem until the problem is eliminated.

May 3

Let Christ Be Magnified in Your Body

For I know that this will turn out for my deliverance through your prayer and the supply of the Spirit of Jesus Christ, according to my earnest expectation and hope that in nothing I shall be ashamed, but with all boldness, as always, so now also Christ will be magnified in my body, whether by life or by death.
—Philippians 1:19-20

My Prayer for Today

Father, I trust in You with all of my heart. Your precepts are tried and true. (Psalm 12:6.) You never give me cause to be ashamed or give up on my faith. I know that if I can believe, all things are possible for me. (Mark 9:23.) So I will not give in to wavering thoughts of doubt. My expectation is fixed and immovable. I shall have the things that I say in Jesus' name. (Mark 11:24.)

My Confession for Today

I remain in eager expectation with the full assurance of hope. I persevere through every trial and stand my ground regardless of the circumstances. I never cower in shame because of my faith. My walk with Jesus is one of persistent courage and unwavering boldness. (1 Corinthians 16:13.) I refuse to give up on my faith, for I know that He who promised is faithful. (Hebrews 10:23.) He will do what He said He would do.

You Are Justified and God Is Satisfied

My Prayer for Today

Therefore, having been justified by faith, we have peace with God through our Lord Jesus Christ.
–Romans 5:1

Father, I thank You that I now have perpetual peace with You. You have erased my sin and caused me to be accepted in Your sight. (Acts 3:19; Ephesians 1:6.) What's more is You initiated it all. It was You who made the decision to save me and draw me unto Yourself. (Romans 2:4; John 6:44; 12:32.) If it weren't for You, I would have no hope. My total dependence is upon You in every way. My rest is perfect and unshakable. (Acts 2:26; Hebrews 4:9-10.) In You, I have absolute acquittal, complete justification, eternal security, and everlasting peace. (Romans 3:27; Psalm 19:23 NLT.)

My Confession for Today

I am justified, acquitted, declared righteous, and given right standing with God through faith. (Romans 8:30,33.) I now have peace with God through Jesus Christ my Lord. He is the surety of my salvation and the confidence by which I presently stand. (Hebrews 7:22.) I have the clarity of mind to understand these things and declare them in faith.

May 5

Faith Gives You Access to the Security of God's Grace

Through whom also we have access by faith into this grace in which we stand, and rejoice in hope of the glory of God.
–Romans 5:2

My Prayer for Today

Father, Your grace is more precious to me than the riches of a thousand kingdoms. You call me into Your presence despite my character flaws and deficiencies. The only favor that is acceptable for me in Your sight is a favor unmerited and undeserved. All that You require of me is that I receive what You have freely given. It is through faith that I have access into this grace by which I stand. All praise be to Your holy name.

My Confession for Today

I have unconditional access into God's incessant and unmerited favor by which I stand. I am now welcomed with open arms whenever I enter the throne room of God. (Hebrews 4:16.) I greatly rejoice in the fact that I can now both see and experience His glory in my life. The barriers to my receiving have been removed and I can now boldly claim all that God wants me to have. (Ephesians 2:13-14.)

Perseverance Leads to Hope—and Victory

My Prayer for Today

Father, with You as my everlasting partner, I am not afraid of the troubles that I must face. I know that in this world I will suffer tribulation, but I also know that I am built for victory. (John 16:33.) With Your help, I persevere under every hardship and adverse circumstance. My faith is my victory. I am a world overcomer. A single word can change a life forever, and a single life can change the world forever. Father, help me change the world for Your glory.

My Confession for Today

I remain full of joy when I encounter trials and sufferings, for I know that through faith and patience I shall emerge triumphant. (Hebrews 6:12.) For trials produce perseverance and endurance in me; and perseverance and endurance develop a maturity of character in me; and the maturity of character in me yields a harvest of joyful and confident hope. This hope never disappoints me, for God's love is shed abroad in my heart through the Holy Spirit who is within me. Through Him, I stand victorious in every situation.

Not only that, but we also glory in tribulations, knowing that tribulation produces perseverance; and perseverance, character; and character, hope. Now hope does not disappoint, because the love of God has been poured out in our hearts by the Holy Spirit who was given to us.
–Romans 5:3-5

May 7

Find Triumph in His Righteousness, Not Your Own

And be found in Him, not having my own righteousness, which is from the law, but that which is through faith in Christ, the righteousness which is from God by faith.
–Philippians 3:9

My Prayer for Today

Father, if I ever fail to approach You because of some sin or personal weakness, shake that nonsense out of me. There is only one way to approach You that is acceptable in Your sight, and that is through the blood of Jesus. (Romans 3:25.) He alone is my strength and righteousness, and only through Him do I have free access to Your throne. (Hebrews 4:15-16.) Father, to focus on myself is to find limitation, fault, and ever-present sin. To focus on You is to find power, possibility, and perpetual holiness. So I choose to be found in You, not having my own righteousness, but that which is through faith in Christ Jesus.

My Confession for Today

Any good that I find within me that comes from my own power is worthless to me. I have set it all aside, putting absolutely no trust in it, so that I can have the overwhelming blessing of knowing my Lord Jesus. I have given up everything in order to have Him in my life. All that I am and all that I have I consider as dung, that I may gain Christ (Philippians 3:8) and be found in Him, not having my own righteousness which comes from obeying the regulations of the Law, but that which comes through faith in Christ.

Abound in Faith with Thanksgiving

My Prayer for Today

As you therefore have received Christ Jesus the Lord, so walk in Him, rooted and built up in Him and established in the faith, as you have been taught, abounding in it with thanksgiving.
—Colossians 2:6-7

Father, You make it so easy to be thankful. The blessings that You have given me are beyond number. Counting them is like counting the stars in the endless galaxies. None of the difficulties of this life can compare to the eternal blessings that are presently mine. (Romans 8:18.) What's more is that You place no cap on the blessings. In You, I have the open-ended promise that You will give me the desires of my heart. (Psalm 37:4.) Father, You make it so easy to love You. I am Yours forever.

My Confession for Today

I live my life in Jesus in the exact same way in which I received Him: by faith. I am rooted, built up and strengthened in my faith through sound teaching, and the fruit that is produced causes a flood of praise and thanksgiving to flow forth from within me. I see right past the natural and take hold of the image in my mind's eye. It is that image, in line with God's will, that becomes my experience in this world.

May 9

Eagerly Expect Your Harvest

For we were saved in this hope, but hope that is seen is not hope; for why does one still hope for what he sees? But if we hope for what we do not see, we eagerly wait for it with perseverance.
—Romans 8:24-25

My Prayer for Today

Father, I recognize that my faith is a spiritual force within me. When I speak in faith, I immediately have the things that I say, and yet the things that I say can seldom be seen with the natural eye. (Mark 11:24.) Therefore, I walk by faith and not by sight. (2 Corinthians 5:7.) I believe in what I do not see based on the authority of Your Word, which gives me hope. I need no further evidence. When I speak to the mountain and maintain unwavering belief that what I have said has come to pass, the mountain must obey. (Mark 11:23.)

My Confession for Today

My faith is the substance of things I hope for and the evidence of things I do not see. (Hebrews 11:1.) I do not hope for the things that I already see, but patiently wait for the things I do not see, continually expressing my firm, confident belief that they are presently mine. What I see with my natural eye is neither truth nor fact. True reality is first and foremost spiritual. Therefore, I have what I believe I have received regardless of what the physical evidence is showing.

You Are God's Greatest Treasure

My Prayer for Today

Father, help me to see the value that You place not only on me, but on all of Your children. Help me to see the world through other people's eyes. Help me to cherish myself and others as You cherish us. (Mark 12:31.) You have placed us here to be a family, to glorify You as our Father, and to share our gifts with each other. No one person is more important or more valued than the next. All are unique, exceptional, and irreplaceable. Bring us together, Lord. Make us one with You and one with each other. (John 17:21-23.)

Are not five sparrows sold for two copper coins? And not one of them is forgotten before God. But the very hairs of your head are all numbered. Do not fear therefore; you are of more value than many sparrows.
–Luke 12:6-7

My Confession for Today

When I look at the sparrow, I know I am looking at a creature that my Father loves and watches over very carefully. Yet, when the Father looks at me, He sees someone worth more than many flocks of sparrows. He holds me so close to His heart that He even numbers the very hairs on my head. (Isaiah 40:11.) With such a loving Father to guide and protect me, I have absolutely nothing to fear.

May 11

Believe What God Says About You

The Angel of the LORD appeared to him, and said to him, "The LORD is with you, you mighty man of valor!" Then the LORD turned to him and said, "Go in this might of yours, and you shall save Israel from the hand of the Midianites. Have I not sent you?"
—Judges 6:12, 14

My Prayer for Today

Father, one of the greatest joys of life is to do what others say is impossible. Therefore, help me to thwart the enemy's "you can't" or "hath God said?" accusations. (Genesis 3:1 KJV.) With You, Father, nothing is impossible. (Mark 10:27.) Every word that You speak comes to pass and every promise You have made has within it the power of fulfillment. (Psalm 33:9; 2 Corinthians 1:20.) You make me strong in the power of Your might. (Ephesians 6:10.) You guide me in Your wisdom and prepare me for battle. (Psalm 119:98; 144:1.) In You I have fixed and certain victory and You never forsake me for any reason. (1 Corinthians 15:57; Hebrews 13:5.) All praise be to Your holy name.

My Confession for Today

I am a warrior in the army of God. (2 Timothy 2:3.) I am intrepid — full of courage and valor — and the Lord is with me in everything that I do. (Joshua 1:9.) I do not allow circumstances to direct my faith. I go forward fearlessly in the will and power of Almighty God. It is my Father, the God of the entire universe, who has sent me to do His work. (Colossians 1:15; Luke 2:49; Philippians 2:13.) He has ordained me in my calling. (Jeremiah 1:5.) I am anointed and well able to do what He has called me to do.

Fulfill the Good Pleasure of His Goodness

My Prayer for Today

Father, I commit myself to run this race with endurance. (Hebrews 12:1.) I am elated that You have counted me worthy of Your calling and that You fulfill my faith with Your immeasurable power. However, enthusiasm is useless without persistence. Therefore, train me for endurance, Father. Teach me how to stand fast against temptation, ignore circumstances, and maintain my belief no matter what my eyes may see. (1 Peter 5:12 NIV; 1 Corinthians 10:13; 2 Corinthians 5:7.)

My Confession for Today

My heavenly Father has counted me worthy of His calling. He has chosen me from among all the people of the earth to be His own son/daughter. By His power, which works so mightily within me, He fulfills every good purpose I have set my hand to perform and every act prompted by my faith. The name of Jesus is glorified in me, and I in Him, according to the grace of my God and Lord, Jesus Christ.

Therefore we also pray always for you that our God would count you worthy of this calling, and fulfill all the good pleasure of His goodness and the work of faith with power, that the name of our Lord Jesus Christ may be glorified in you, and you in Him, according to the grace of our God and the Lord Jesus Christ.
–2 Thessalonians 1:11-12

Be Satisfied in Jesus

On the last day, that great day of the feast, Jesus stood and cried out, saying, "If anyone thirsts, let him come to Me and drink. He who believes in Me, as the Scripture has said, out of his heart will flow rivers of living water." But this He spoke concerning the Spirit, whom those believing in Him would receive; for the Holy Spirit was not yet given, because Jesus was not yet glorified.
–John 7:37-39

My Prayer for Today

Father, I thank You for the Holy Spirit. He is my Comforter, Counselor, and strength. (John 14:16-17, 26.) I thank You that He speaks to me in the midst of the darkness and guides me by the light of the Word. (Psalm 119:105.) I thank You that His power flows in and through me so that I can receive all that You want me to have and be all that You want me to be. But most of all, Father, I thank You for His friendship and companionship. He is the joy of my morning and my rejoicing through the obligations of my day. (Psalm 30:5; 89:16.)

My Confession for Today

I have come to Jesus and have drunk deeply of His provision. He gives me not only that which refreshes, but that which replenishes as well. He has sent the Holy Spirit Himself to dwell within my own spirit to produce rivers of living water which both plentifully and constantly flow forth from me. His currents overwhelm and drown out all doubts and fears, and the fountain of His waters brings forth a shower of blessings into my life. (Ezekiel 34:26.)

Remember Who Is on Your Side

My Prayer for Today

Father, I know that in this life tribulations are inevitable. (John 16:33.) There are many who oppose the truth. Yet, Father, by faith in the name of Jesus I can carry Your power to a hurting world. Despite the efforts of my detractors, may I speak Your Word with boldness and carry Your message with signs and wonders following.

My Confession for Today

When I speak the Word to the problem, all of hell breaks loose. It is written in Psalm 2:1-4, that when the heathen rage against me and plot my destruction and the kings of the earth

Now, Lord, look on their threats, and grant to Your servants that with all boldness they may speak Your word, by stretching out Your hand to heal, and that signs and wonders may be done through the name of Your holy Servant Jesus.
—Acts 4:29-30

(spiritual ruling powers of darkness) assemble themselves against the Lord and His anointed (me), He who sits in heaven laughs. God Himself observes their threats and takes His stand with me. He is on my side! (Psalm 118:6.) Therefore, I declare His Word fearlessly, in the name of Jesus, and He stretches out His hand to perform signs, wonders, and miracles on my behalf!

May 15

The Law of Righteousness Is Already Fulfilled in You

What shall we say then? That Gentiles, who did not pursue righteousness, have attained to righteousness, even the righteousness of faith; but Israel, pursuing the law of righteousness, has not attained to the law of righteousness. Why? Because they did not seek it by faith, but as it were, by the works of the law. For they stumbled at that stumbling stone.
–Romans 9:30–32

My Prayer for Today

Father, purge from me every speck of legalism mentality. Help me to see clearly that the righteousness that You find acceptable is the righteousness that comes through faith. With You, righteousness is a matter of law. Either I work to maintain it and be forever flawless by my own power, or I can receive the righteousness of the flawless One who gave Himself for me. I choose the latter, Father. I claim Jesus' righteousness and not my own.

My Confession for Today

I have obtained a righteousness that is not my own. My righteousness comes from God through the avenue of my faith. All of my ongoing works are wrought within the righteousness of God. Despite my shortcomings, I am accepted by God and fully worthy to receive His assistance and many blessings.

The Lord Satisfies Your Every Desire

My Prayer for Today

Father, I acknowledge that You alone are the provider of all things. Though I sweat and pound the pavement to make a living, it is You who uphold me through it all. I can do nothing aside from Your will and power. It is through Your partnership alone that I prosper and achieve greatness in this earth.

My Confession for Today

My Father loves me and is faithful to perform all of His promises to me. When I fall, He upholds

The LORD upholds all who fall, and raises up all who are bowed down. The eyes of all look expectantly to You, and You give them their food in due season. You open Your hand and satisfy the desire of every living thing.
—Psalm 145:14–16

me in His arms. When I am bowed down, He lifts me up and bids me to hold my head high and be proud of what He has made me to be. He is always there to provide me with whatever I need. I am a vessel of His favor. His hand is always opened to satisfy my every desire.

May 17

Your Faith Has Omnipotent Support

So Samuel grew, and the LORD was with him and let none of his words fall to the ground.
—1 Samuel 3:19

My Prayer for Today

Father, I know that You hear every word that I speak and are committed to fulfill them. By the words that I speak, I provide the rudder that drives my course in life. (James 3:4-5.) Therefore, set a guard over my mouth and remind me of Your Word in every circumstance. (Psalm 141:3.) Help me to maintain my course on the path of Your perfect will. (Psalm 16:11.)

My Confession for Today

The Lord is with me in everything that I do. He lets none of the words that I speak in faith fall short of their intended purpose. So I say with all boldness that everything I do today is anointed with His power and will prosper without fail. Creative ideas come to me in abundance. (Proverbs 8:12 KJV.) I am a blessing to family, friends, peers, and business associates. My healing springs forth speedily, and I have excess energy to complete the day's work. (Isaiah 58:8; Deuteronomy 33:25.)

Wage the Good Warfare

My Prayer for Today

Father, keep me on the path of Your perfect will. Help me to always recognize when my faith is taking a wrong turn. I know that Your will for me is to fulfill the desires of my heart and that when I am personally fulfilled I am best prepared to be of service to others. (Psalm 37:4.) So, help me to be the person You created me to be. (Psalm 139:14-16.) Help me to reject the path that is driven by ungodly influences so that my journey of faith may never suffer shipwreck.

My Confession for Today

I follow the instruction of my fathers and mothers in the faith, so far as what they teach me is in keeping with the Word and the prophecies which have been spoken about me and which God has confirmed within my spirit. I fight the good fight, holding on to my faith and a good conscience. (1 Timothy 6:12.) I maintain a straight course on the path of God's will.

> *This charge I commit to you, son Timothy, according to the prophecies previously made concerning you, that by them you may wage the good warfare, having faith and a good conscience, which some having rejected, concerning the faith have suffered shipwreck.*
> *—1 Timothy 1:18-19*

May 19

Follow God with All of Your Heart

Elijah came to all the people, and said, "How long will you falter between two opinions? If the LORD is God, follow Him; but if Baal, follow him." But the people answered him not a word.
—1 Kings 18:21

My Prayer for Today

Father, my complete trust is in You. You alone are God. (Psalm 86:10.) You created all that I can touch and see as well as what I cannot touch and see. (Colossians 1:16.) You formed galaxies so vast and enormous that it would take a trillion lifetimes to explore them. You alone are the worthy One. Therefore, You have my allegiance. I will not falter between two opinions. You are God. Lead me where You want me to go and make the path clear so that I can walk it without stumbling. (Psalm 27:11.)

My Confession for Today

I am fixed and steadfast in my faith. I do not waiver between opposing opinions. My heavenly Father is God. There is no other. I turn my back on the forces of darkness and follow my God with all of my heart. When I am ridiculed for my faith, I turn my attention to the Word. The world must see evidence in order to believe. I, on the other hand, believe first and I create the evidence with my faith. (John 20:29.)

Do Not Focus on Riches, but Fulfillment in Christ

My Prayer for Today

Father, it is abundantly clear that riches are an ungodly pursuit. It is not Your will for riches to be the end goal of my faith. They are a mere by-product of living in Your righteousness. My number one pursuit is simply to become whom You created me to be. To be true to myself is to serve You and to advance Your kingdom. By living productively, doing what I love and do best, I become a magnet for provision. You made me unique among all of creation and designed me to fill an individualized purpose. (Ephesians 1:11.) Help me to see that clearly, Father. Help me to pursue the right things so that I do not fall into temptation and a snare.

And having food and clothing, with these we shall be content. But those who desire to be rich fall into temptation and a snare, and into many foolish and harmful lusts which drown men in destruction and perdition.
–1 Timothy 6:8-9

My Confession for Today

I am content in all circumstances, knowing full well that God, my Father and Provider, is always with me and I am never without His provision. (Hebrews 13:5.) I am calm and stress free in any and every situation. I do not set my mind on money and riches, forgetting the fact that I have a heavenly Father who loves me and is caring for me; for I know that those who focus on money and riches fall into many temptations and are taken in many traps, get-rich-quick schemes, and unethical pursuits. Through such focus, they enter into many foolish and harmful desires that plunge them into ruin and destruction.

May 21

Avoid Sorrows and Just Be You

The love of money is a root of all kinds of evil, for which some have strayed from the faith in their greediness, and pierced themselves through with many sorrows.
–1 Timothy 6:10

My Prayer for Today

Father, money is but a thing. It is a tool to achieve a purpose. It is necessary to life in this world, but not for life in the Spirit. So keep greed far from me. Keep me from desiring abundance only to consume it on my lusts. The only possible way to be truly happy is to live according to Your will, Father. You designed me to be me and to have no other gods before You. (Exodus 20:3.) Therefore, money shall not be my god. I will advance, increase, and live in abundance simply by fulfilling my place in the kingdom, being true to myself, and doing Your will.

My Confession for Today

I am fully focused on living according to the will of God for my life. I do not love money and power. I remain humble, gracious, and generous, reflecting the character of my Father in all things. If I gained control of all of the world's riches, and lavished myself with all manner of luxury, it would not bring me fulfillment. I am fulfilled by being me. I am created for a purpose and a mission and I intend to fulfill it. (Ephesians 1:11.) Therein is my greatest service to God and the key to a happy and prosperous life.

Fight the Good Fight

My Prayer for Today

Father, train me to be a good soldier in Your army. (2 Timothy 2:3.) Help me to reject worldly pursuits and chase after only those things that are conducive to a godly life. Help me to see that true joy is only found in You. (Psalm 16:11.) Warn me against religious traditions and manmade opinions that are clueless of Your purposes. Father, there is no greater thief of joy in the earth than man-centered religious ideas. (James 1:26-27.) Shield me against them, Father. Help me to gain the pleasures of a truly godly life. (Psalm 16:11.)

My Confession for Today

But you, O man of God, flee these things and pursue righteousness, godliness, faith, love, patience, gentleness. Fight the good fight of faith, lay hold on eternal life, to which you were also called and have confessed the good confession in the presence of many witnesses.

—1 Timothy 6:11-12

I am a man/woman of godly faith. I flee youthful lusts and the pursuit of riches and power. My chief aim is to fulfill my calling and be the person I am created to be. I seek to know myself and how I am designed so that I can take my place and be of greatest service to others. I pursue wisdom, righteousness, godliness, faith, love, gentleness, and endurance. I fight the good fight of faith, taking hold of the eternal life to which I was called when I made my good confession in the presence of many witnesses.

May 23

Speak Boldly in the Lord

Therefore they stayed there a long time, speaking boldly in the Lord, who was bearing witness to the word of His grace, granting signs and wonders to be done by their hands.

–Acts 14:3

My Prayer for Today

Father, my only truly effective witness to the world is the fruit that I produce with my faith. Therefore, make me a powerful witness. Pour Your power through my focused and unwavering belief. Take notice of the hope that is within me and manifest it in my life. Make me an example for others to follow. Bear witness to the word of Your grace granting signs and wonders to be performed by my hands.

My Confession for Today

I speak fearlessly and boldly for the Lord. He continually bears testimony to the Word of His grace (divine enabling) by granting signs and wonders to be performed through my hands. I am a powerful person with abilities far above the natural world: I am able to bless others and bring God's glory and provision into their lives. I am the very ambassador of heaven and the carrier of God's power to a lost and hurting world. (2 Corinthians 5:20; Mark 16:15.)

Let All that You Do Be Done with Love

My Prayer for Today

Watch, stand fast in the faith, be brave, be strong. Let all that you do be done with love.
–1 Corinthians 16:13-14

Father, You make me fearless. Armies could be arrayed against me and I would not be afraid. (Psalm 27:3.) You are on my side and no enemy has a chance against You. (Psalm 118:6.) You make it easy to be brave, Father. Help me to be productive this day so that I may advance Your kingdom and spread Your love to a hurting world.

My Confession for Today

I am constantly alert and on guard against the attacks of the enemy. I stand firm and fearless in my faith—a man/woman of courage, strengthened with all might by the Holy Spirit who is within me — and all that I do is centered in love. (Colossians 1:11.) I am aware of the plight of others, and I focus my faith to meet their needs. I use my gifts and talents for acts of service and have a spirit of generosity toward my fellow man.

May 25

You Have Great Faith!

The centurion answered and said, "Lord, I am not worthy that You should come under my roof. But only speak a word, and my servant will be healed. For I also am a man under authority, having soldiers under me. And I say to this one, 'Go,' and he goes; and to another, 'Come,' and he comes; and to my servant, 'Do this,' and he does it." When Jesus heard it, He marveled, and said to those who followed, "Assuredly, I say to you, I have not found such great faith, not even in Israel!"

—Matthew 8:8-10

My Prayer for Today

Father, You have given me Your authority and placed me in the earth to govern and control it. (Luke 10:19.) Help me to be productive in this capacity. It is You who causes the elements to respond to my faith. Therefore, increase my power that I may bear witness to the truth. Cause what I birth in the spirit to manifest in the natural in increased measure to the praise of Your glory.

My Confession for Today

When I speak the Word of God, His healing power occupies my words and is carried in the direction that I send it. (Isaiah 55:11.) When I speak to a situation, it must conform to my intended purpose. (2 Corinthians 4:13.) The elements are subject to my authority. Words are my servants and the carriers of my faith to a hurting world.

Have Faith in the Word

My Prayer for Today

Father, no truly noble person is of two minds about anything. (James 1:6-8.) Train me to be strong in faith. Fill me with understanding of Your precepts and promises. You have given Your Word for a purpose. It has within it the very power of fulfillment. Help me to profit from it. Open my eyes and make me wise in the ways of faith. Cause Your power to flow in abundance as I express my unwavering belief and move forward to do Your will in this earth.

> *For indeed the gospel was preached to us as well as to them; but the word which they heard did not profit them, not being mixed with faith in those who heard it.*
> *—Hebrews 4:2*

My Confession for Today

I fully realize that I will not be able to enter into God's rest if I do not believe. (Hebrews 4:3,11 KJV.) If I allow doubt and unbelief to enter in, I open the door for all kinds of fear, anxiety, and turmoil to enter in as well. Therefore, my heart's concern is to hold fast to God's promises so that I will not fall short of entering into His rest. When I believe and speak, I remain focused and single-minded. (2 Corinthians 4:13.) Every word that I speak in faith is a present reality that will soon manifest in my circumstances. (Hebrews 11:1.)

May 27

Don't Stress, It's Already Done

For we who have believed do enter that rest, as He has said: "So I swore in My wrath, 'They shall not enter My rest,'" although the works were finished from the foundation of the world.

—Hebrews 4:3

My Prayer for Today

Father, You have provided all that I need to live a blessed and prosperous life. Everything was set in place from the foundation of the world. Science has proven that Your precepts of faith are woven into the fabric of creation. Therefore, teach me how to maintain my belief. Show me what I can do to focus my attention properly and project my thoughts in accordance with Yours. Partner with me so that I manifest my desires with unfailing accuracy.

My Confession for Today

The message I have heard is of no value to me unless I combine it with faith. It is through my belief that I have entered into God's rest. It is faith that brings forth His provision from the spirit realm. In the spirit, all things are already provided and through believing they become a present fact in my life.

Believe and Be Established

My Prayer for Today

Father, help me to believe despite the tribulations I endure. Help me to hold Your Word as the final authority in every circumstance. A person's true character is not tested when times are good, but in times of failure, tragedy, disappointment, and loss. I am determined, Father, that no matter what I face, no matter what the odds or the circumstance, I will believe.

The head of Ephraim is Samaria, and the head of Samaria is Remaliah's son. If you will not believe, surely you shall not be established.
–Isaiah 7:9

My Confession for Today

I stand firm, fixed and unwavering in the battle of faith. I endure through testing, ridicule, and mockery. (James 5:11.) I overcome all obstacles, setbacks, and hindrances. (1 John 5:4.) Those who set themselves up as my enemy fall by their own devices. (Psalm 9:16.) I am a fierce faith warrior and an impossible foe. When this fight is over, I will be the one standing.

May 29

Jesus Already Did His Part, Now Do Yours

The righteousness of faith speaks in this way, "Do not say in your heart, 'Who will ascend into heaven?'" (that is, to bring Christ down from above) or, "Who will descend into the abyss?'" (that is, to bring Christ up from the dead).
—Romans 10:6-7

My Prayer for Today

Father, I thank You for the revelation that the righteousness of faith speaks. It is the anointed One, and His anointing within me, that provides the power to achieve my goal. (1 John 2:20.) I live in Christ and His words live in me. By this, I know that I can ask what I will and it will be done for me. (John 15:7.)

My Confession for Today

My righteousness is founded on faith. It is totally unnecessary for me to try to bombard the gates of heaven in order to be saved or receive from God. I am always welcome at my Father's throne. (Hebrews 4:16.) It is also ludicrous for me to expect Jesus to suffer over and over again every time I mess up. His sacrifice has made me righteous once and for all. (1 Peter 2:24; Hebrews 10:10.) His work is finished, and I am perfected for all of eternity. (John 17:4,23.)

Keep the Word on Your Lips and in Your Heart

My Prayer for Today

Father, Your Word dwells within me in all of its rich abundance. What I believe in my heart and confess with my mouth is accomplished in Jesus' name. I purpose in my heart to be a believer, Father. With Your assistance, I am steadfast, immovable, and unshakable. (1 Corinthians 15:58.) Nothing can keep me from the salvation that You have provided.

My Confession for Today

The way of justification, salvation, healing, and blessing is not put at a distance from me. The Word is on my lips and in my heart. I make my confession by the Word of faith. Jesus rose from the dead and He is now my Lord. I am saved and delivered from every circumstance beginning with salvation from spiritual death; for it is with my heart that I believe unto justification and righteousness, and it is with my mouth that I confess, bringing forth my salvation and deliverance.

But what does it say? "The word is near you, in your mouth and in your heart" (that is, the word of faith which we preach): that if you confess with your mouth the Lord Jesus and believe in your heart that God has raised Him from the dead, you will be saved. For with the heart one believes unto righteousness, and with the mouth confession is made unto salvation.
—Romans 10:8-10

May 31

He Will Not Allow You to Be Ashamed

The Scripture says, "Whoever believes on Him will not be put to shame."
—Romans 10:11

My Prayer for Today

Father, You are the God of my success. Success comes to the person who sees a mall when looking at a pile of rocks, a world leader when looking at a homeless child, an executive when looking at a tattooed gangster, and a priceless treasure to Your very heart when looking at a mirror. I am made for something special, Father, and to glorify You is to fulfill it in its fullest measure. (Isaiah 43:7.)

My Confession for Today

I am fully convinced that anyone who puts their faith in the Lord shall never be put to shame. Through the process of faith, He richly blesses me with all things. My unwavering belief is the springboard for a satisfying, abundant, and prosperous life. I behold, as if a mirror the image of my future, and speak of it in the present tense. (2 Corinthians 3:18.) By this process, the power of the Spirit within me brings my desires into this natural world.

The Word Will Not Return Void

My Prayer for Today

Father, Your Word is faithful. Nothing that You have promised ever falls short of Your intent. All that You require is that I believe. I commit myself to this end, Father. Regardless of what my eyes see, what my body feels, or what the circumstances are showing, I believe. Your Word is my final authority. It is mine to receive and its benefits are mine to enjoy.

> *So shall My word be that goes forth from My mouth; it shall not return to Me void, but it shall accomplish what I please, and it shall prosper in the thing for which I sent it.*
> *—Isaiah 55:11*

My Confession for Today

As rain and snow fall from heaven to water the earth and make it bring forth seed for the sower and bread for the eater, so it is with God's Word. (Isaiah 55:10.) He has sent it to me for a purpose and it will accomplish that purpose in my life. It is continually on my lips as a seed and it brings me a perpetual harvest of good things. What a joy it is to be led forth in such peace and assurance! (Isaiah 55:12.) The mountains and the hills burst forth into song before me, and I enjoy the goodwill of all who see God's favor in my life. (Isaiah 55:12; Proverbs 3:3-4.)

June 2

God Is Quick to Respond to You

Shall God not avenge His own elect who cry out day and night to Him, though He bears long with them? I tell you that He will avenge them speedily. Nevertheless, when the Son of Man comes, will He really find faith on the earth?
—Luke 18:7-8

My Prayer for Today

Father, true faith has been scarce on the earth. Too many of us have spoken out of both sides of our mouths. One minute we declare our unwavering faith and the next we agree with the circumstance. Not I, Father. I choose to believe in spite of what I see or feel. I know that You are always working with me to create the kind of life that I desire to live. (Colossians 1:29) You never fail me, Father, so train me thoroughly so that I will never fail You. (Isaiah 58:11)

My Confession for Today

My heavenly Father never neglects me. He is always with me to guide, defend, and even avenge me. (Isaiah 35:4) When I call upon Him, He answers. He takes up my cause as His own and honors my faith. I will not let Him down. When Jesus returns, He will find me living by faith in this earth.

Seedtime and Harvest Is Working Today

My Prayer for Today

While the earth remains, seedtime and harvest, cold and heat, winter and summer, and day and night shall not cease.
—Genesis 8:22

Father, help me to always realize that everything I do is a seed that will produce a harvest. For every effect there is a cause, and for every result there is a root foundation that brought it forth. Every choice I make this day will yield a return. So, guide me in Your wisdom, Father. Teach me how and when to act. Disciple me to be a son/daughter who pleases You and makes You proud.

My Confession for Today

While the earth remains, I can absolutely count on seedtime and harvest, cold and heat, summer and winter, and day and night. These fixed and certain laws remain in the earth. Therefore, I know beyond shadow of doubt that I will reap what I have sown. When I sow my seed, I can count on a harvest.

June 4

You Were Chosen for Such a Time as This

"If you remain completely silent at this time, relief and deliverance will arise for the Jews from another place, but you and your father's house will perish. Yet who knows whether you have come to the kingdom for such a time as this?"

–Esther 4:14

My Prayer for Today

Father, knowing You is the one thing that ensures my constant victory. You cause all that I do to be conformed to the standards of Your will. (Psalm 143:10.) When I face adversity, You bring people into my life to steer me in the direction You want me to go. You are my ever-present help in time of trouble or in the day of prosperity. (Psalm 46:1.) Show me the direction to take, Father. Reveal Your purpose for placing me here for such a time as this. (Ephesians 1:11.)

My Confession for Today

God chose me for a specific purpose. In His infinite wisdom, He has placed me in His kingdom for such a time as this. I am His ideal choice to carry out what He has called me to do. He has given me a mission to fulfill, and I intend to fulfill it. I am the best that He has to fulfill my calling. I will not dishonor Him by forcing others who are less capable to do my work for me.

Seek Wise Counsel

My Prayer for Today

Father, teach me to walk in the counsel of Your will and reject the ways of the ungodly. Your wisdom declares that what is gained by deceit becomes a drain on the soul. (Proverbs 20:17.) The more one gains, the emptier they get. So, keep me within the boundaries of Your precepts. (Psalm 119:27.) Open my mind to know how, why, and when to do things. Everything I do is a seed that will produce a harvest. (Genesis 8:22.) Make my harvest plentiful, Father, but only within the boundaries of Your will.

My Confession for Today

I move forward in life in happiness and peace. I am keenly focused on the guidance of the Spirit. My delight, gratification, and satisfaction are in the Word of the living God. In it I meditate—speaking it to myself day and night—engrafting and rooting it deeply into my spirit. By this, my way is made prosperous, and I achieve tremendous success. (Joshua 1:8.) I am like a tree that is planted beside fresh water springs. I bear the best of fruit in my life. Everything about me exudes life, and everything that I set my hand to do prospers.

Blessed is the man who walks not in the counsel of the ungodly, nor stands in the path of sinners, nor sits in the seat of the scornful; but his delight is in the law of the LORD, and in His law he meditates day and night. He shall be like a tree planted by the rivers of water, that brings forth its fruit in its season, whose leaf also shall not wither; and whatever he does shall prosper.
–Psalm 1:1-3

June 6

Your Harvest Is Constantly Flowing

Your threshing shall last till the time of vintage, and the vintage shall last till the time of sowing; you shall eat your bread to the full, and dwell in your land safely.
—Leviticus 26:5

My Prayer for Today

Father, under Your blessing there is always enough with plenty to spare. By Your power, all that I have is increased so that my life is filled with Your abundance. What's more, You cover me with Your hedge of protection so that I can enjoy Your provision free from worry and anxiety. (Job 1:10; Psalm 139:5.) Your precepts provide wisdom and direction so that I don't squander my wealth. By Your counsel, I maintain my increase until I leave a substantial inheritance for my children and grandchildren. (Proverbs 13:22.)

My Confession for Today

I am never without provision. I thresh the fruit of my harvest from the time of gathering through to the time of planting. My harvest is constantly flowing. I reap it every day of my life. I am blessed with God's abundance, enjoy all that I desire, and dwell in safety in the land.

The Lord Sustains You

My Prayer for Today

Father, I thank You for providing my sustenance. You are with me at all times and in every circumstance. No matter what I face, You are there to fill me with strength to endure and prosper. You are the first to confront the enemy on my behalf, and You always see to it that I am never overwhelmed. With You as my faithful partner, I cannot fail.

My Confession for Today

I stretch myself out to sleep in perfect peace, free of all anxiety. When my rest is complete, I awake again and find the Lord at my side, keeping guard over my life. He is an ever-present sentinel who never fails to protect me from the attacks of my enemies. I will not fear even tens of thousands drawn up against me, for I am never alone. The Lord of hosts is my companion and ally. He strikes my enemies down in a fierce display of His power. His mighty fist shatters their teeth. So let the enemy bark all he wants. His bite is nothing to me.

I lay down and slept; I awoke, for the LORD sustained me. I will not be afraid of ten thousands of people who have set themselves against me all around. Arise, O LORD; save me, O my God! For You have struck all my enemies on the cheekbone; You have broken the teeth of the ungodly.
–Psalm 3:5-7

June 8

God Never Lets Go of Your Hand

Where can I go from Your Spirit? Or where can I flee from Your presence? If I ascend into heaven, You are there; if I make my bed in hell, behold, You are there. If I take the wings of the morning, and dwell in the uttermost parts of the sea, even there Your hand shall lead me, and Your right hand shall hold me.

—Psalm 139:7-10

My Prayer for Today

Father, Your mercy and grace make Your omnipresence a comfort. You are never harsh with me nor do You look for reasons to condemn me. No matter where I am or what I am doing, You always see what is best in me. (1 Corinthians 13:7) I can always count on You to encourage, strengthen, and assist me through the many storms of this life. When I am in the worst of conditions, You never let go of my hand. (Isaiah 41:13.) I never have to worry or hide my face from You. Your unconditional love always leads me on to victory. (1 Corinthians 15:57.)

My Confession for Today

My Father is with me wherever I go. (Joshua 1:9.) Whether I rise on the wings of the dawn or settle at the far side of the sea, God is there to guide me—His right hand holds me securely and His love bolsters my confidence in my success. (Jeremiah 31:3.)

Abide in His Love

My Prayer for Today

Father, show me the depths of Your love for me. Instruct me in the ways of love that I may be a reflection of Your love to a lost world. Teach me to see the world through other people's eyes. Fill my life with the fruit of love so that Your joy may remain in me and that my joy may be full. Make love the center point of all that I do so that my faith is always aligned with Your will.

My Confession for Today

Jesus loves me in the same way that the Father loves Him. I am like a prized treasure filling His heart with joy. I abide in His love—always recognizing and remembering it in all that I do. I keep my mind focused on the best things in life. I pay attention to the Word and do all that it commands me to do. God's joy and delight are in me, and my joy and delight are made complete in Him.

> *As the Father loved Me, I also have loved you; abide in My love. If you keep My commandments, you will abide in My love, just as I have kept My Father's commandments and abide in His love. These things I have spoken to you, that My joy may remain in you, and that your joy may be full.*
> *–John 15:9-11*

God Is Your Faithful Advocate

You are near, O LORD, and all Your commandments are truth. Concerning Your testimonies, I have known of old that You have founded them forever. Consider my affliction and deliver me, for I do not forget Your law. Plead my cause and redeem me; revive me according to Your word.
—Psalm 119:151-154

My Prayer for Today

Father, I thank You that You didn't choose to dwell far off so that I would have to send my prayers to heaven or some other distant place. You chose to dwell in the closest and most intimate place possible: within my heart. (1 Corinthians 3:16.) I am now one with You and You are one with me. (John 17:21-23.) All that I do in this world I do together with You. As my loving Father, plead my cause, fight my fight, and keep me on the path of Your will. (Psalm 139:24.)

My Confession for Today

My Father considers my afflictions and delivers me according to His Word. When I speak it, life and health flood into my body. (Proverbs 4:20-22.) I remember the power of the Word. It remains in the forefront of my thoughts. God has given it to me to keep my life safe and provide healing and security for me in times of trouble. The fullness of His blessings comes to me through His Word, and His mercy toward me endures forever. (Romans 15:29; Psalm 107:1.)

You Are the Friend of God

My Prayer for Today

Father, I thank You that I am no longer a servant, but a son/daughter. You have brought me into Your family. I am now Your own child with gifts and talents that are precious to the kingdom. Show me what You want me to do today, Father. Reveal to me the path where my talent is most needed so that Your kingdom can advance in the way that You have intended.

My Confession for Today

There is no greater love in existence than the love that Jesus has for me. I am one of His close friends. I listen for His instruction and do all that He commands me to do. He reveals to me His intimate secrets and makes me a vital part of His plans and purposes. It wasn't me who chose Him, but He chose me. (John 15:16.) Before the beginning of time, He picked me to be His friend and brother/sister. (Ephesians 4:1; Romans 8:29.) I am now one with Him in Spirit and through Him I bear an abundance of lasting and eternal fruit. (John 17:21.)

Greater love has no one than this, than to lay down one's life for his friends. You are My friends if you do whatever I command you. No longer do I call you servants, for a servant does not know what his master is doing; but I have called you friends, for all things that I heard from My Father I have made known to you.
—John 15:13-15

June 12

The Lord Is Your Keeper

He will not allow your foot to be moved; He who keeps you will not slumber. Behold, He who keeps Israel shall neither slumber nor sleep. The LORD is your keeper; the LORD is your shade at your right hand. The sun shall not strike you by day, nor the moon by night. The LORD shall preserve you from all evil; He shall preserve your soul. The LORD shall preserve your going out and your coming in from this time forth, and even forevermore.
—Psalm 121:3-8

My Prayer for Today

Father, by the authority of Your will I claim You as my Father and my friend. It is You who bids me to walk by faith declaring that if I can see myself as being what I desire, then I am that very thing. (2 Corinthians 5:7; Proverbs 23:7.) You understand my struggles and patiently help me with every new step that I take. I rest in the shadow of Your wings as You preserve my coming and going now and forevermore. (Psalm 63:7.)

My Confession for Today

The world may turn to the psychiatrist, the psychic, and the politician for help, but my help comes from the Creator of heaven and earth. (Colossians 1:16.) My destiny is fixed and I am resolved to attain it. I am not praying for opportunities; I am preparing for them. They are presently mine. The One watching over me is tenacious. He never sleeps or even blinks an eye. He is the shade at my right hand so that nothing can even come close to harming me. My Father watches over my coming and my going and everything in between, both now and forevermore!

You Are Filled with Power

My Prayer for Today

Father, do not allow my faith to be empty. Let me not speak empty words, but words of power that change the world to make it a better place to live. May every action that I take be within the confines of my faith goals. Keep me from wavering even a little to the right or to the left. (Joshua 23:6.) Make my path straight before me in a single-minded pursuit of my dreams. (Isaiah 45:2.)

My Confession for Today

By faith, I produce an abundance of good works and have a steadfast endurance inspired by hope in my Lord Jesus Christ. My Father chose me out of the world to be His own son/daughter. (John 15:16.) He sought me out, found me, and made me what I am today. If ever I begin to think that God doesn't want me around, or that He is fed up with me, I will remember that He is the One who sought me out and chose me to be His child. I did not go running to Him; He came running for me. He knew everything that I would do, even after receiving Jesus, and He still wanted me to be His son/daughter. Therefore, knowing that He loves me so much, I will do my best to live a life pleasing to Him in every way. (Jeremiah 31:3; 2 Corinthians 5:8.)

Knowing, beloved brethren, your election by God. For our gospel did not come to you in word only, but also in power, and in the Holy Spirit and in much assurance, as you know what kind of men we were among you for your sake.
—1 Thessalonians 1:4-5

June 14

He Will Prosper Your Career

We urge you...that you also aspire to lead a quiet life, to mind your own business, and to work with your own hands, as we commanded you, that you may walk properly toward those who are outside, and that you may lack nothing.
—1 Thessalonians 4:10-12

My Prayer for Today

Father, help me to be industrious in Your kingdom. Help me to wade through the failures in order to obtain the blessings. Build in me a resilience that will withstand any attack the enemy brings against me. (Luke 10:19.) I know that the most successful people in the world are those who have failed the most, simply because they have done the most. May I never let obstacles or setbacks hinder me or shy me away from the prize that is set before me. (Micah 7:8; 1 Corinthians 9:24.)

My Confession for Today

I make it my heart's ambition to live a peaceful life, no matter how many devil heads I have to stomp to attain it. (Psalm 91:13; James 4:7.) I mind my own business, attend to my own affairs and needs, and work with my own hands to build a foundation for my prosperity. (Psalm 1:1-3.) I am dependent upon no man to meet my needs. I am never found begging for money or support. (Psalm 37:25.) In this way, my life wins the respect of those who are outside of faith.

Your Harvest Constantly Increases

My Prayer for Today

Father, You know my struggles and failures. You see all that I have suffered, much of which was from my own hand. Help me turn it around, Father. Bring me back from captivity. Cause my mistakes to become tools to help me organize my victory. Make my weeping a memory, Lord. Flood my life with the harvest of my hope.

My Confession for Today

My Father restores my fortunes like the raging streams of the Negev. (Psalm 126:4 NIV.) I have sown my seed and shall reap an abundant harvest. Through hardship and turmoil I have gathered my seed, and I have sown it in the midst of life's troubles. But, oh, my latter end! What I have sown in tears, I will reap with joy! I gather my harvest in bundles so large they cannot be carried! Perseverance always smiles in the end, and I'm smilin' big. (Romans 5:4-5.)

> *Bring back our captivity, O LORD, as the streams in the South. Those who sow in tears shall reap in joy. He who continually goes forth weeping, bearing seed for sowing, shall doubtless come again with rejoicing, bringing his sheaves with him.*
> *—Psalm 126:4-6*

June 16

The Lord Prepares Your Heart for His Instructions

LORD, You have heard the desire of the humble; You will prepare their heart; You will cause Your ear to hear, to do justice to the fatherless and the oppressed, that the man of the earth may oppress no more.
—Psalm 10:17-18

My Prayer for Today

Father, I am fully aware that You did not create one person to be more important than another. I realize that everyone I meet is in some way my superior, and that I, in some way, am theirs. Everyone is gifted and talented, and everyone has a divine mission to fulfill. Prepare me for mine, Father. Train me as a coach trains a prized athlete. (2 Timothy 2:5 NLT.) Cause my ear to hear and my heart to understand. (Psalm 143:8.)

My Confession for Today

The Lord has prepared my heart for His fellowship. His ear is attentive to the sound of my voice and He has prepared Himself to guide me in my way. (Psalm 73:24.) Those who oppress me shall now meet His justice. He has risen in my defense so the oppressor can oppress me no more.

God Richly Gives You All Things to Enjoy

My Prayer for Today

Father, never let me forget what matters most in life. Though I may prosper in every way and have all that I need and more, let it not be my first focus. Riches are fleeting and fully unworthy of my trust. You alone are my everlasting provision and safeguard against turmoil and disaster.

My Confession for Today

I am in complete self-control. I do not trust in uncertain riches, but in the counsel of my God. He richly provides me with good things of every kind to enjoy. I am not only rich in possessions, but rich in good deeds as well, being ever generous and always willing to share. Through my acts of generosity, I lay up for myself an abundance of treasures in heaven as a firm foundation for my future. (Matthew 6:20.) In this, I have taken hold of the life that is truly life—the very life that God desires for me to live. (Deuteronomy 30:19; John 20:31 NIV.)

Command those who are rich in this present age not to be haughty, nor to trust in uncertain riches but in the living God, who gives us richly all things to enjoy. Let them do good, that they be rich in good works, ready to give, willing to share, storing up for themselves a good foundation for the time to come, that they may lay hold on eternal life.
—1 Timothy 6:17–19

June 18

Your Heavenly Father Finds No Reason to Reject You

All that the Father gives Me will come to Me, and the one who comes to Me I will by no means cast out. For I have come down from heaven, not to do My own will, but the will of Him who sent Me. This is the will of the Father who sent Me, that of all He has given Me I should lose nothing, but should raise it up at the last day.
–John 6:37-39

My Prayer for Today

Father, I thank You for the security that I enjoy in Christ Jesus. In Him, I have eternal life and will never see destruction. (John 3:15-16.) I have Your promise that You will find no reason to cast me from Your presence. None of my security is placed in my own power. All of it, first to last, is placed in the blood of Jesus and sealed by the Holy Spirit. (1 John 1:7; Revelation 12:7; Ephesians 1:13.) Worry for my future has become a thing of the past. I can now live freely, by faith, and receive every blessing that You so desire to give. (John 8:36; Psalm 68:19.)

My Confession for Today

My heavenly Father has entrusted my eternal security to Jesus. I have turned to Him and pledged my endless devotion. (Romans 10:9.) He has given me His Word that He will find absolutely no reason to reject me. I have come to Him and have given Him my life, so from now on I don't need to fear. This is the Father's will: that I should never be lost again. I have been given new life and shall be raised up on the last day. (2 Corinthians 5:17.)

Jesus Became What You Are, that You Might Become What He Is

My Prayer for Today

Father, I thank You that in Christ Jesus I have become rich beyond measure. Worldly wealth cannot be compared to the true riches of becoming one with You. (John 17:21.) I am now an heir of heaven. (Ephesians 3:6; Romans 8:17.) This very day, people who have gone there before me will walk by my heavenly mansion and know that it was built for me. (John 14:2-3.) Even in this earth I am Your covenant partner through Jesus' blood. (Genesis 17:2-5; Ephesians 2:13-14.) I have every promise and Christ's own anointing. (2 Corinthians 1:20; 1 John 2:20,27.) I thank You for it all, Father. Help me to live in it according to Your perfect will.

For you know the grace of our Lord Jesus Christ, that though He was rich, yet for your sakes He became poor, that you through His poverty might become rich.
–2 Corinthians 8:9

My Confession for Today

I know the grace of my Lord Jesus, that though He was rich, for my sake He became poor, so that I, through His poverty, could become rich. I am continually and abundantly supplied with all good things. (Philippians 4:19; Psalm 84:11.) By faith I receive all that I desire and more. (Hebrews 11:1; Proverbs 10:24.) My imagination paints the canvas of my future, and I do not let go of that image until I hold the reality of it in my very hands.

June 20

God Looks Favorably upon You and Is Pleased to Prosper You

For I will look on you favorably and make you fruitful, multiply you and confirm My covenant with you. You shall eat the old harvest, and clear out the old because of the new. I will set My tabernacle among you, and My soul shall not abhor you.
—Leviticus 26:9–11

My Prayer for Today

Father, this day is a good day. I have You on my side prospering everything I set my hand to do. (Psalm 1:3) I have Your strength, fellowship, counsel, and assistance. This is a stress-free day, for You are looking upon me favorably, making me fruitful, multiplying me, and confirming Your covenant with me. Every day brings new gifts for me to enjoy. What a pleasure it is to serve You, Father. I am Yours forever.

My Confession for Today

The Lord looks upon me with favor. He causes everything that I do to be fruitful and prosperous. He multiplies me in all good things and in every good way. He sets me apart unto Himself, establishing and ratifying His covenant with me. I am living in the fullness of His abundance. My increase is continual, so that I must regularly clear out the old to make room for the new. (Psalm 115:14.)

You Are Blessed to Be a Blessing

My Prayer for Today

Father, I thank You for giving me the blessing. (Deuteronomy 28:8.) All of Your ability to prosper is within me at this very moment. (Ephesians 3:20; 1 John 3:2.) Therefore, as the key to my promotion is to always be worth more than I am paid, pour out such a blessing on me that those in my circle of influence see me not only as a blessing, but as an essential element of their own success. Every good leader sees themselves as a servant. (John 13:3-7.) So make me a good leader, Father. Help me to serve others and meet the needs of many in a shower of Your abundance. (Ezekiel 34:26.) According to Your Word, bless me that I may be a blessing to others.

I will make you a great nation; I will bless you and make your name great; and you shall be a blessing. I will bless those who bless you, and I will curse him who curses you; and in you all the families of the earth shall be blessed.
—Genesis 12:2-3

My Confession for Today

I have been called by God to fulfill the destiny that He has for my life. He has made me great and has blessed me with an abundance of all good things. All of my needs and desires are fully met in Him. (Ephesians 3:20.) God's blessing upon me makes me of ever-increasing value to those around me. I am created for regular promotion. (Psalm 75:6-7 KJV.) I am blessed and I am a blessing. In this awesome prosperity that I enjoy from my heavenly Father, I have plenty for myself, with an abundance left over.

June 22

The Word Is Your Defense

The devil said to Him, "If You are the Son of God, command this stone to become bread." But Jesus answered him, saying, "It is written...." Now when the devil had ended every temptation, he departed from Him until an opportune time.
–Luke 4:3–4, 13

My Prayer for Today

Father, train me in the ways of the Word and shield me from the deceptions of the enemy. Teach me to properly balance Your precepts and only move forward in ways that will bring You glory. (Psalm 119:27.) My life is not my own. I have given it to You in full understanding that You alone know what is best for me. I wish to be nothing more and nothing less than what You have created me to be. Make my life a self-actualizing journey of faith that glorifies You in every way.

My Confession for Today

I am a son/daughter of God led by the Spirit of God. (Romans 8:14.) When I am tempted by the devil, I use the Word of God as my defense. I understand that Satan and his demons know the Word well and will twist it to their own benefit. But I am a man/woman of the Word. It is rooted and grounded within my spirit in all wisdom and understanding. (Isaiah 11:2.) When the devil attacks, I rout him with it. (Ephesians 6:17; Hebrews 4:12.)

He Shall Give You the Desires of Your Heart

My Prayer for Today

Father, You are my joy and my delight. In You I have wisdom, freedom, everlasting supply, and unending love. (1 Corinthians 1:30; Luke 4:18; Philippians 4:19; Jeremiah 31:3.) I commit my life to You in every way. Only by Your guidance am I guaranteed success. Take Your heavenly machete and carve a path for me in this jungle. (Ephesians 6:17; Psalm 73:24.) Lead me to treasures that only You can find. Bring me into the land of excitement, everlasting joy, and absolute fulfillment. (Psalm 16:11.)

My Confession for Today

I trust in the Lord, and I do what is good. I dwell in the land and feed on His faithfulness. I delight myself in Him and He gives me the desires of my heart. I commit my way to Him and He ensures my success. He causes my righteousness to shine forth as the light and my justice as the noonday.

Trust in the LORD, and do good; dwell in the land, and feed on His faithfulness. Delight yourself also in the LORD, and He shall give you the desires of your heart. Commit your way to the LORD, trust also in Him, and He shall bring it to pass. He shall bring forth your righteousness as the light, and your justice as the noonday.
–Psalm 37:3-6

June 24

Your Burden Has Been Removed

I will walk among you and be your God, and you shall be My people. I am the LORD your God, who brought you out of...Egypt, that you should not be their slaves; I have broken the bands of your yoke and made you walk upright.
—Leviticus 26:12-13

My Prayer for Today

Father, thank You for freeing me from the yoke of bondage. You didn't create me to be a slave, but a son/daughter. You've made me Your own. By Jesus' sacrifice, I now have You as my closest companion. (Galatians 1:4; Hebrews 13:5.) You have removed my burden and made me to walk uprightly as one who is free. You have given me life and purpose. (John 10:10; Ephesians 1:11.) You bid me to walk as You walk and to live as You live. You mentor me through life's trials and see to it that I am never overwhelmed. You are a good Father and worthy of my praise.

My Confession for Today

The Lord has set His dwelling place within me and has given me His Word that He will never leave me nor forsake me. (1 Corinthians 3:16; Hebrews 13:5) His Spirit is ever with me and is indeed within me. He walks with me and His presence surrounds me. (Psalm 125:2.) He is my closest companion in this earth. He has broken the bars of the yoke of slavery that were once on my shoulders. He dashed them to pieces and declared that I am free! Through faith and perseverance I make sport of difficulties and disappointments and bring my Father glory in this earth.

Remember What God Has Done for You

My Prayer for Today

Father, help me to be aware of what I am doing and how it affects my life and spiritual walk. Help me to always remember what You have done for me. Fuse Your works onto the tablet of my heart and bring them to my remembrance that I may teach them to my posterity. (Proverbs 3:3; John 14:26.) There is an eternity at stake, Father. So, open the eyes of my children. Give them revelation of Your will and purpose for them. Cause them to know and understand Your precepts and to respond to the call You have placed on their lives.

Only take heed to yourself, and diligently keep yourself, lest you forget the things your eyes have seen, and lest they depart from your heart all the days of your life. And teach them to your children and your grandchildren,
–Deuteronomy 4:9

My Confession for Today

I attend and give my complete attention to all that the Lord has done for me. I do not let it slip from my mind. I keep these things in the midst of my heart all the days of my life. (Proverbs 4:21.) I teach them to my children and my grandchildren as long as I have breath within me.

June 26

He Will Bring Your Soul Out of Trouble

*Revive me, O
LORD, for Your
name's sake! For
Your righteousness'
sake bring my soul
out of trouble. In
Your mercy cut off
my enemies, and
destroy all those
who afflict my
soul; for I am
Your servant.*
—Psalm 143:11-12

My Prayer for Today

Father, I enlist Your assistance this day to help me fight this battle of faith. (1 Timothy 6:12.) Revive me and restore my strength. (2 Corinthians 12:9.) Cut off my enemies and eliminate those who afflict my soul. Create in me a powerforce that not only withstands every attack, but counters with dynamic, focused, and unstoppable faith. (Ecclesiates 4:12; Ephesians 6:13.)

My Confession for Today

God teaches me to do His will on the earth. (Psalm 143:10.) His Spirit leads me on a level ground, free of the bumps and potholes of confusion. (Romans 8:14; 1 Corinthians 14:3.) I am His own child and have taken the surname (family name) of God. (Ephesians 3:14-15; Isaiah 43:6-7.) For the sake of His name, He preserves my life and delivers me from trouble. (Psalm 121:7-8.)

If He Is Holy, so Are You

My Prayer for Today

Father, I submit myself to You in all things and in every way. I joyfully acknowledge my total dependence upon You for salvation, power, and blessing. I know that when I trust the One within, I never go without. I am now grafted into the tree and have become a partaker of its root and its fatness. I am as blessed as heaven itself and have within me all power to do all things. (2 Corinthians 4:7 NLT.) I do not support the root, but the root supports me.

My Confession for Today

Jesus is the Vine and I am a branch of the Vine. (John 15:5.) If the Vine is holy, I am holy as well. In this, I do not make an arrogant boast, just a statement of fact. It is a declaration of my total and complete dependency upon Jesus. It is the Vine that gives life to the branch. Without Jesus, I am nothing. It is not me who supports the Vine, but the Vine who supports me.

For if the firstfruit is holy, the lump is also holy; and if the root is holy, so are the branches. And if some of the branches were broken off, and you, being a wild olive tree, were grafted in among them, and with them became a partaker of the root and fatness of the olive tree, do not boast against the branches. But if you do boast, remember that you do not support the root, but the root supports you.
—Romans 11:16–18

June 28

Do Not War According to the Flesh

Though we walk in the flesh, we do not war according to the flesh. For the weapons of our warfare are not carnal but mighty in God for pulling down strongholds, casting down arguments and every high thing that exalts itself against the knowledge of God, bringing every thought into captivity to the obedience of Christ.
–2 Corinthians 10:3-5

My Prayer for Today

Father, I thank You that I have weapons of the spirit to fight against the devil's horde. (Ephesians 6:10-18.) I have the spiritual force of faith to change my circumstances and make things right. You did not place me on this earth to be a helpless victim of the enemy's attacks. To the contrary, You command me to be strong and courageous, and to overcome the world through faith. (Deuteronomy 31:6; 1 John 5:4.) Faith can never be divorced from courage. Therefore, I will live my life fearlessly and take my dominion over all that exalts itself against You.

My Confession for Today

Though I live in the world, I do not wage war as the world does, for the weapons of my warfare are not carnal, but spiritual. I have the very power of Christ to demolish every stronghold that has been raised up against the things of God. I tear down and refute all arguments, theories, reasonings and every proud and lofty thing that exalts itself above the knowledge of God. I take every thought captive to the obedience of Christ.

The Word and the Name Are Supreme

My Prayer for Today

Father, I fully understand that for me to worship toward Your holy temple is to worship toward myself. (1 Corinthians 3:16.) You now dwell within my heart. All of your strength, wisdom, and ability are right now within me. Every promise in Your Word is mine for the asking. When I present one to You, You respond with "yes" and "amen". (2 Corinthians 1:20.) In Your presence I have endless provision and strength to conquer the day. You make it easy to be courageous, Father. With You as my partner I cannot fail.

My Confession for Today

God has exalted His name and His Word above all things. (Philippians 2:9-11.) They are the keys that open the door of certainty to all of my prayers. I am bold and stouthearted enough to enter into the very throne room of God and fully expect Him to fulfill His Word on my behalf. (Hebrews 4:16.)

I will worship toward Your holy temple, and praise Your name for Your lovingkindness and Your truth; for You have magnified Your word above all Your name. In the day when I cried out, You answered me, and made me bold with strength in my soul.
—Psalm 138:2-3

June 30

Seek the Lord With Your Whole Heart

> But from there you will seek the LORD your God, and you will find Him if you seek Him with all your heart and with all your soul.
> —Deuteronomy 4:29

My Prayer for Today

Father, I know that You are not far from me. (Acts 17:27.) I do not have to call out to You from afar and hope that You hear my voice. I do not have to climb a mountain in order to find You or get You to recognize me. You are always here with me. You never leave me nor forsake me, despite my shortcomings. (Hebrews 13:5.) I have found You within me. You are my very heart and soul and the source of all my joy and fulfillment. (Psalm 16:11.)

My Confession for Today

I set my face like flint to seek my Father with all of my heart. (Isaiah 50:7.) With every fiber of my being I cling to Him, thirsting for His fellowship, for I know that it is His good pleasure to make Himself known to me. (Ephesians 1:9.) When I seek Him, I find Him, if I seek Him with all of my heart.

Give God Your Best Time

My Prayer for Today

Father, fill me with Your power as I draw near to You in faith. (1 Chronicles 29:11-12; James 4:8.) Restore to me any strength that I have unwittingly lost. Build me up, Father. Edify me and establish me on heights I have never known. (Habakkuk 3:19 KJV.) Reveal to me new strategies and show me things I have never seen. (John 16:13.) Help me to believe what I do not see, that I may see what I have believed. (John 20:29; Hebrews 11:1; 2 Corinthians 5:7; Mark 11:23-24.)

The report went around concerning Him all the more; and great multitudes came together to hear, and to be healed by Him of their infirmities. So He Himself often withdrew into the wilderness and prayed.
—Luke 5:15-16

My Confession for Today

I regularly and consistently take the time to go to an isolated place, free of distraction, to pray and fellowship with my heavenly Father. I am not moved by need, nor do I focus on how much work there is to do. (Psalm 16:18.) I am moved by design, doing things the way that God has commanded. (Proverbs 16:9.) I am wise to go to my Father for rest and rejuvenation.

July 2

Hope in God

Why are you cast down, O my soul? And why are you disquieted within me? Hope in God, for I shall yet praise Him for the help of His countenance.
–Psalm 42:5

My Prayer for Today

Father, though the world is in chaos, my faith is steady. You are above all—omniscient and omnipotent. None can succeed as Your enemy. And You are on my side. (Psalm 118:6.) I have Your Word that You will never leave me nor forsake me. (Hebrews 13:5.) You have promised that You will find no reason to cast me out. (John 6:37.) Therefore, I can find no valid reason to be worried or alarmed. If You are for me, who can succeed against me? (Romans 8:31.)

My Confession for Today

I refuse to be depressed about any circumstance or situation I find myself in. I always keep in mind that my heavenly Father loves me with all of His heart and is caring for me every second of every day. (1 Peter 5:7; Jeremiah 31:3.) He commands His loving-kindness in the daytime and at night His song remains with me. (Psalm 92:2.) My Father never fails to be there for me. He is my Comforter who restores to me the joy of my salvation. (John 14:26; Psalm 51:12.)

God's Name Is upon You

My Prayer for Today

Father, I thank You for giving me Your blessing.
What You have blessed is blessed forever. In
You, I have no reason to give up. Under Your
constant coaching and persistent guidance
my temperament has become fashioned for
endurance. My faith prevails through the blackest
storm. Though troubles surround me and the
enemy sends ruthless attacks, I remain steadfast
and unwavering. (Psalm 27:3.) I am always
conscious of Your presence within me. That alone
is enough to alleviate all fear. I acknowledge,
Father, that Your name is upon me and Your
blessing shall prevail. (Proverbs 18:10.)

*"The LORD bless
you and keep you;
the LORD make
His face shine
upon you, and be
gracious to you;
the LORD lift up
His countenance
upon you, and
give you peace."
So they shall
put My name
on the children
of Israel, and I
will bless them.*
—Numbers 6:24–27

My Confession for Today

The Lord has conferred upon me every blessing that heaven has
to offer. His eyes are trained upon me and He relentlessly watches
over me to insure my safety. (Psalm 34:15; 121:5 NIV.) He is my
ever-present Helper who supports me in all that I do. (John 14:26.)
His face shines upon me to enlighten my way and show me mercy,
kindness, and an abundance of favor. I bear His name as His own
child, have His permanent stamp of approval, and live in His
continuous peace.
(Psalm 84:11.)

July 4

The Truth Shall Make You Free

Then Jesus said to those Jews who believed Him, "If you abide in My word, you are My disciples indeed. And you shall know the truth, and the truth shall make you free."
–John 8:31-32

My Prayer for Today

Father, Your Word is truth; open the eyes of my understanding that I may comprehend its precepts. (John 17:17; Psalm 119:27.) Reveal to me its hidden treasures and cause me to be perceptive of its power and value. (Psalm 119:18; Hebrews 1:3.) Make me to be a disciple who imitates You in every way, and help me to blaze a trail of faith that will one day be the highway on which my children travel. (Ephesians 5:1-2.)

My Confession for Today

I am a true disciple of Jesus. I remain focused on His Word, continually meditating upon it, speaking it, and living according to its precepts. I know the truth and the truth has made me free. The hindrance of unworthiness has been removed from my life. (John 3:16; 2 Corinthians 5:19.) I now have free access to the treasuries of heaven, and I am welcomed as a son/daughter and heir of the kingdom. (Titus 3:5-7.)

Plant a Seed to Meet Your Need

My Prayer for Today

Father, thank You for revealing to me the methods of creation. You have caused all things to respond to the principles of seedtime and harvest. (Genesis 8:22.) Whatsoever I sow, that shall I also reap. (Galatians 6:7.) When I give, it is given back to me good measure, pressed down, shaken together, and running over. In this You prove that You are not the God of "just enough to get by." You are the God of abundance. (2 Corinthians 9:8.) It is Your perfect will that I increase more and more. (Psalm 115:14.) With You, there is always enough. You have not put a cap on my dreams, but bid me to continuously ask and receive that my joy may be full. (John 16:24.)

Give, and it will be given to you: good measure, pressed down, shaken together, and running over will be put into your bosom. For with the same measure that you use, it will be measured back to you.
—Luke 6:38

My Confession for Today

I live my life in a spirit of generosity. I always look for ways to give to others. When I give, God causes His favor to flow into my life so that I will receive the same kind of blessings in return. He takes the measure that I have given, anoints it with the power of increase, and then gives it back to me in an overflow of His abundance. (Psalm 65:11.)

July 6

He Will Guide You to Your Desired Haven

Then they cry out to the LORD in their trouble, and He brings them out of their distresses. He calms the storm, so that its waves are still. Then they are glad because they are quiet; so He guides them to their desired haven.
—Psalm 107:28-30

My Prayer for Today

Father, You are my strength and my shield. (Psalm 28:7.) You surround me with round-the-clock protection. You guide me through every trial and still the storm that rages against me. You bring me joy in the midst of suffering and heal all of my hurts. You encircle me with everlasting favor that attracts increase into my life. (Psalm 5:12; 18:35.) You know exactly what will make me happy and You faithfully guide me to my desired haven.

My Confession for Today

When troubles come my way, I call to God for assistance and He draws me from their grasp. In His great love for me, He stills the storms to a whisper and silences the raging waves of the sea. He restores my joy as praises fill my mouth. He then takes me by the hand and guides me to the realization of my dreams.

Use Your Emotions

My Prayer for Today

> *Then the Spirit of God came upon Saul when he heard this news, and his anger was greatly aroused.*
> *—1 Samuel 11:6*

Father, I know that You did not create me to live a cowardly life. Therefore, train me for battle. (Psalm 144:1.) Make me a faith warrior who conquers kingdoms and brings Your goodness on the scene. (2 Timothy 2:3; Romans 8:37.) Stir up my spirit against evil and give me wisdom for the fight. (Proverbs 2:7.) Help me to feel what You feel, and react the way that You react. Make my actions inspire other Christians to discover the kingly qualities that are hidden within them so that we may build a powerful force for good in this earth.

My Confession for Today

I am not built for apathy or complacency, but for action-packed faith. When reports come that are contrary to the will and purpose of God, I stir myself up against them. I pour the power of emotion into my faith to change the situation to the praise of God's glory. When I speak, I mean what I say and fully expect what I say to come to pass. When Satan raises his head in my direction, he knows he's got a fight on his hands.

July 8

Fill Your Heart With Good References

My heart is overflowing with a good theme; I recite my composition concerning the King; my tongue is the pen of a ready writer. You are fairer than the sons of men; grace is poured upon Your lips; therefore God has blessed You forever.
—Psalm 45:1-2

My Prayer for Today

Father, light my candle with the flame of Your mentorship. (Psalm 18:28.) Make my heart overflow with a good theme that I may speak words of faith and give birth to Your blessings. May Your grace be poured out upon my lips, Father. May every word that I speak be filled with Your love and perfect will.

My Confession for Today

My spirit is stirred and elated within me as I speak these words to my King. My tongue is as the pen of a ready writer to proclaim His praises today. I call to reference every good thing that is in me in Christ Jesus. He has made me to be the most excellent of men/women, and by His divine enabling, my lips carry His powerful anointing to the world.

You Have All Power and Authority in Jesus

My Prayer for Today

Father, I thank You that I have power and authority over and above all demons. I am in Jesus and He is in You. We three are one. (John 17:21.) Therefore, I have You there to back every word that I speak and every act of Your will that I perform. I have the power from You to heal the sick and cure diseases. By faith I can make mountains move and cause absolute turmoil in Satan's camp. (Mark 11:23-24.) His day has ended as far as I am concerned. This day I will move forward to repair what he has destroyed.

Then He called His twelve disciples together and gave them power and authority over all demons, and to cure diseases. He sent them to preach the kingdom of God and to heal the sick.
–Luke 9:1-2

My Confession for Today

Jesus has given me power and authority over all demons and to cure sicknesses and diseases of every kind. He has sent me out to proclaim the present fact of the Kingdom of God and to bring healing to a hurting world. The words that I speak are not empty. They are empowered with unwavering belief and they accomplish what I send them forth to do. (Isaiah 55:11.)

July 10

You Have an Awesome Inheritance

O LORD, You are the portion of my inheritance and my cup; You maintain my lot. The lines have fallen to me in pleasant places; yes, I have a good inheritance. I will bless the LORD who has given me counsel; my heart also instructs me in the night seasons. I have set the LORD always before me; because He is at my right hand I shall not be moved.
—Psalm 16:5-8

My Prayer for Today

Father, You are the source of my supply. You, are the very Creator of the universe who gives life to the dead and calls those things that be not as though they were (Romans 4:17); the very One who loves me so much that You chose to make Your home within my heart (Galatians 2:20); the One who provides for my every need. (Philippians 4:19.) Truly the lines have fallen to me in pleasant places. I am blessed above all that I can ask or imagine. (Ephesians 3:20.) I choose to let my imagination run wild, Father. Meet all of my needs and fulfill the desires of my heart according to Your Word.

My Confession for Today

My heavenly Father has assigned me my share of His inheritance and my cup overflows continually. (Psalm 23:5 NIV.) He has set my boundaries in a spacious and pleasant land, and has given me a delightful endowment. I praise the Lord for His counsel. Even at night, my spirit guides me in His way. With Him at my right hand, I stand strong in every circumstance.

He Is Your Shield and Exceedingly Great Reward

My Prayer for Today

After these things the word of the LORD came to Abram in a vision, saying, "Do not be afraid, Abram. I am your shield, your exceedingly great reward."
—Genesis 15:1

Father, it is easy to become distracted by the things of this life. The ways of this world are contrary to Your ways. To most of us, seeing is believing. To You, believing is seeing. I submit to You this day that I choose to live Your way. I walk by faith and not by sight. (2 Corinthians 5:7.) Though I have a long way to go in my spiritual growth, I will not use it as an excuse for inaction. As a great novel begins with a single word, so does a walk of faith begin with a single small faith step. Be my guide, Father. Coach me to become a powerforce in this earth.

My Confession for Today

I am afraid of nothing! God, the Creator of the universe, is my shield. He grants me abundance to the extreme. My reward, in Him, is exceedingly great. Everything that I do is covered in His anointing. I succeed in the midst of turmoil, and increase despite what the world is suffering. (Psalm 115:14; 22:19; 37:19.)

July 12

He Preserves You and Fills Your Heart's Desire

The LORD is near to all who call upon Him, to all who call upon Him in truth. He will fulfill the desire of those who fear Him; He also will hear their cry and save them. The LORD preserves all who love Him, but all the wicked He will destroy.
—Psalm 145:18-20

My Prayer for Today

Father, I thank You that I have passed from judgment into life. (Romans 5:18.) I have been translated from the kingdom of darkness into the kingdom of Your dear Son. (Colossians 1:13.) I am no longer as I once was. I am now in the royal line. You are my Father, Jesus is my Brother, and the Holy Spirit is my Instructor. Therefore, nothing can block the path of my success.

My Confession for Today

My heart belongs to God and His to me. We bring great joy to each other in this life. He fulfills my every desire and is always there to take His stand at my side. His eyes never leave me, nor do mine leave Him. (1 Peter 3:12.) We two are dedicated to our covenant and our love for each other will never run dry.

The Spirit Gives Life to the Natural

My Prayer for Today

It is the Spirit who gives life; the flesh profits nothing. The words that I speak to you are spirit, and they are life.
–John 6:63

Father, lead me again this day on the path of Your will. (Psalm 25:5.) Help me to perform the small tasks as if each one would buy me the life of my dreams. Take not adversity from me, but guide my hand to carve a path through it for others to follow. Show me the ways of Your Spirit and teach me the precepts that will set the captives free. (Psalm 25:4; Luke 4:18.)

My Confession for Today

The Spirit is what quickens things and brings them to life. (John 6:63 KJV.) The flesh does not renew or prevail over anything of lasting value. God quickened me into this new life by the Spirit, through the living Word. My spirit has been renewed and re-created with the very nature of God. (2 Peter 1:4.) I fully understand that the Word of God is spirit material. In the same way that Jesus used His words to bring things to life, I use His Word and principles to bring things to life as well. (Psalm 119:50.)

July 14

Keep Away from the Path of the Destroyer

You have tested my heart; You have visited me in the night; You have tried me and have found nothing; I have purposed that my mouth shall not transgress. Concerning the works of men, by the word of Your lips, I have kept away from the paths of the destroyer [the violent and lawless].
—Psalm 17:3-4

My Prayer for Today

Father, Your Word is my light and my salvation. (Psalm 119:81,105.) It is a sure guide through the darkness where the destroyer sets his snares. (Psalm 91:3.) Keep me in the security of Your grace, Father. Guide me in the ways of wisdom and protect me from the pitfalls of transgression. Strengthen me in the power of Your might. (Ephesians 6:10.) Help me to learn from my mistakes and to see the path of opportunity each one creates.

My Confession for Today

I am determined that the words of my mouth will be pure and in perfect agreement with the Word of God. When I set my faith goal, test it by the Word, believe in its fulfillment, and speak it forth into my life, I know that I shall have what I say. (Mark 11:24.) My faith is more powerful than my situation. (1 John 5:4.) I am never a victim of circumstances. God gave me the power to control my circumstances and to create the kind of life that brings Him glory in every way. (Romans 5:13; Ephesians 3:16 NIV.)

The Lord Delivers You from the Wicked

My Prayer for Today

Father, You are the God of my protection. I do not trust in the power of sword or shield, but in the strength of Your might. (2 Chronicles 20:6.) No matter what the odds or the enemy I have You as my security. You confront the enemy and cast him down before me. You deliver my life from the wicked and cause me to prosper in the midst of disaster. All that I am and all that I have greatly increases because of You, Father. (Psalm 115:14.) All praise be to Your glorious name.

My Confession for Today

I am held secure in the arms of my Father. (Isaiah 40:11.) When I call to Him, He hears me and rescues me from all oppression. (Psalm 40:1; Jeremiah 20:13.) He keeps me as the apple of His eye and hides me in the shadow of His wings. (Deuteronomy 32:10; Psalm 57:1.) When my enemies surround me and plot my ruin, God intervenes on my behalf. He draws His sword and clears the way before me. He takes the attack personally and delivers me with mighty acts of judgment.

> *They have closed up their fat hearts; with their mouths they speak proudly. They have now surrounded us in our steps; they have set their eyes, crouching down to the earth, as a lion is eager to tear his prey, and like a young lion lurking in secret places. Arise, O LORD, confront him, cast him down; deliver my life from the wicked with Your sword.*
> *—Psalm 17:10-13*

You Shall Be Satisfied

With Your hand from men, O LORD, from men of the world who have their portion in this life, and whose belly You fill with Your hidden treasure. They are satisfied with children, and leave the rest of their possession for their babes. As for me, I will see Your face in righteousness; I shall be satisfied when I awake in Your likeness.
—Psalm 17:14-15

My Prayer for Today

Father, this life is nothing compared to what You have prepared for me in heaven. Yet, everything I do in this life will be felt for eternity. This moment is of utter importance. Help me make it count, Father. Help me to convert my ideas into need fillers. Prepare me for increased power that I may be a blessing in this earth.

My Confession for Today

The Lord cherishes me and holds me dear to His heart. He stills my hunger and supplies me with an abundance of provisions. (Philippians 4:19.) My children live copiously with an unlimited supply of good things and I store up great wealth as an inheritance for each of them. (Proverbs 13:22.) I live under the commanded blessing of God and all that I do prospers without fail. (Deuteronomy 28:8; Psalm 1:3.)

God Will Fulfill His Word

My Prayer for Today

> The LORD said to Moses, "Has the LORD's arm been shortened? Now you shall see whether what I say will happen to you or not."
> —Numbers 11:23

Father, I thank You for making me unique among all of Your creation. (Psalm 139:14.) I am created for a purpose and a mission, one that You say will prosper me and give me hope and a future. (Ephesians 1:11; Jeremiah 29:11 NIV.) Lead and guide me, Father, and direct my steps.(Psalm 37:23; 119:133.) Reveal to me what to do and I will do it with all of my might. Help me to create more opportunities than I can find. Show me the path of dominion and make me wise to walk in it. (Jeremiah 6:16.)

My Confession for Today

The Lord's hand is not shortened and His ability ever remains the same. His Word to me is accomplished and I will see the results with my own eyes. Every good promise of the covenant is mine to receive. (1 Kings 8:56; 2 Corinthians 1:20.) I am blessed to live a stress-free and prosperous life. God's anointing is ever-present within me. No matter what I face, I am destined for victory. (1 Corinthians 15:57.)

July 18

Your Heavenly Father Speaks to You

He declares His word to Jacob, His statutes and His judgments to Israel. He has not dealt thus with any nation; and as for His judgments, they have not known them. Praise the LORD!
—Psalm 147:19-20

My Prayer for Today

Father, I thank You for giving me insight and understanding of Your precepts. By the power of Your promise, fill me with Your anointing and cause the words that I speak to come to pass. (Ephesians 1:17-23; Mark 11:23-24.) Bless me as only Your child can be blessed. You have not set a ceiling on my benefits. I am limited only by what I can believe I have received. Your Word declares that if I can believe, all things are possible for me. (Mark 9:23.) Therefore, give me Your wisdom and help me to create an inheritance that will be felt for generations to come. (Proverbs 13:22.)

My Confession for Today

God favors me so highly that He has determined to reveal to me what the world can never truly know: His Word. (Mark 4:11.) He gives me special knowledge and keen insight into its deepest meanings. I find great treasure in His promises and rejoice that each one is mine to receive. Whenever a need arises, I can rest assured that God has filled it in Jesus' name. (Philippians 4:19.)

He Lights up the Path Before You

My Prayer for Today

Father, light the lamp of my understanding. Enlighten my darkness and give me wisdom to make right decisions. Fill me with the benefits of Your promises. Give me what I desire that is in line with Your Word, and the time and energy to enjoy it. (Psalm 37:4.) Strengthen me in the power of Your might. Set me on high places and secure me there within the hedge of Your protection. (Psalm 139:5.)

My Confession for Today

God's Word flows through me in all of its perfection, as my shield, sword, and protective refuge. God arms me with His strength and makes my way flawless before Him. By His power I prevail through every battle. He trains me in the art of spiritual warfare and enables me to do what the world thinks impossible. (Ephesians 6:10-18; Mark 10:27.) The Lord has broadened my path so that in me there is no shadow of turning. (James 1:17.)

You will light my lamp; the LORD my God will enlighten my darkness. For by You I can run against a troop... I can leap over a wall. As for God, His way is perfect; the word of the LORD is proven; He is a shield to all who trust in Him.... God... arms me with strength, and makes my way perfect. He makes my feet like the feet of deer, and sets me on my high places. He teaches my hands to make war.... You have also given me the shield of Your salvation; Your right hand has held me up, Your gentleness has made me great. You enlarged my path under me, so my feet did not slip.
—Psalm 18:28-36

July 20

Encourage Yourself in the Lord

Now David was greatly distressed, for the people spoke of stoning him, because the soul of all the people was grieved, every man for his sons and his daughters. But David strengthened himself in the LORD his God.
—1 Samuel 30:6

My Prayer for Today

Father, You are my strength and my refuge. (Psalm 46:1.) In You, I have safety from those who plot my destruction. Grant me wisdom this day. Fill my mind with ideas to prosper not only myself, but those around me as well. (Proverbs 8:12.) Bless me that I may be a blessing, and train me that I may train others and provide them a sound example to follow. (Genesis 12:2.)

My Confession for Today

When turmoil comes in like a flood, I encourage myself in the Lord. I look to God and His Word for my confidence. (Proverbs 3:26.) When others fail me and forsake me, God takes His stand on my behalf. He sees to it that my provision is restored. Together, we overcome any and every problem that I may face. (1 John 4:4.)

All of the Covenant Blessings Are Yours

My Prayer for Today

Father, as I am blessed this day, in turn, make me a blessing to others. Let me not be self-centered, self-absorbed, and egotistical. I know I am blessed, and I thoroughly enjoy and appreciate it, but I want the same for others. Make me a blessing, Father. Make me to be like You. Your hand is open to the just and the unjust alike. (Matthew 5:45.) You own everything, yet You offer it all to anyone who will receive it. (Luke 12:29-32.) Give me the same attitude, Father. Teach me to be just like You.

My Confession for Today

By the Word of the Lord I am set high above all worldly people. (Deuteronomy 28:1.) All of His covenant blessings have come upon me and overtaken me. I am blessed (given divine favor, good fortune, happiness, prosperity, and good things of every kind) in the city and I am blessed in the country. Blessed are my children, my animals, and my garden. Blessed are my produce and my gatherings. I am blessed when I come in and blessed when I go out.

> *"Blessed shall you be in the city, and blessed shall you be in the country. Blessed shall be the fruit of your body, the produce of your ground and the increase of your herds, the increase of your cattle and the offspring of your flocks. Blessed shall be your basket and your kneading bowl. Blessed shall you be when you come in, and blessed shall you be when you go out."*
> *—Deuteronomy 28:3-6*

July 22

You Live Under God's Commanded Blessing

The LORD will cause your enemies who rise against you to be defeated before your face; they shall come out against you one way and flee before you seven ways. The LORD will command the blessing on you in your storehouses and in all to which you set your hand, and He will bless you in the land which the LORD your God is giving you.
—Deuteronomy 28:7–8

My Prayer for Today

Father, You are my covenant associate and friend. There is no power to bless but that which You grant, and there is no power to curse but that which You allow. As we are bound by our covenant, protect me with all the power that You possess. Command Your blessing upon me and establish me. Use Your influence to increase and prosper all that I set my hand to do.

My Confession for Today

The Lord causes my enemies who rise up against me to be defeated before my face. They rise up against me in one direction, but flee from me in seven directions. The Lord commands blessings on all of my treasuries and on everything that I set my hand to do. He gives me abundant prosperity in the land which He has given me. I am established in holiness and set apart unto the Lord. (Ephesians 4:24; Psalm 4:3.) He makes His declaration that I am His and under His guardianship. (Isaiah 43:1; 1 Peter 2:25 NLT.)

You Are Supposed to Have More than Enough

My Prayer for Today

Father, I thank You that people recognize Your presence in me. I thank You for pouring Your unlimited supply into my life so that I am never in want in any way. All of my needs are fully met. (Philippians 4:19.) Help me to use what You have given to glorify Your name. Keep me from squandering Your provision. Make me wise in all things. Help me to hold myself to a higher standard than what others expect of me, and may my previous best be my only competition.

My Confession for Today

All of the people of the world clearly see that I am called by the name of the Lord. They recognize that I am in His family. I am His son/daughter and heir, and His blessings are evident in life. (Romans 8:16-17.) This fact sparks terror in the hearts of my enemies. The Lord gives me a tremendous surplus of prosperity for my home and family. The fruit of my body, the young of my cattle, and the produce of my ground are blessed with His abundance.

Then all peoples of the earth shall see that you are called by the name of the LORD, and they shall be afraid of you. And the LORD will grant you plenty of goods, in the fruit of your body, in the increase of your livestock, and in the produce of your ground, in the land of which the LORD swore to your fathers to give you.
—Deuteronomy 28:10-11

God's Treasure Is Your Inheritance

The LORD will open to you His good treasure, the heavens, to give the rain to your land in its season, and to bless all the work of your hand. You shall lend to many nations, but you shall not borrow. And the LORD will make you the head and not the tail; you shall be above only, and not be beneath, if you heed the commandments of the LORD your God, which I command you today, and are careful to observe them.
–Deuteronomy 28:12–13

My Prayer for Today

Father, I thank You for the unfailing provision that I now enjoy. You bless all of the work of my hands and cause me to live free of the bondage of debt. You bring associations into my life who are conducive to my success. You cause me to be a light to those in the darkness and You assist me as I lead them on the path of their dreams. (Matthew 5:16.)

My Confession for Today

My Lord gives rain to my land precisely when I need it. He has opened to me His heavenly treasury. With perfect timing, He rains it down upon me and blesses all the work of my hands. I am a lender and not a borrower. I lend to many and borrow from none. I am the head and not the tail, above only and not beneath. I am destined to take the lead in any enterprise I undertake. My Father has placed me at the top and never at the bottom, for I keep His Word and I am careful to adhere to His statutes.

Give the Lord First Place in Your Life

My Prayer for Today

Father, help me to be true to Your Word and the purpose that You have placed within me. (Ephesians 1:11.) Reveal to me the mysteries of Your precepts and their specific purpose in my life. (Ephesians 1:9; 6:19.) I know that I am here to have fellowship with You as well as with those in our entire family, the body of Christ, who are in my sphere of influence. (1 John 1:3,7.) Our purpose is to enjoy each other and be of service to one another. Clarify my purpose and make me a self-actualized individual. Show me the gifts and hidden talents that make me unique among all of creation. Help me to know myself totally that I may bring the best of service to all.

So you shall not turn aside from any of the words which I command you this day, to the right or the left, to go after other gods to serve them.
–Deuteronomy 28:14

My Confession for Today

I do not reject any of my Father's requirements. I do not steer away from them even a little to the right or to the left. I set them firmly in my heart and place my complete trust in them regardless of what my eyes may see or what other gods—the lusts of this world—may offer. The righteous requirement of the Law is fulfilled in me. (Romans 8:4.) I have been made the very righteousness of God in Christ Jesus. (2 Corinthians 5:21.) My trust is firmly planted in Him.

July 26

God Makes Good on His Word

God is not a man, that He should lie, nor a son of man, that He should repent. Has He said, and will He not do? Or has He spoken, and will He not make it good?
—Numbers 23:19

My Prayer for Today

Father, You make good on Your every promise to me. Your ways are infinitely higher than those of men. (Isaiah 55:9.) Everything You do is filled with honor and integrity, encouragement and blessing, and unconditional love. Make me like You, Father. Mold my life into a mirror reflection of Your character and nature. (2 Corinthians 3:18.) Show me everything I need to know to glorify You in all that I do.

My Confession for Today

My Father is not a man that He would lie to me. He does not shrink back from any of His promises. What He has said, He does. What He has spoken comes to pass in my life. He presents to me every good promise of His Word, and gives me assurance that He will bring it to pass. I am a truly blessed man/woman with a destiny that defies the imagination. (1 Corinthians 2:9.)

He Blesses You and Multiplies You in Every Way

My Prayer for Today

Father, I thank You for the blessing that You have given me. I am blessed spirit, soul, and body. You fill me with inspiration for every area of my life. Your friendship and partnership enlightens my life in every way. (Psalm 18:28.) All that I do is a joint venture with the God of all creation! Ideas flood my mind for new goals and dreams. (Proverbs 8:12.) Help me not to plant my ideas in pots, Father, but in fertile fields. Give me wisdom to flourish. Cause me to increase in a shower of abundance that I may be a blessing in this earth. (Ezekiel 34:26.)

My Confession for Today

With the blessing of Abraham, my Father blesses me. With the multiplying of Abraham, my Father multiplies me. My faith brings me all that I desire from the treasury of God's promises. Through Abraham's Seed [Jesus] I possess the gates of my enemies. (Galatians 3:16; Genesis 24:60; Romans 8:37.) In Him, I have received happiness, peace, prosperity and good things of every kind.

Blessing I will bless you [Abraham], and multiplying I will multiply your descendants as the stars of the heaven and as the sand which is on the seashore; and your descendants shall possess the gate of their enemies. In your seed all the nations of the earth shall be blessed, because you have obeyed My voice.
—Genesis 22:17-18

July 28

Rejoice in the Advancement of God's Kingdom

They sang responsively, praising and giving thanks to the LORD: "For He is good, for His mercy endures forever toward Israel." Then all the people shouted with a great shout, when they praised the LORD, because the foundation of the house of the LORD was laid.
–Ezra 3:11

My Prayer for Today

Father, I thank You that You are always good to me. I never have to worry about Your wrath, or whether You might harm me in order to teach me something. You are good and all that You do is good. (Psalm 145:9.) Teach me to always remember Your goodness, Father. Help me lay a foundation where I can build a joyful life. Help me learn from yesterday, that I may do what I can today to create a better tomorrow.

My Confession for Today

The Lord is my foundation. His is the immovable base on which I rest and the surety that I will stand. He is not good to me only some of the time, He is good to me all of the time. His love for me endures forever. (Hebrews 13:5.) His grace and mercy have hedged me in so that His power will never be taken from me. (Psalm 139:5.) I will praise Him with great shouts of joy all the days of my life.

To Know God Is to Love Him

My Prayer for Today

> *Then they said to Him, "Where is Your Father?" Jesus answered, "You know neither Me nor My Father. If you had known Me, you would have known My Father also."*
> *–John 8:19*

Father, the moment I received Jesus as my Savior, You came to dwell within my heart. I am known by You, and as I have read Your Word and spent time with You, I have come to know You and love You. You are my Father forever and no power in the universe can ever separate us. (Romans 8:35, 39.) As Jesus is in You, I am in Him, and we three are one. (John 17:21.) What a wonder! What a joy! What a privilege it is to be an actual son/daughter of the living God. (John 1:12.) I cherish You, Father. I thank You that I am Your child, friend, student, and partner, now and forevermore.

My Confession for Today

Jesus has brought me into an intimate relationship with Himself. I love Him; He is my Friend, my Lord, my Savior, and my Brother. I both know Him and am known by Him. I know our Father intimately as well. He is my Dad (Abba) and is ever watching over me. (Romans 8:15; Psalm 34:15.) He is my ever-present trainer in the ways of faith. He shows me how to maintain my belief and project it to change my circumstances and live the kind of life that is a reflection of heavenly royalty. (1 Peter 2:9.)

July 30

You Have a Helper

Nevertheless I tell you the truth. It is to your advantage that I go away; for if I do not go away, the Helper will not come to you; but if I depart, I will send Him to you. And when He has come, He will convict the world of sin, and of righteousness, and of judgment: of sin, because they do not believe in Me; of righteousness, because I go to My Father and you see Me no more; of judgment, because the ruler of this world is judged.
—John 16:7-11

My Prayer for Today

Father, I thank You for giving me the ever-present assistance of the Holy Spirit. With Him as my chief mentor, my success is inevitable. His wisdom has become my wisdom and His strength has become my strength. (Ephesians 1:17-20.) Nothing that I think or do is separate from His influence—it is swayed in the direction of Your will.

My Confession for Today

It is to my advantage that Jesus has gone on to heaven to take His place at the right hand of the Father. His going has brought the Holy Spirit—my Comforter, Counselor, and Strength—to me. He is ever with me in close fellowship, revealing to me all that I need to know. (John 16:13.) It's He who has revealed to me my deliverance from sin and right standing in God's eyes. (Romans 5:21 NLT.) He gives me a direct revelation of Satan's defeat and a full understanding of my rights, privileges, and authority in Jesus.

God's Word Is Perfect

My Prayer for Today

Father, the precepts and principles You have shown me in Your Word are perfect. They are a guide to me to keep me from stumbling. (Jude 1:24.) Their wisdom makes me wise; they enlighten the eyes of my understanding so that I can make the right decisions in my walk of faith. (Ephesians 1:18.) Open Your precepts up to me more and more, Father. Teach me the way that I should go and guard me against taking the wrong path in life. (Psalm 27:11; 25:20 NIV.)

My Confession for Today

My wisdom comes from the Word of my Father. The perfection of His ways has revived my soul and given joy to my heart. (Psalm 18:5; 119:25; Jeremiah 15:16.) The radiance of His commands is the light by which I see. (Psalm 119:105.) The Word is more precious to me than the purest of gold and sweeter to me than honey from the comb. (Psalm 19:9-10; 119:103.) By it, I am warned of all pending danger and in keeping the statutes therein, I store up the greatest of rewards. (Hebrews 11:7; Deuteronomy 28:1-2.)

The law of the LORD is perfect, converting the soul; the testimony of the LORD is sure, making wise the simple; the statutes of the LORD are right, rejoicing the heart; the commandment of the LORD is pure, enlightening the eyes; the fear of the LORD is clean, enduring forever; the judgments of the LORD are true and righteous altogether.
—Psalm 19:7-9

August 1

It Will Go Well with You and Your Children After You

You shall therefore keep His statutes and His commandments which I command you today, that it may go well with you and with your children after you, and that you may prolong your days in the land which the LORD your God is giving you for all time.
—Deuteronomy 4:40

My Prayer for Today

Father, You are the power behind a long and prosperous life. Your precepts are flawless. By following Your will, I am guaranteed success. (Joshua 1:7-8.) Lead me, Father. (Psalm 139:24.) Teach me Your ways. (Psalm 25:4.) Instill within me the knowledge that I need that it may go well with me and my children after me, and that I may prolong my days.

My Confession for Today

I know, understand, and give my complete attention to the fact that my heavenly Father is the one true God in heaven above and on earth beneath. (1 Corinthians 8:6.) There is no other. He is my Father, my Lord, my Master, my Teacher, and my Example. I obey all of His commands, for by them it goes well with me and with my children after me. He has engrafted His Word into my heart so that I may prolong my days in a full and abundant life in the land that He has given me as an inheritance for all of eternity.

He Carried It All

My Prayer for Today

Father, thank You for choosing me to be Your child. (John 15:16.) Thank You for turning me from the path of destruction and setting me on a highway of prosperity. (Proverbs 8:20-21.) Thank You for making Jesus my substitute so that I may enjoy life the way You intended for it to be lived. (Romans 5:8; John 10:10.) You have left no shortage of supply. (Philippians 4:19.) All that I need in spirit, soul, and body are now mine to receive by faith, and I thank You for it all in Jesus' name.

My Confession for Today

Jesus bore my sicknesses and carried my pains. He was smitten, afflicted, and pierced through the hands and feet because of my transgressions. He was bruised and battered because of my wickedness. He became sick with my sicknesses and suffered excruciating pain on my account. He took my punishment upon Himself and gave me His peace. Because of His wounds, I am made well. I am now totally healed spirit, soul, and body, and I have God's promise that He will never turn His back on me. (Hebrews 13:5.)

Surely He has borne our griefs and carried our sorrows; yet we esteemed Him stricken, smitten by God, and afflicted. But He was wounded for our transgressions, He was bruised for our iniquities; the chastisement for our peace was upon Him, and by His stripes we are healed. All we like sheep have gone astray; we have turned, every one, to his own way; and the LORD has laid on Him the iniquity of us all.
—Isaiah 53:4-6

August 3

Trust God, Not Riches

Why should I fear in the days of evil, when the iniquity at my heels surrounds me? Those who trust in their wealth and boast in the multitude of their riches, none of them can by any means redeem his brother, nor give to God a ransom for him— for the redemption of their souls is costly, and it shall cease forever.
–Psalm 49:5-8

My Prayer for Today

Father, I recognize that the redemption of my soul was costly. You sacrificed more than reason can explain. (1 Corinthians 6:20; 1 Peter 2:24.) I gave You no cause to want me, and yet You pursued me with relentless passion. You have always reached out to me in love. Even in the midst of my sin, Your grace surrounded me and Your mercy protected me. (Genesis 19:19.) You chose me, drew me to Yourself, and caused me to understand Your precepts. (John 6:44; 15:16; Psalm 119:27.) I will forever be grateful for this, Father. All praise be to Your precious name.

My Confession for Today

I refuse to be afraid in days of adversity. When times are bad and the world is in turmoil, I remain confident. (Psalm 27:3.) When iniquity surrounds me and snaps at my heels, I remain steadfast and stable. I do not trust in my wealth to provide my security. My hope is wholly in God. (Psalm 43:5.) He alone gives me certainty for the future. He alone is my redemption and shelter in this life. (Psalm 61:3.)

You Are Like an Aloe Planted by the Lord

My Prayer for Today

Father, as Your child and heir to Your kingdom you have made me to be blessed above all the world. (James 2:5.) You cause my influence to be felt abroad. You give me strength like that of a wild ox and make me to prevail over my enemies. (Numbers 24:8; Psalm 18:29,34,37.) Your blessing is upon my house and Your anointing of increase encompasses all that I do. With Your assistance, I progress more and more, moving in grace and faith, and flourishing so abundantly that I become the envy of kings.

My Confession for Today

I am like a garden beside a flowing river — like an aloe planted by the Lord. I live in a beautiful home. I have my own sources of riches and plenty — an endless provision from my heavenly Father. My children dwell within the flood of His abundance. I am poised and prepared to conquer life's difficulties. I am as a couched lion that no enemy dares to arouse. My partnership with God is evident and my provision flows like a geyser in a desert land. (Isaiah 43:19.)

How lovely are your tents, O Jacob! Your dwellings, O Israel! Like valleys that stretch out, like gardens by the riverside, like aloes planted by the LORD, like cedars beside the waters. He shall pour water from his buckets, and his seed shall be in many waters. His king shall be higher than Agag, and his kingdom shall be exalted.
–Numbers 24:5-7

August 5

God Thinks Good Thoughts Toward You

For I know the thoughts that I think toward you, says the LORD, thoughts of peace and not of evil, to give you a future and a hope. Then you will call upon Me and go and pray to Me, and I will listen to you. And you will seek Me and find Me, when you search for Me with all your heart.
–Jeremiah 29:11-13

My Prayer for Today

Father, I know the thoughts that You have for me are always for good and never for evil. You hold me in the palm of Your hand and shield me from the violent attack. (Isaiah 49:16; 2 Samuel 22:3.) You prosper me in the midst of famine and despair, and rescue me from all oppression. (Psalm 37:19; Daniel 6:27.) Under Your banner of protection I enjoy good things of every kind. (Exodus 17:15.) Keep me close to You, Father. Help me to see the path that You want me to take.

My Confession for Today

All of God's thoughts for me are for good and never evil. His plan for my life is to make me prosperous, give me hope, and provide for me a glorious future. He has hand-picked everything that is best for me in life and presents it to me with great joy. His desire for me is to live in His abundance. (John 10:10.) My call brings a smile to my Father's face and He listens to me with great concern. (Psalm 4:6 NLT; 1 John 5:14.) He has rescued me from the powers of darkness and is now enjoying my continual companionship. (Colossians 1:13.)

The Lord Shall Enlighten Your Darkness

My Prayer for Today

Father, thank You for Your unfailing guidance. You enlighten my way before me and cause me to understand the direction that I must take. By You, I can conquer any enemy and overcome any hardship. You are within me, Your ability has become my ability. (John 17:23; 14:12.) Nothing is impossible to me so long as I believe. (Mark 9:23.) You are the strength by which I live and the power behind all of my victories. (1 Corinthians 15:57.)

My Confession for Today

My ears are opened to the Lord's instruction, and I remain firmly on the path of His perfect will. He Himself lights my way before me. By Him, I have victory over every enemy. I run through a garrison and leap over their fortified walls. My Father is my Shield, Refuge, Rock, and Fortress! He walks in front of me to clear my path. I live a hindrance-free life. Success comes to me with an ease that seems almost effortless.

You are my lamp, O LORD; the LORD shall enlighten my darkness. For by You I can run against a troop; by my God I can leap over a wall. As for God, His way is perfect; the word of the LORD is proven; He is a shield to all who trust in Him. For who is God, except the LORD? And who is a rock, except our God? God is my strength and power, and He makes my way perfect. He makes my feet like the feet of deer, and sets me on my high places.
–2 Samuel 22:29–34

He Trains You for Battle

[The Lord] teaches my hands to make war, so that my arms can bend a bow of bronze. You have also given me the shield of Your salvation; Your gentleness has made me great. You enlarged my path under me; so my feet did not slip.

—2 Samuel 22:35-37

My Prayer for Today

Father, You are forever my mentor and my guide. You are my master trainer who instructs me in the art of war. In You, I can do the impossible and cause blessing to flow in the midst of desolation. (Luke 1:37; Exodus 17:6.) You enlarge Your path beneath me so that my feet do not slip. Every day my strength is renewed so that I may overcome the battles that I must endure. (Deuteronomy 33:25; John 16:33.) You have made it so that nothing can keep me from receiving Your blessings by faith.

My Confession for Today

The Lord trains my hands to do battle so that my arms can bend a bow of bronze. He has given me the shield of His salvation.   By His grace, He came down to my level that I may be lifted up to His level. He has enlarged my steps under me to keep me from falling. His greatness is within me and by His strength I destroy the enemy. I refuse to turn back until my enemies are consumed. (2 Samuel 22:38.) I keep them at bay and they shall not arise! (Psalm 41:11; Deuteronomy 28:7.) My Lord has girded me with strength for the battle. (1 Samuel 2:4.) I see nothing but the backs of my enemies as they turn tail and run from me utterly terrified! (Exodus 23:27.)

Through Jesus There Is Plentiful Provision

My Prayer for Today

Father, thank You for drawing me to Yourself through Jesus. (John 12:32.) He is the door by which I have found salvation. Through Him I have found a pasture where my faith can flourish. Because of what Jesus did for me, I have a position that almost seems too good to be true. I am Your actual son/daughter, a new creation, a partaker of the covenant, and a recipient of the promises. (Romans 8:17; 2 Corinthians 5:17; 2 Peter 1:4.) By faith I can receive all the desires of my heart. (Mark 11:24; Psalm 37:4.) I am ever so deeply grateful for this, Father. All praise to Your holy name.

Then Jesus said to them again, "Most assuredly, I say to you, I am the door of the sheep. All who ever came before Me are thieves and robbers, but the sheep did not hear them. I am the door. If anyone enters by Me, he will be saved, and will go in and out and find pasture."
–John 10:7-9

My Confession for Today

Jesus is the Door for the sheep. I enter into God's blessings and salvation through Him alone. I am one of the true sheep. I neither listen to, nor obey the voice of a thief. It is through Jesus that I have entered into this mighty covenant communion with God that I now enjoy. (Galatians 3:17.) In Him, I enjoy true freedom and liberty, and find such pasture that whatever the circumstance, good or bad, I have all that I need and more.

August 9

Jesus Gave You Abundant Life

The thief does not come except to steal, and to kill, and to destroy. I have come that they may have life, and that they may have it more abundantly.
—John 10:10

My Prayer for Today

Father, far be it from me to ever accuse You of causing the hardships and difficulties that I face. You are the giver of abundant life. What You do is good and all that You give is good. (Genesis 1; Psalm 73:1.) Destruction is not in Your nature. Your perfect will is to fill my life with good things of every kind. (Joshua 23:14; Matthew 7:11.) Partner with me, Father, and instruct me as to how to receive. Be my tutor in the ways of faith so that my life will glorify You in every way.

My Confession for Today

I am living the abundant life. God has poured His unfailing provision upon me and I never have to go without. Jesus Himself is my shepherd. He so loves me that He willingly laid down His life to provide for me all that He has and all that He is. (John 10:17-18.) He bought God the right to recreate me as His own child. (1 Corinthians 6:20; 2 Corinthians 5:17-18.) I am now an heir of the kingdom and a recipient of its blessings. (Romans 8:11.)

God Wants to Make You Prosperous Beyond Measure

My Prayer for Today

Father, Your Word is a powerful declaration of Your desire to bless. Under Your anointing I can reap a hundred fold in the same year I have sown. You do not put a ceiling on how much I can receive. The more I sow, the more I prosper. (Galatians 6:7.) Father, I glory in Your anointing for increase. Yet, I also remember Your warnings. Keep my heart from the love of money and keep my purposes within Your perfect will. (1 Timothy 6:10-11.)

My Confession for Today

The Lord has blessed me with abundance. His favor finds a home in me. He receives the seed that I have sown and blesses it so that it will bring forth the maximum yield. He has taken hold of me in His powerful arm and promoted me. (Isaiah 40:11; Psalm 75:6-7 KJV.) In Him, I find wealth and position. I have been separated from the world. (John 17:16.) He has placed within me extraordinary qualities that are unlike any other. As I live according to my gifts, I become a magnet for prosperity and provision.

> *Then Isaac sowed in that land, and reaped in the same year a hundredfold; and the LORD blessed him. The man began to prosper, and continued prospering until he became very prosperous; for he had possessions of flocks and possessions of herds and a great number of servants. So the Philistines envied him.*
> —Genesis 26:12-14

August 11

Seek Wisdom and Understanding

Yes, if you cry out for discernment, and lift up your voice for understanding, if you seek her as silver, and search for her as for hidden treasures; then you will understand the fear of the LORD, and find the knowledge of God. For the LORD gives wisdom; from His mouth come knowledge and understanding; He stores up sound wisdom for the upright; He is a shield to those who walk uprightly; He guards the paths of justice, and preserves the way of His saints.
—Proverbs 2:3–8

My Prayer for Today

Father, You are the giver of wisdom and the purveyor of knowledge. Therefore, fill me with these in an abundant supply. Teach me Your ways that I may live my life like You in every possible way. (Psalm 86:11.) Be my shield against error and my safeguard against misdirection. Guard my path and preserve my way before me.

My Confession for Today

The search for wisdom is of prime importance in my life. I understand the fear of the Lord and have personal and intimate knowledge of God. It is the Lord's good will to grant me wisdom; therefore, I know that when I seek it out, He will make certain that I find it. Through God's Word I gain tremendous knowledge and understanding. He holds victory in reserve for me and stands guard with me in every circumstance and endeavor that I undertake. (1 Corinthians 15:57.)

He Gives You Favor with the Authorities

My Prayer for Today

Father, I place Your will above all things. To please You and honor You is my first ambition. In You alone I find true blessing. To walk with You is to surround myself with favor. (Psalm 5:12.) According to Your promise, Father, cause those in authority to look favorably upon me. Set me in positions where my gifts are needed and lead me to acts of service for which I am best suited.

My Confession for Today

I take courage to do all that the Lord has commanded. He has given me favor with the rulers of this world and with their officials. He has set me in a position of high honor among them. By the anointing of the Lord, I attract favor and good fortune into my life. Therefore, I am bold to take my place in His army and go forward to do His work. (2 Timothy 2:3.)

Blessed be the LORD God of our fathers, who has put such a thing as this in the king's heart, to beautify the house of the LORD which is in Jerusalem, and has extended mercy to me before the king and his counselors, and before all the king's mighty princes. So I was encouraged, as the hand of the LORD my God was upon me; and I gathered leading men of Israel to go up with me.
–Ezra 7:27-28

August 13

He Causes Your Enemies to Fear You

This day I will begin to put the dread and fear of you upon the nations under the whole heaven, who shall hear the report of you, and shall tremble and be in anguish because of you.
—Deuteronomy 2:25

My Prayer for Today

Father, I thank You that You always have my back. If anyone desires to come against me, they must come through You first. You are my sentinel and warrior advocate who never fails to protect me. (Psalm 27:1.) As I move through this day, I recognize that You have gone before me. (Deuteronomy 31:8.) You have placed fear and dread in the hearts of my enemies. You cause them to hear Your report of me and to be in anguish because of me.

My Confession for Today

God Himself has gone before me to clear the way for my victory. He causes me to have favor with my peers and associates, and shields me from adversity. (Psalm 5:12.) This day He has put the fear and dread of me in the hearts of my enemies. They hear His report of me and cancel their plans to destroy me. They see me as one to be avoided and even grant me favor to keep in my good graces.

The Holy Spirit Is Your Guide

My Prayer for Today

Father, I thank You that You have not left me in this earth without a guide. (John 14:26.) By the Holy Spirit within me I can know what to do and how to react in any situation that I face. It is He who reveals to me my inheritance in Christ Jesus. He reminds me of Your promise and even shows me things to come. By His constant supervision, I prosper and succeed in every endeavor I undertake.

My Confession for Today

The Holy Spirit is within me, leading and guiding me through the paths of this life. He tells me what He hears from the Father and trains me in the ways of faith. He even warns me of things to come so that I am not taken by surprise. With Him as my Counsel, I am guaranteed success in all that I do. It is He who reveals to me the vast inheritance that I have in Christ Jesus and He trains me to receive it now in this life. (Ephesians 1:10-11.) All that the Father has belongs to Jesus and He freely gives it all to me through the Holy Spirit who dwells within me.

When He, the Spirit of truth, has come, He will guide you into all truth; for He will not speak on His own authority, but whatever He hears He will speak; and He will tell you things to come. He will glorify Me, for He will take of what is Mine and declare it to you. All things that the Father has are Mine. Therefore I said that He will take of Mine and declare it to you.
—John 16:13–15

August 15

The Lord Will Make You Abound in Every Good Way

The LORD your God will make you abound in all the work of your hand, in the fruit of your body, in the increase of your livestock, and in the produce of your land for good. For the LORD will again rejoice over you for good as He rejoiced over your fathers.
—Deuteronomy 30:9

My Prayer for Today

Father, I thank You for giving me an anointing to abound in all things. Everything I set my hand to do prospers without fail. (Psalm 1:3.) Help me to always understand that You rejoice when I prosper. (Psalm 35:27.) You are not the God who takes pleasure in sickness and poverty. (3 John 2.) You never use adversity to cause me harm. Your hand is always open to me so that I can receive the desires of my heart through faith. (Mark 11:24; Psalm 37:4.)

My Confession for Today

My Father takes great pleasure in the abundance of my prosperity. He prospers my children, my land, and my cattle. As His born again recreated child, I am set apart from the rest of the world and given the right to receive from His stores of abundance. (Psalm 4:3.) I am one who has been singled out to be a recipient of His blessings and His goodness. I follow His instruction and treasure His commands. (Psalm 119:111-112.)

The Word Gives You Favor and High Esteem with God and Man

My Prayer for Today

Father, You are perfect in all of Your ways. Every word from Your lips must be fulfilled. (Numbers 23:19.) Your precepts give life and bring prosperity, protection and peace to those who receive them. (John 5:24.) I fuse them to my heart and never allow them to depart from my lips.(Isaiah 59:21.) By them, I find favor and high esteem with You and with men. You are the Lord and King of my life, and I trust You with all of my heart. I commit my path to You and I am confident in the direction that You show me.

My Confession for Today

I am a wise son/daughter of the living God. I understand and willingly submit to His ways in order to be a success in life. My life is prolonged and is a joy to live. Love and faithfulness guide my decisions; favor prevails in my life, and I obtain a good and honorable name in the sight of God and men. I always am God-inside minded and never cease to acknowledge His presence to guide me in all I do. With Him at the point, all of my paths are made straight.

Do not forget my law, but let your heart keep my commands; for length of days and long life and peace they will add to you. ...bind [mercy and truth] around your neck, write them on the tablet of your heart, and so find favor and high esteem in the sight of God and man. Trust in the LORD with all your heart, and lean not on your own understanding; in all your ways acknowledge Him, and He shall direct your paths.
–Proverbs 3:1-6

August 17

Put Your Trust in the Right Place

Do not be wise in your own eyes; fear the LORD and depart from evil. It will be health to your flesh, and strength to your bones. Honor the LORD with your possessions, and with the firstfruits of all your increase; so your barns will be filled with plenty, and your vats will overflow with new wine.
—Proverbs 3:7–10

My Prayer for Today

Father, You alone are my wisdom and my strength. I claim no authority of my own to get me through this life. All that I am and all that I have comes from You. My entire life is in Your hands. Therefore, I pledge myself to You in every way. All of my possessions and the increase of my substance are Yours to govern. Let me know what You want me to do, Father, and I will do it. Show me how to live, how to prosper, and how to honor You with my life. (Psalm 25:4.)

My Confession for Today

I am a strong and healthy man/woman who enjoys God's abundant provision. I would have nothing if it weren't for my heavenly Father. Therefore, I will honor Him with my wealth and the best part of all of my increase. I am a generous soul and a cheerful giver. Because of this, everything that I set my hand to do is blessed and brings forth an abundant harvest. (Psalm 1:3.) My storage places are filled to overflowing and my vats brim over with new wine.

The Lord Wants You to Increase

My Prayer for Today

Father, open the eyes of my understanding that I may know what it means to be Your child. (Ephesians 3:18.) Show me the glory of the house of God. Reveal to me the depths of security, prosperity, and love that are now mine in Christ Jesus. All that I am and all that I have are found in You, Father. And all that You are and all that You have are found in me. (John 17:22-23.)

My Confession for Today

The Spirit of the Lord dwells within me and His Word, in all of its power, is continually on my lips.(Psalm 119:11,13.) So I have been established in this earth with supernatural power and authority. I rule in righteousness and in reverence for my God. He has made me like the light of the morning at sunrise on a cloudless day—like the brightness after the rain that brings forth grass from the earth. I am safe, secure, and well established. I am protected and provided for under the provisions of God's covenant. All things in my life are ordered aright so that my success is absolutely guaranteed.

He shall be like the light of the morning when the sun rises, a morning without clouds, like the tender grass springing out of the earth, by clear shining after rain. Although my house is not so with God, yet He has made with me an everlasting covenant, ordered in all things and secure. For this is all my salvation and all my desire; will He not make it increase?
–2 Samuel 23:4-5

You Are a Vital Part of His Army

A people come, great and strong, the like of whom has never been; nor will there ever be any such after them, even for many successive generations. A fire devours before them, and behind them a flame burns; the land is like the Garden of Eden before them, and behind them a desolate wilderness; surely nothing shall escape them. Their appearance is like the appearance of horses; and like swift steeds, so they run.
—Joel 2:2-4

My Prayer for Today

Father, lead me to the people with whom I should associate. Show me the crowd to which I should belong. Since there is power in partnership and strength in numbers, number me with the elite and partner me with the strong. I know that shared vision is a highway to greatness, Father. So as like attracts like and light has fellowship with light, set me in partnership with those who love You and are focused on doing Your will. (2 Corinthians 6:14.)

My Confession for Today

I am a vital member of the Lord's army. I am part of a strong and daring breed, born again in the bloodline of the King. (John 3:5; 6:5.) I have come into God's kingdom for such a time as this. Because of what He has done in me, what appears to be impossible has become the inevitable in my life. I am unique and specially chosen to be God's ambassador and soldier in His army in these last days. (2 Corinthians 5:20; 2 Timothy 2:3; 3:1.) So I stand firm and stately as a stallion and move forward with the force of the heavenly cavalry. I consider this the greatest day to be alive!

You Are a Powerful Force for Good

My Prayer for Today

Father, give me peers who are fearless and wise. Cause me to be in vital union with those who are moving forward in faith and love and are not given to self-absorbed ambitions. Partner me with those who hear Your voice and obey Your commands. Keep me from arrogant glory seekers who do not have a heart for Your presence. Draw strong, focused, goal-oriented people into my life who are changing the world for Your glory.

My Confession for Today

I charge like a warrior and scale every obstacle like a well-trained soldier. (Psalm 18:29.) I do not vie for position, but march steadily in the ranks, moving straight ahead and plunging through defenses. I am a part of an irresistible and invulnerable force in this earth. I obey the voice of my Commander as He leads me on to victory. (Joshua 5:14; 1 Corinthians 15:57.) I take my place as a vital part of a force unlike any other before or since. I carry forth God's Word into the earth as His loyal soldier and deadly enemy of the devil.

They do not push one another; every one marches in his own column. Though they lunge between the weapons, they are not cut down. They run to and fro in the city, they run on the wall; they climb into the houses, they enter at the windows like a thief. The earth quakes before them, the heavens tremble; the sun and moon grow dark, and the stars diminish their brightness. The LORD gives voice before His army, for His camp is very great; for strong is the One who executes His word.
–Joel 2:8-11

August 21

Keep the Word on Your Lips

You shall love the LORD your God with all your heart, with all your soul, and with all your strength. And these words which I command you today shall be in your heart. You shall teach them diligently to your children, and shall talk of them when you sit in your house, when you walk by the way, when you lie down, and when you rise up.
—Deuteronomy 6:5-7

My Prayer for Today

Father, I love You with all of my heart. Your commands are my delight, for I know that they are life to me in abundance. All of Your desires for me are for my good. You always know what is best for me and never try to keep me from enjoying Your many blessings. I have Your Word that I am to be blessed. (Revelation 22:14.) I shall dwell in beautiful buildings filled with heavenly treasures. (John 14:2-3; Psalm 23:6.)

My Confession for Today

I love my heavenly Father with all of my mind, all of my spirit, and all of my physical strength. His Word is implanted and deeply rooted in my mind and in my heart. I whet and sharpen the Word within me that it may pierce through to my mind and my spirit. (Hebrews 4:12.) I talk of God's precepts when I sit in my house, when I walk by the wayside, when I lie down and when I rise up. I bind them as a sign on my hand and as an ornament before my eyes. (Deuteronomy 11:18.) I write them on the doorposts of my house and upon my gates. (Deuteronomy 11:20.)

Remember Where the Power Comes From

My Prayer for Today

Father, I thank You that You fill my house with all good things. You cause me to thrive in the power of Your anointing. (Hebrews 1:9.) You rescue me from bondage and establish me as Your own. (Deuteronomy 29:13.) Forever I will enjoy Your presence and be filled with provision from Your matchless bounty. (Psalm 21:6.)

My Confession for Today

By the promise of God, I receive an abundance of blessings. (John 1:16 AMP; 2 Corinthians 9:8 AMP.) I am brought into a prosperous dwelling. My home is supplied with good things of every kind. I receive it all by grace through faith. (Ephesians 2:8.) It is the Lord who prospers me and gives me an inheritance of things that I did not provide. I will not forget what He has done for me.

So it shall be, when the LORD your God brings you into the land of which He swore to your fathers, to Abraham, Isaac, and Jacob, to give you large and beautiful cities which you did not build, houses full of all good things, which you did not fill, hewn-out wells which you did not dig, vineyards and olive trees which you did not plant—when you have eaten and are full—then beware, lest you forget the LORD who brought you out of the land of Egypt, from the house of bondage.
–Deuteronomy 6:10-12

Live Worry Free

Therefore I say to you, do not worry about your life, what you will eat or what you will drink; nor about your body, what you will put on. Is not life more than food and the body more than clothing? Look at the birds of the air, for they neither sow nor reap nor gather into barns; yet your heavenly Father feeds them. Are you not of more value than they?
—Matthew 6:25-26

My Prayer for Today

Father, Your grace is all that I need to live a worry-free life. (2 Corinthians 12:9.) You do not care for me because of my performance, but because of the value that You have placed on me. In Your eyes I am worth the very blood of Jesus. (Luke 22:20.) Therefore, knowing that You love me so much and that everything You give I can receive by grace through faith, I never have a need to worry or be afraid.

My Confession for Today

I refuse to be worried about provision for my life. I have plenty to eat and drink and plenty of clothes to wear. My Father considers my life precious in His sight and will not force me to go without the things that I need. I look to the birds of the air and I am reminded that God provides for me. I am considered far more important in my Father's eyes than the birds. Therefore, I can look to them and know with certainty that my provision is signed, sealed, and delivered without fail.

Your Father Takes Good Care of You

My Prayer for Today

Father, You are my counsel and strength; I have no reason to be afraid. (Psalm 16:7; 28:7.) You never leave me nor forsake me.(Hebrews 13:5.) Even if I fail and stumble in my walk, You are always there to lift me up and encourage me to move on. (Isaiah 41:10.) You never cause Your provision to stop because of my shortcomings, but are always there to bless me with Your abundance. I am more important to You than anything in Your vast creation, and I can be assured that You will provide for my every need. (Ephesians 3:20.)

My Confession for Today

I cast worry far from me and live in God's peace and security. I look to the flowers, which neither toil nor spin, but are arrayed in such beauty that even Solomon in all of his glory did not compare to them. When I see how wonderfully they are clothed, I look at myself. My Father blesses all the work of my hands. (Psalm 90:17.) He considers me far more important than the flowers. So if He beautifully clothes flowers, which are here today and gone tomorrow, He'll clothe me, His eternal son/daughter, in the finest apparel.

Which of you by worrying can add one cubit to his stature? So why do you worry about clothing? Consider the lilies of the field, how they grow: they neither toil nor spin; and yet I say to you that even Solomon in all his glory was not arrayed like one of these. Now if God so clothes the grass of the field, which today is, and tomorrow is thrown into the oven, will He not much more clothe you, O you of little faith?
–Matthew 6:27-30

August 25

Seek First the Kingdom

Therefore do not worry, saying, "What shall we eat?" or "What shall we drink?" or "What shall we wear?" For after all these things the Gentiles seek. For your heavenly Father knows that you need all these things. But seek first the kingdom of God and His righteousness, and all these things shall be added to you."
—*Matthew 6:31-33*

My Prayer for Today

Father, I am the son/daughter who has captured Your heart. You are the perfect parent to me. You never cause me to beg or go without, but nourish me and provide for me daily. Within Your house there is safety and prosperity. (Psalm 68:6.) Your kingdom is filled with the best of all blessings. Why should I fear or worry about the future when I am an eternal heir to the kingdom? (Romans 8:17.) Today and every day, now and forevermore all of my needs are met according to Your riches in glory by Christ Jesus. (Ephesians 3:20.)

My Confession for Today

I absolutely refuse to worry! I have plenty to eat, drink, and wear. I rejoice in the present fact of my Father's provision. My first thought in all things is the advancement of His kingdom through the force of faith. With this mindset and spiritual stronghold, all of my physical and material needs shower into my life in a flood of abundance. (Ezekiel 34:26.) I serve the great I AM who is ever in the present. (Exodus 3:14; Psalm 139:7-10; Matthew 28:20.) So as a good and loyal son/daughter, I focus my attention on what I can do in the present to magnify my heavenly Father and bring glory to His name.

God Likes a Scrapper

My Prayer for Today

Father, build within me such strength of character that I persevere under any circumstance. You are obviously One who honors persistence. Therefore, fill me with Your unstoppable power and give me a tenacity that makes the devil cringe. (John 1:12; James 4:7.)

My Confession for Today

I am a scrapper when it comes to the things of God. Only the brave are effective in faith. Therefore, I make myself stubborn against feelings of fear, doubt, and insecurity. I am a conqueror who receives all that God desires for me to have. (Romans 8:37.) Through faith, I achieve all of my goals and live the life that I am created to live. (Jeremiah 29:11.)

Then Jacob was left alone; and a Man wrestled with him until the breaking of day. Now when He saw that He did not prevail against him, He touched the socket of his hip; and the socket of Jacob's hip was out of joint as He wrestled with him. And He said, "Let Me go, for the day breaks." But he said, "I will not let You go unless You bless me!" So He said to him, "What is your name?" He said, "Jacob." And He said, "Your name shall no longer be called Jacob, but Israel; for you have struggled with God and with men, and have prevailed."
—Genesis 32:24–28

August 27

Your Reaping and Sowing Can Be Simultaneous

"Behold, the days are coming," says the LORD, "When the plowman shall overtake the reaper, and the treader of grapes him who sows seed; the mountains shall drip with sweet wine, and all the hills shall flow with it."
–Amos 9:13

My Prayer for Today

Father, I believe that I am living in the day of Your accelerated blessing. I know that I have reaped what I have sown. (Galatians 6:7.) What I did in the past is what caused me to be where I am today, and what I am doing in the present is what will determine my future. Help me to make the right choices and sow the appropriate seed, then cause that seed to flourish with accelerated growth so that my harvest comes swiftly.

My Confession for Today

I am living in the day of God's inconceivable blessings. His abundance is accelerating on my behalf. My harvest springs up all around me even as I am sowing my seed. The mountains around me drip with new wine and the hills pour out God's blessings making my harvest one of matchless quality and value.

He Encircles You and Instructs You

My Prayer for Today

Father, it is an awesome thing to know that I am the apple of Your eye. You favor me above all creatures and care for me in every situation that I face. You surround me with Your love and supply me with Your provision. (Psalm 5:12 NLT; Philippians 4:19.) I take refuge under Your wings. (Psalm 91:4.) As my only mentor and guide, You make me ride on the heights of the earth, eat from the choicest crops, and draw oil from the granite crag. Through faith in You, I live my life blessed, accomplish the extraordinary, and enjoy the fruits of Your righteousness. (Acts 19:11 NIV; Philippians 1:11.)

My Confession for Today

God has encompassed me and drawn me unto Himself. I find refuge in His arms. He keeps watch over me with unfailing devotion and guards me as the apple of His eye. He alone leads and guides me. He makes me to ride upon the high places of the earth. He bids me to eat from His abundance. He gives me honey from the rock and oil from the flinty crag. In Him, I enjoy the fullness of every good thing that life has to offer. (Psalm 84:11.)

"He...encircled him, He instructed him, He kept him as the apple of His eye. As an eagle stirs up its nest, hovers over its young... taking them up... on its wings, so the LORD alone led him, and there was no foreign god with him. He made him ride in the heights of the earth, that he might eat the produce of the fields; He made him draw honey from the rock, and oil from the flinty rock."
–Deuteronomy 32:10-13

August 29

Do Not Despise the Day of Small Beginnings

For who has despised the day of small things? For these seven rejoice to see the plumb line in the hand of Zerubbabel. They are the eyes of the LORD, which scan to and fro throughout the whole earth.

—Zechariah 4:10

My Prayer for Today

Father, I pledge myself to live by Your example. Though I am small in the eyes of many, I wield the very creative power of the universe. (1 Corinthians 3:16.) Even as a mustard seed grows into a plush tree, by faith I accomplish the extraordinary. (Matthew 17:20.) I do not look to what is seen, for then I may despise the day of small beginnings. (2 Corinthians 4:18.) I know that every great venture begins with a single step, but a step taken with a resolve to persevere is a dream realized. No matter how small the step or how lofty the goal, You cause all of my dreams to come true. (Psalm 37:4-5.)

My Confession for Today

I do not despise, nor mock, the day of small beginnings. I have a thorough understanding that even the tiniest of seeds can become a great tree. I know that the eyes of the Lord go to and fro throughout the earth seeking someone through whom He can show Himself strong. (2 Chronicles 16:19.) I have consecrated myself to be that person.

You Are Like a Green Olive Tree in the House of God

My Prayer for Today

Father, Your works concerning this world were accomplished at its foundation. (Matthew 25:34; Hebrews 4:3.) Such is the reality of faith. What is to be obtained in the future must be presently received. (Hebrews 11:1.) I know I will never be what I think I will become, but only what I think I already am. Therefore, I say with absolute faith that I am like a green olive tree in the house of God. I flourish at the height of heavenly abundance, and everything I do prospers without fail. (Psalm 1:3.)

> *But I am like a green olive tree in the house of God; I trust in the mercy of God forever and ever. I will praise You forever, because You have done it; and in the presence of Your saints I will wait on Your name, for it is good.*
> *—Psalm 52:8-9*

My Confession for Today

I am like a green olive tree in the house of God. Everything that I do prospers and I never fail to bear good fruit. (Psalm 1:3.) Opportunities for advancement regularly come my way. (Psalm 75:6-7 KJV.) From this day to eternity, I can count on receiving nothing but blessing from my great Father God. Forever will I praise His name!

God Is Fighting for You

> You must not fear them, for the LORD your God Himself fights for you.
> –Deuteronomy 3:22

My Prayer for Today

Father, I thank You for taking a stand against my enemies. When they seek to destroy me, You are the first to confront them. You fight for me as a good Father defending his child. Therefore, I have nothing to fear. You cannot be defeated and so I cannot be defeated. (2 Corinthians 2:14.) This day I will move forward in boldness, sowing seeds on my journey and reaping the harvest of Your abundance. (Galatians 6:7.)

My Confession for Today

I have absolutely no fear of my enemies, for it is the Lord who goes before me. He is the first to confront the enemy on my behalf. He fights for me, routes my enemies, and grants me the victory. Every step that I take is ordered by the Lord. (Psalm 37: 23.) He causes me to have the advantage in every situation. With His guidance it is easy for me to be prosperous and successful. (Joshua 1:8; Proverbs 16:3 NLT.)

Speak His Word and He Will Back It for You

My Prayer for Today

Father, Your Word is faithful in all things. It is the single most solid foundation for my faith. The integrity of Your promises brings forth the expected end for which I have placed my trust. (Jeremiah 29:11 KJV.) I know that You will do what You have said, therefore, I rejoice. (Psalm 33:9.) I have presently received the desires of my heart. (Psalm 37:4.) In the name of Jesus, I say my amen to the praise of Your glory.

Know now that nothing shall fall to the earth of the word of the LORD which the LORD spoke concerning the house of Ahab; for the LORD has done what He spoke by His servant Elijah.

–2 Kings 10:10

My Confession for Today

Not one Word of the Lord spoken from my mouth goes unfulfilled. (1 Kings 8:56.) All of His promises and blessings are in my life. Each one that I believe and receive is manifested for me. (1 Thessalonians 2:13; Mark 11:24.) I ascend the ladder of success and my finances are increased with God's anointing for abundance. His blessing is on all of my accounts. (Philippians 4:17.) I am anointed for increase (2 Corinthians 1:21; Deuteronomy 28:2) and everything I do prospers. (Psalm 1:3.)

September 2

You Must Believe

Jesus answered them, "I told you, and you do not believe. The works that I do in My Father's name, they bear witness of Me. But you do not believe, because you are not of My sheep, as I said to you. My sheep hear My voice, and I know them, and they follow Me."
–John 10:25-27

My Prayer for Today

Father, I thank You that I am a member of Your flock. I am presently Your workmanship created in Christ Jesus. (Ephesians 2:10.) You have made me to be one who hears Your command and is quick to obey. I have consecrated my heart to believe in You. Guide me through this day, Father. Be the voice I hear behind me keeping me on the path of Your righteousness. (Isaiah 30:21.)

My Confession for Today

The works that I do are evidence that I am in Jesus. All of the power that works in and through me comes through His name. (Matthew 28:18-19; Ephesians 1:19-22.) I am in Christ. As Jesus is One with the Father, I am in Jesus, and so have become one with the Father as well. (John 17:21-23.) My total and complete reliance for the sustenance of my new life is upon Jesus alone. I am part of His fold—a standing and valued member of His family.

You Are Created to Hear His Voice

My Prayer for Today

Father, Your presence is the embodiment of joy and peace. (Psalm 16:11.) To know You is to love You and to love You is to obey You. (John 14:15.) You are my anthem, Father. You are my strength, my song, and my eternal salvation. (Exodus 15:2.) In You I have perfect security. Throughout this life I am held in Your hand for safekeeping. None can pluck me out of it or even get near me to try. My spirit is quiet within me as I rest in Your embrace. (Psalm 61:3-4.)

My Confession for Today

My ears have been opened and I continually listen to the Lord's voice. He knows me personally, and I follow Him relentlessly. He has given me eternal life and I shall never lose it. I am held secure under His tender care from now through eternity. My Father, who is greater than all, has placed His seal upon me and has committed me to Jesus' care. (2 Corinthians 1:21-22.) No one can snatch me out of my Father's hand. I am in Jesus, just as Jesus is in the Father. We are all one. (John 17:21-23.)

My sheep hear My voice, and I know them, and they follow Me. And I give them eternal life, and they shall never perish; neither shall anyone snatch them out of My hand. My Father, who has given them to Me, is greater than all; and no one is able to snatch them out of My Father's hand. I and My Father are one.
–John 10:27-30

September 4

He Sends His Assistance to You

He shall send from heaven and save me; He reproaches the one who would swallow me up.... God shall send forth His mercy and His truth. My soul is among lions; I lie among the sons of men who are set on fire, whose teeth are spears and arrows, and their tongue a sharp sword. Be exalted, O God, above the heavens; let Your glory be above all the earth.
–Psalm 57:3-5

My Prayer for Today

Father, it is pure joy to be Your child. I am safe under the shadow of Your wings. (Psalm 57:1.) Though many rise against me, they are like chaff in the wind. I know that You see their contempt for Your Word and their plans to restrain me, but they cannot succeed. (Psalm 63:9.) You are the God of my strength and my very ability to overcome. (1 John 4:4.) I thrive like a green leaf even in drought. (Jeremiah 17:8.) When all is said and done, You will be exalted and Your glory will shine over all the earth.

My Confession for Today

The glory of my Father is revealed in me. I am in the midst of lions and I dwell among the raging beasts—I must deal with men who have teeth like spears and arrows and tongues that lash out like swords—yet God's glory won't be contained. From His throne on high, He sends me a host of fierce warring angels to deliver me from those who would trample me down and swallow me up. All who rise against me are routed without remedy, while I am taken aside to enjoy the benefits of God's mercy and loving-kindness.

Turn Your Face to the Wall

My Prayer for Today

Father, I turn my eyes from anything that would distract me from my faith goals. I know that You always hear me and that You honor my faith. (John 9:31.) No matter what the circumstances show, life must yield itself to what I believe. What I see will only change through my belief in what I cannot see. (Hebrews 11:1.) The unseen is the true reality. It is the first cause of what I see and the foundation of all that I desire to accomplish.

My Confession for Today

I refuse to lay claim to an evil report. Any and every report that contradicts the Word of my God I consider to be false and misleading. I know the power of God that is at work within me. (Ephesians 3:20.) He is faithful and what He has spoken will come to pass in my life. (1 Corinthians 1:9; Joshua 21:45.) So when the evil report comes, I set my face to the wall: I do not look upon, nor listen to, that which is contrary to the Word. I will accept nothing less than what God has promised.

He turned his face toward the wall, and prayed… saying, "Remember now, O LORD, I pray, how I have walked before You in truth and with a loyal heart, and have done what was good in Your sight." And Hezekiah wept bitterly. And…the word of the LORD came to [Isaiah], saying, "Return and tell Hezekiah the leader of My people, 'Thus says the LORD… "I have heard your prayer, I have seen your tears; surely I will heal you. On the third day you shall go up to the house of the LORD.""

–2 Kings 20:2-5

September 6

You Are Extremely Gifted and Skilled

Chenaniah, leader of the Levites, was instructor in charge of the music, because he was skillful.
—1 Chronicles 15:22

My Prayer for Today

Father, I thank You for making me unique among all of Your creation. I am specially created to serve a purpose and a mission in this life. (Ephesians 1:11; Jeremiah 29:11.) My greatest service to You is to fulfill who I am made to be. I am not an imitator of others. (Ephesians 5:1.) I am distinct and peerless when it comes to my individuality. I am an integral part of the body of Christ, designed for a specific function. (1 Corinthians 12:27; Ephesians 4:12.) Help me to know that function perfectly, Father, and to be the very person You created me to be.

My Confession for Today

I am skilled in what God has called me to do. He has anointed me with great expertise on the job and in the work of the kingdom. (Luke 4:18; Psalm 90:17.) I face every situation with the God-given ability to perform extraordinarily well. My life is a pleasure to live. As I walk in my gifting I draw close to God and find more joy and fulfillment than I ever dreamed possible. (Psalm 16:11.)

He Is with You to Make this Day a Success

My Prayer for Today

Father, thank You for the favor that You pour into my life. Your blessing is upon me at home and on the job. Your powerful anointing makes my calling easy to perform. It is normal for me to do what You desire for me to do. I am perfectly fitted for the task. It is literally the fulfillment of who I am. Yet, You cause that which is natural for me to be supernaturally blessed. You cause Your influence to go before me in all that I do so that my progress is not only unhindered, but abundantly prosperous. (Psalm 126.)

My Confession for Today

The Lord is always with me to make me prosperous and very successful. Those who have been appointed as my supervisors can clearly see that the Lord is with me. They see how He makes everything that I set my hand to do thrive and prosper. He grants me abundant favor with those in authority over me. They look upon me as one who is called to lead and, for my sake, the Lord blesses them and all that they have.

The LORD was with Joseph, and he was a successful man; and he was in the house of his master the Egyptian. And his master saw that the LORD was with him and that the LORD made all he did to prosper in his hand. So Joseph found favor in his sight, and served him. Then he made him overseer of his house, and all that he had he put under his authority. So… from [that] time… the LORD blessed the Egyptian's house for Joseph's sake; and the blessing of the LORD was on all that he had in the house and in the field.
—Genesis 39:2-5

September 8

The Lord Loves You and Will Always Be There for You

When my father and my mother forsake me, then the LORD will take care of me. Teach me Your way, O LORD, and lead me in a smooth path, because of my enemies.
—Psalm 27:10–11

My Prayer for Today

Father, You are a true and faithful friend. You never leave me nor forsake me no matter how much I deserve it. (Hebrews 13:5.) You are always there leading me and guiding me on the hard paths of this life. Others may forsake me, but You never leave my side. I cling to You as my one true love, Father. Lead me on a plain path for Your name's sake. (Psalm 23:3.) Take notice of my enemies and make me powerful to overcome them.

My Confession for Today

Even if my father and mother were to forsake me, the Lord would take me in. He loves me just the way that I am and receives me with great joy and gladness. All of my oppressors present no problem for me, for the Lord is my Guide. He teaches me His ways and leads me on a clear path toward victory. He is the very director of my thoughts and the protector of my dreams. (Philippians 4:8; Proverbs 10:24; 11:23 NIV; Luke 18:27.)

He Enlightens Your Understanding

My Prayer for Today

Father, I thank You for giving me a spirit of wisdom and revelation in the knowledge of You. I thank You for opening the eyes of my understanding that I may know the expected end of my calling. I thank You for revealing to me the riches that are now mine as Your child and heir. (Romans 8:16-17.) In You, I am well-equipped and able to accomplish the task set before me. (Numbers 13:30; Philippians 4:13.)

My Confession for Today

My heavenly Father has given me a spirit of wisdom and revelation, of insight into mysteries and secrets in the deep and intimate knowledge of Himself. (Mark 4:11.) My spirit has been enlightened with a flood of understanding so that I can know and comprehend the hope of my calling and the immense riches of this glorious inheritance that has become my own.

That the God of our Lord Jesus Christ, the Father of glory, may give to you the spirit of wisdom and revelation in the knowledge of Him, the eyes of your understanding being enlightened; that you may know what is the hope of His calling, what are the riches of the glory of His inheritance in the saints.
–Ephesians 1:17–18

September 10

The Power Within You Is Unstoppable

What is the exceeding greatness of His power toward us who believe, according to the working of His mighty power which He worked in Christ when He raised Him from the dead and seated Him at His right hand in the heavenly places, far above all principality and power and might and dominion, and every name that is named, not only in this age but also in that which is to come. And He put all things under His feet, and gave Him to be head over all things to the church, which is His body, the fullness of Him who fills all in all.
—Ephesians 1:19-23

My Prayer for Today

Father, I thank You for pouring Your powerful anointing into me. This very moment I am filled with the power that You wrought in Christ when You raised Him from the dead. Right now I have authority over and above all of the power and authority of the enemy. (Luke 10:19.) Give me wisdom to walk in this revelation, Father. Make me a wise disciple who places Your will first in all that I do.

My Confession for Today

I have complete understanding of the exceeding greatness of God's power toward me. The power residing and working within me is the very power that God wrought in Christ when He raised Him from the dead. I am the fullness of Jesus as He fills me in every way. All things are placed under my feet and every power and dominion must obey me as I apply the power of attorney that Jesus gave me to use His name. (John 14:14.)

His Eyes and Heart Are with You Perpetually

My Prayer for Today

Father, I know Your character and Your resolve. You never, ever give up on me or find reasons to turn away from me. Your eyes and Your heart are with me perpetually, regardless of how many times I fail You. You hear my every prayer and cause all things to yield to the voice of my faith. I humble myself before You, Father, as a student to an honored teacher. Teach me what You know and make me like You in every possible way. (Psalm 25:4; 2 Corinthians 3:18.)

My Confession for Today

The land that I dwell on is subject to my dominion. When I humble myself and seek the face of my Father, He hears from heaven and brings healing to the land. His ears are ever opened to my prayers and His eyes never leave me. He has chosen me and set me apart as an ambassador of the kingdom. (2 Corinthians 5:20.) He has placed His name upon me and His eyes and heart are with me both now and forevermore.

If My people who are called by My name will humble themselves, and pray and seek My face, and turn from their wicked ways, then I will hear from heaven, and will forgive their sin and heal their land. Now My eyes will be open and My ears attentive to prayer made in this place. For now I have chosen and sanctified this house, that My name may be there forever; and My eyes and My heart will be there perpetually.
–2 Chronicles 7:14–16

September 12

Rip Your Inheritance out of the Devil's Hands

From the days of John the Baptist until now the kingdom of heaven suffers violence, and the violent take it by force.
—Matthew 11:12

My Prayer for Today

Father, teach me to make war with my faith. (2 Corinthians 10:3-4.) Help me to understand the strategies of the enemy so that I can defeat him at every turn. Show me what You want me to accomplish and how to achieve the goals You place before me. You have revealed that if I desire something, I must often fight to get it. Therefore, make me a skilled fighter—a faith warrior to bring glory to Your name. (1 Corinthians 6:12.)

My Confession for Today

I am a spiritually violent man/woman when I need to be. I am willing to fight the enemy, Satan, and his forces on any ground. I seize the blessings of the kingdom with skillful force, exerting all of my resources in a blaze of fury that sends the devil reeling. (Ephesians 6:10-18.) I take up the weapons of spiritual warfare and plow down every obstacle that would hinder me from living the life that God has ordained for me to live.

Be the Best that You Can Be

My Prayer for Today

> I beseech you therefore, brethren, by the mercies of God, that you present your bodies a living sacrifice, holy, acceptable to God, which is your reasonable service.
> *–Romans 12:1*

Father, You have made me what I am. My only true fulfillment is to do what I am called to do. Therefore, I offer myself in service to You. Teach me Your perfect will and show me the path that You want me to take. (Psalm 25:4.) Reveal to me my greatest joy, for no one can do what You created me to do. (Jeremiah 29:11 NIV.) Only I can fulfill the task to the standard that You have set, but without Your partnership I can neither know it nor fulfill it. (John 15:55.) So make me wise, Father. Show me the way that I should go in Jesus' name. (Psalm 143:8.)

My Confession for Today

In view of God's mercy, I dedicate my body as a living sacrifice, holy and well pleasing to Him. This is my spiritual worship. I follow the ways of the spirit as I am led by the Holy Spirit. (Romans 8:14.) I do not conform to the ways of the world, but am transformed by the renewing of my mind so that I may demonstrate the good, acceptable, and perfect will of God. (Romans 12:2.)

September 14

He Is Your Everything

But of Him you are in Christ Jesus, who became for us wisdom from God—and righteousness and sanctification and redemption—that, as it is written, "He who glories, let him glory in the LORD."
–1 Corinthians 1:30-31

My Prayer for Today

Father, I thank You that I am in Christ Jesus. In Him, I live and move and have my being. (Acts 17:28.) He is my substitute in all things. (1 Peter 2:24.) He is my everything—my wisdom, my righteousness, my sanctification, and my redemption. He is my sonship and my right to approach Your throne without any sense of inadequacy. (Hebrews 4:14-16.) He alone has made me worthy. He alone is my holiness. (Romans 11:16.)

My Confession for Today

My heavenly Father has given me new life in Christ Jesus my Lord. Jesus has become my wisdom, righteousness, sanctification, and redemption. Therefore, I set myself in agreement with what is written and make my boast in Him, proudly rejoicing and giving Him glory! (Psalm 44:8.) I am wise, righteous, sanctified, and redeemed. I am complete in Christ Jesus my Lord. (Colossians 2:10.)

Build and Prosper

My Prayer for Today

Father, You are my provider and my never-failing source of supply. (Genesis 22:14; Philippians 4:19.) In You I have found my rest. No enemy has the power to overwhelm me or cause me to fail. I am one with the Anointed One and I have His anointing. (John 17:21; 2 Corinthians 1:21.) Every promise is now mine. (2 Corinthians 1:20.) His blessing has become my blessing. His status is now my status. His place in Your heart, Father, is now my place in Your heart. (John 17:23, 26.)

My Confession for Today

The Lord grants me His peace in every circumstance. I have put my complete faith and trust in Him. I seek Him, longing for His fellowship with all of the passion that is within me. He has given me rest in the comfort of His mighty arms. I work and build wondrous dwellings for His glory and enjoy the splendor of His prosperity.

He built fortified cities in Judah, for the land had rest; he had no war in those years, because the LORD had given him rest. Therefore he said to Judah, "Let us build these cities and make walls around them, and towers, gates, and bars, while the land is yet before us, because we have sought the LORD our God; we have sought Him, and He has given us rest on every side." So they built and prospered.
–2 Chronicles 14:6-7

September 16

Guard Your Heart with All Diligence

Keep your heart with all diligence, for out of it spring the issues of life. Put away from you a deceitful mouth, and put perverse lips far from you. Let your eyes look straight ahead, and your eyelids look right before you. Ponder the path of your feet, and let all your ways be established. Do not turn to the right or the left; remove your foot from evil.
—Proverbs 4:23-27

My Prayer for Today

Father, teach me to guard my heart, for it is the seat of my spirit out of which flows the issues of life. Train my mouth to speak in faith. Show me the path of single-mindedness so that my ways may be established and I can enjoy success in all that I do.

My Confession for Today

Above all else, I diligently guard my heart, for it is the wellspring of my life. I do not speak perverse, obstinate, or wicked talk. Negative and corrupt language does not come out of my mouth. My eyes look straight ahead. They are fixed on the prize set before me. (Philippians 3:14.) I achieve my goals without distraction or wavering. I deliberate and premeditate over every step that I take. I only move forward in ways that are stable and well-established.

He Gives You Favor in Every Circumstance

My Prayer for Today

Father, I thank You that You are with me showing me mercy and granting me Your unmerited favor. You cause those in authority over me to trust my judgment. They know that they do not need to continually check on me, for You are with me prospering all that I set my hand to do. (Proverbs 1:3.) By Your favor, Father, I receive promotions, raises, and ever-increasing authority, in Jesus' name.

My Confession for Today

No matter what the circumstances may be in my life, I prosper, for the Lord is with me to show me mercy, loving-kindness, and an abundance of favor with all of those I come in contact with. I have favor with my employers, my pastors, my teachers and my administrators. They see that I am called to be a leader and the Lord makes everything that I am put in charge of to prosper.

Then Joseph's master took him and put him into the prison, a place where the king's prisoners were confined. And he was there in the prison. But the LORD was with Joseph and showed him mercy, and He gave him favor in the sight of the keeper of the prison. And the keeper of the prison committed to Joseph's hand all the prisoners who were in the prison; whatever they did there, it was his doing. The keeper of the prison did not look into anything that was under Joseph's authority, because the LORD was with him; and whatever he did, the LORD made it prosper.
—Genesis 39:20–23

September 18

God Dwells Within You

Do you not know that you are the temple of God and that the Spirit of God dwells in you?
—1 Corinthians 3:16

My Prayer for Today

Father, what a wonder it is to know that You are dwelling within me. I do not have to pray toward heaven when the King of heaven is right now inside of me. You are the key to a perfect walk of faith. You are the author and finisher of it—the very architect who drew up the blueprints from the imaginations of Your mind. (Hebrews 12:2.) With you as my partner, mentor, and guide, all of my plans succeed and nothing is impossible for me to accomplish. (Luke 1:37.)

My Confession for Today

I am the very temple of God and His Spirit dwells within me. His power is working in me mightily. (Colossians 1:29.) It attaches itself to my words and causes the image in my mind to be manifested in my circumstances. What I believe I have received is what I experience in my life. (Mark 11:24.) I achieve every goal without wavering. It is God's power within me that causes all that I desire to come to pass in Jesus' name.

You Are One Spirit with the Lord

My Prayer for Today

He who is joined to the Lord is one spirit with Him.
—1 Corinthians 6:17

Father, I am amazed that You would choose to become one spirit with me. You have joined us together in such a perfect partnership that we are as one person. As Jesus is in You, I am in Him, and we three are one. (John 17:21-23.) When I walk into a room, the Lord of heaven and earth walks into the room. When I use my faith, You join Yours with mine. There is nothing that I do that You are not part of, Father. Therefore, no matter what, I am destined to succeed.

My Confession for Today

I am united with the Lord and have become one spirit with Him. In all that I do, I display His character and integrity. (2 Corinthians 3:18.) I can easily perform any task I am given. He causes me to always be in the right place at the right time. All of His benefits are with me. (Psalm 68:19.) His favor causes people to go out of their way to do nice things for me. (Proverbs 3:4.) By His anointing within me I can receive all things and do all things. (2 Corinthians 1:21; 1 Timothy 6:17; Ephesians 3:20.)

September 20

He Gives You Insight into Visions and Dreams

He sought God in the days of Zechariah, who had understanding in the visions of God; and as long as he sought the LORD, God made him prosper.
–2 Chronicles 26:5

My Prayer for Today

Father, You are my first love. Your Word declares that You draw near to me as I draw near to You. (James 4:8.) You see past all of my weaknesses and keep no account of my sin. (Psalm 103:12.) In Your eyes I am clean, pure, and holy with full authority to approach Your throne whenever I so please. (Hebrews 4:16.) You make Your love for me Your chief motivation. (John 3:16.) Your desire for my companionship is my life's thrill. To do Your will is to just be me. That is the principle on which You base my mission and my career.

My Confession for Today

I stand on the Lord's promise that as long as I seek Him, He will give me success in all that I do. His power within me is the attracting force that brings into manifestation all that I need to live the life of my dreams. (Deuteronomy 28:2; Psalm 68:19.) I relentlessly pursue God's will, for it is the only way I can find happiness and fulfillment. (Psalm 37:4.) God's favor goes before me to open many doors of opportunity. (Proverbs 3:4.) My personality radiates with confidence and my joy draws the lost to seek my Father's love.

Jesus Is the Way

My Prayer for Today

Father, I fully recognize that only through Jesus do I have access to You. You are perfectly holy, just, and good, and only the holy can approach You. Therefore, if I rely on my own power I find myself to be completely unworthy. Yet Jesus is entirely worthy and through Him my access is guaranteed. He is my sanctification, justification, and righteousness. (1 Corinthians 1:30; Romans 5:18.) I know You only through Him, and through Him I know the power to overcome this world. (John 16:33.)

My Confession for Today

I know the way into my Father's presence. It is through Jesus alone. He is the way, the truth, and the life. There is no way for me to reach the Father, but through Him. In Jesus, I have a perfect revelation of the Father. Through Him, I can both see and know the heart of God. If ever I wonder what God thinks of me, I can look to Jesus and all of my wondering will be laid to rest.

"Where I go you know, and the way you know." Thomas said to Him, "Lord, we do not know where You are going, and how can we know the way?" Jesus said to him, "I am the way, the truth, and the life. No one comes to the Father except through Me. If you had known Me, you would have known My Father also; and from now on you know Him and have seen Him."
–John 14:4-7

September 22

Run Your Race to Win

Do you not know that those who run in a race all run, but one receives the prize? Run in such a way that you may obtain it. And everyone who competes for the prize is temperate in all things. Now they do it to obtain a perishable crown, but we for an imperishable crown. Therefore I run thus: not with uncertainty. Thus I fight: not as one who beats the air.
—1 Corinthians 9:24-26

My Prayer for Today

Father, train me as a coach trains a gifted athlete. Teach me to discipline myself so that spirit, soul, and body work in harmony to achieve my faith goals. Show me proper technique and discipline me for the long run. (Hebrews 12:6 NIV.) Speak to me in my corner as I fight this fight of faith to which I am called. (1 Timothy 6:12.)

My Confession for Today

I live my life for Jesus as if I were a runner in a race who gives his all, knowing that only one will win and obtain the crown of victory. I run to win. I freely submit myself to the rigors of strict training, subduing my mind, body, and spirit, so that I can be the best that I can possibly be. I run with passion and purpose, with a clear goal and objective. I am a well-disciplined and willingly suffer through the pain of hard training. My eyes are fixed on the finish line and that crown of victory. (1 Corinthians 15:57.)

The Lord Searches Your Heart

My Prayer for Today

Father, through Jesus I have come to know You deeply and intimately. I know Your love, character, and nature. You are the most perfect friend that I could ever have. I commit myself to You wholly, serving You with a loyal heart and a willing mind. You have drawn me to Yourself in tender compassion, and now You dwell within me with power and purpose. (John 6:44; Romans 8:9.) This day I recognize these things and act upon them in accordance with Your will.

My Confession for Today

I know my great Father God and I appreciate Him. I have personal and intimate knowledge of Him. I understand Him and hear Him. I serve Him with all of my heart and with a willing mind. He is the first and most vital necessity in my life. I am His forever.

"As for you, my son Solomon, know the God of your father, and serve Him with a loyal heart and with a willing mind; for the LORD searches all hearts and understands all the intent of the thoughts. If you seek Him, He will be found by you; but if you forsake Him, He will cast you off forever."
–1 Chronicles 28:9

September 24

Your Words Shall Feed Many

In the multitude of words sin is not lacking, but he who restrains his lips is wise. The tongue of the righteous is choice silver; the heart of the wicked is worth little. The lips of the righteous feed many, but fools die for lack of wisdom.
—Proverbs 10:19–21

My Prayer for Today

Father, teach me to use my head before I open my mouth. Teach me to recognize the value and power behind every word that I speak. You have made my tongue like choice silver. It is the starting point of provision for me and everyone in my circle of influence. Fill me with wisdom to speak the right things. Create in me a habit of consistently glorifying You in every way.

My Confession for Today

I am cautious with my words. Every word that I speak is carefully thought out. I am intimately familiar with the power of the spoken word. When I focus my attention on my goal and speak the end from the beginning, I have the things that I say. (Isaiah 46:10; Mark 11:23-24.) Therefore, I make sure that every word is in line with God's will and will produce a harvest of goodness in my life. My words are like choice silver. They nourish, sustain, and supply the needs of many.

Humble Yourself Before the Lord

My Prayer for Today

Father, You are the God who hears and answers prayer. (Psalm 65:2; 138:3.) You never turn a deaf ear to me, but are quick to respond to my requests. It is Your good pleasure to grant me the desires of my heart and supply the provisions to make my dreams come true. (Psalm 37:4; Philippians 4:19.) When I ask, I receive and my joy is made full. (John 16:24.) It is such an honor to serve such a wonderful Father. I commit myself to You eternally. All praise to Your holy name.

My Confession for Today

When distressing days arrive, I remain humble before God and continually seek His favor. God loves me and honors my faith despite my shortcomings. Even when I fall, I draw near to Him, for I have His promise that He will run to me, embrace me in His arms, and restore me to my rightful position in His kingdom. (Luke 15:11-32.)

Now when he was in affliction, he implored the LORD his God, and humbled himself greatly before the God of his fathers, and prayed to Him; and He received his entreaty, heard his supplication, and brought him back to Jerusalem into his kingdom. Then Manasseh knew that the LORD was God.
–2 Chronicles 33:12-13

September 26

God Blesses You Extravagantly

By the God of your father who will help you, and by the Almighty who will bless you with blessings of heaven above, blessings of the deep that lies beneath, blessings of the breasts and of the womb. The blessings of your father have excelled the blessings of my ancestors, up to the utmost bound of the everlasting hills. They shall be on the head of Joseph, and on the crown of the head of him who was separate from his brothers.
–Genesis 49:25–26

My Prayer for Today

Father, I thank You for making me fruitful in all things. You give me strength to endure through the most trying circumstances. You command me to be fearless, and You strengthen me in the power of Your might. (Isaiah 41:10,13; Ephesians 6:10.) You are always with me to help me in any way that I need. (Psalm 46:1.) Your blessings rain upon me, Your love surrounds me, Your grace upholds me, and Your anointing causes me to prevail. (Ezekiel 34:26; Psalm 32:10 NIV; Romans 5:2.)

My Confession for Today

I am a fruitful branch of the Vine. (John 15:5.) My branches scale and cover walls. I stay steady in the midst of adversity. (Psalm 10:6.) My strong arms remain ready, for the hand of my Lord—my Shepherd, my Rock— helps me. (Psalm 23:1; 18:2.) The Almighty blesses me with blessings that come down from heaven and up from the earth. My Father's blessings are greater than all and His bounty mocks the bounty of kings.

Be a Generous Soul

My Prayer for Today

Father, teach me how to be a generous soul. Help me to always recognize that Your blessing is upon me and that I will always have all that I need and more. For me, there is a constant supply of seed to sow and a never-ending harvest to enjoy. It is my heart's desire to do good and be a blessing to others. Pour Your favor upon me, Father, and prosper me in Your abundance so that I flourish like foliage.

My Confession for Today

All of my desires are for good things. I seek good and find good will. I give freely, without restraint, and yet gain even more. My generosity causes a tremendous supply of good things to pour forth into my life. When I refresh others, I also am refreshed. When my hand is ready to give and do good, my head is crowned with the blessings of God. (Ephesians 1:3.) I live in His abundance and thrive like a green leaf.

There is one who scatters, yet increases more; and there is one who withholds more than is right, but it leads to poverty. The generous soul will be made rich, and he who waters will also be watered himself. The people will curse him who withholds grain, but blessing will be on the head of him who sells it. He who earnestly seeks good finds favor, but trouble will come to him who seeks evil. He who trusts in his riches will fall, but the righteous will flourish like foliage.
—Proverbs 11:24–28

September 28

He Satisfies You with the Goodness of His House

Blessed is the man You choose, and cause to approach You, that he may dwell in Your courts. We shall be satisfied with the goodness of Your house, of Your holy temple. By awesome deeds in righteousness You will answer us, O God of our salvation, You who are the confidence of all the ends of the earth, and of the far-off seas.
—Psalm 65:4-5

My Prayer for Today

Father, as I am Your chosen one, I am blessed. You cause me to approach You and to find tranquility in Your presence. All fear is purged from me as I enter Your throne room. By Your blessing, my home and family are filled with good things of every kind. You always answer me when I call, and I find salvation in Your presence. You are the confidence of all the earth, Father. Blessed is the one who puts his trust in You. (Psalm 2:12.)

My Confession for Today

My Father has chosen me and adopted me as His own child. (Romans 8:5 NIV.) He has brought me near to Himself and has given me a place of honor in the courts of His palace. He fills me with all good things so that I am in need of nothing. All I have to do is ask and He freely gives me all that He has. (John 16:24.) My year is crowned with the bounty of the Lord and all of my carts overflow with His abundance. (Psalm 65:11.)

Everything You Have Begins with Him

My Prayer for Today

Father, without You I am nothing, I have nothing, and I can do nothing. (John 15:5.) Without You I am wretched and useless. May I always recognize Your preeminence. All of my power comes from You alone and all that I enjoy is the result of Your giving heart. I can give nothing except what has first come from You, and I can do nothing except by the power You have placed within me. (2 Corinthians 4:7

Who am I, and who are my people, that we should be able to offer so willingly as this? For all things come from You, and of Your own we have given You.
–1 Chronicles 29:14

NLT.) I freely and willingly bow my knee before You in reverence and gratitude for all that You have done for me. (Psalm 84:11; 136:3.)

My Confession for Today

All that I have comes from the Lord. All that I can give was His to begin with. So, all of my strength and ability to give offerings comes from Him alone. I am humbled by the realization that I am a steward, not a proprietor. Therefore, all of my boasting is in Him! (Psalm 34:2.) All of my joy is in Him! I do not give grudgingly, but cheerfully. (2 Corinthians 9:7.) I consider it an honor and a privilege to be able to give for the support of the kingdom. My giving is a declaration that God alone is in charge of my prosperity.

September 30

Love Never Fails

Love suffers long and is kind; love does not envy; love does not parade itself, is not puffed up; does not behave rudely, does not seek its own, is not provoked, thinks no evil; does not rejoice in iniquity, but rejoices in the truth; bears all things, believes all things, hopes all things, endures all things. Love never fails.
—1 Corinthians 13:4-8

My Prayer for Today

Father, Your character is the very nature of love. (1 John 4:16.) You are always patient and kind toward me. You are actively engaged in producing good things in my life. (Psalm 145:9.) You never feel that I am being given too much; You find pleasure in my prosperity and are thrilled when I receive Your abundance. (Psalm 37:27.) You always see the best in me and place all of my sins in a sea of forgetfulness. (Micah 7:19.) What a joy it is to know that You are God. My heart is Yours for You are fully worthy of it.

My Confession for Today

I am patient and kind. I do not envy others, nor boast of the great things I have done. I am not haughty and overbearing, rude (domineering; pushy) or selfish. I am generous with all that I have and willing to give to those in need. I am not easily angered, and I keep no record of wrongs done to me. I do not delight in evil, but rejoice in the manifestation of the truth. I bear up under anything and everything that comes. I always see the best in others and overlook their shortcomings. My hopes always remain high and I endure everything without weakening. As long as I walk in love, I will never fail.

He Will Establish You in Every Good Word and Work

My Prayer for Today

Father, I am bound to always give You thanks. The sheer volume of Your blessings toward me is beyond comprehension. Even before the beginning of time, You chose me for salvation. (Ephesians 1:4.) You knew all that I would ever do wrong and chose me regardless. Knowing that You love me so much drives away all fear. I know that I can absolutely count on Your assistance and that You will establish me in every good word and work.

My Confession for Today

Now may our Lord Jesus Christ Himself, and our God and Father, who has loved us and given us everlasting consolation and good hope by grace, comfort your hearts and establish you in every good word and work.
–2 Thessalonians 2:16-17

I am deeply loved by the Lord. From the beginning, He chose me to be saved through the sanctifying work of the Holy Spirit and through my belief in the truth. (2 Thessalonians 2:13.) He called me to this through the Gospel, so that I might share in the glory of my Lord Jesus Christ. I stand firm and hold fast to the teachings that have been passed on to me. (2 Thessalonians 2:15.) Jesus Himself, and God my Father, encourage my heart and strengthen me in every good deed and word. My Father loves me deeply and by His grace He gives me eternal encouragement and good hope.

October 2

Through the Fire and Water—Unscathed!

You have caused men to ride over our heads; we went through fire and through water; but You brought us out to rich fulfillment.
—Psalm 66:12

My Prayer for Today

Father, I am intimately familiar with hardships and tribulation. I have gone through the fire and the water and have felt their ravaging effects. I recognize the days when seedtime and harvest became my enemy. (Galatians 6:7.) By spiritual law I have reaped what I have sown. (Genesis 8:22.) However, today is a new day. Today I am a new man/woman with an understanding of the laws of faith. (2 Corinthians 5:17.) My focus has returned to You, Father. You can now smile and bring me out to rich fulfillment!

My Confession for Today

Though I have been through hardships by the dozens and have been weighed down by burden after burden; though men have ridden hard over my head and I have gone through the fire and the water, I now put the past behind me and look to the Lord. He has brought me into the spacious province of His abundance so that I may enjoy His kingdom living from this day unto eternity.

God Is Always Listening

My Prayer for Today

Father, I thank You that I am clean through the blood of Jesus. (1 John 1:7.) It was not enough for You to dwell in a man-made temple. Your love for me was too vast and immeasurable. You wanted to be so close to me that You chose to actually take up residence within me. You, the very Creator of heaven and earth, are in love with me. I am Your heart's desire and the very apple of Your eye. (Zechariah 2:8.) You have eradicated all that could keep You from me and now we walk this life together as Father and son/daughter.

My Confession for Today

God's eyes are upon me day and night. He is relentless in His care and concern for me. (1 Peter 5:7.) He has placed His name upon me and His presence is ever with me. He listens to me and answers my every prayer. (Psalm 116:1 NLT.) He has forgiven all of my sins and claimed me as His very own. (Psalm 103:3 NIV; Isaiah 43:1.) By His blessing I now enjoy happiness, favor, good fortune, and good things of every kind.

That Your eyes may be open toward this temple day and night, toward the place where You said You would put Your name, that You may hear the prayer which Your servant makes toward this place. And may You hear the supplications of Your servant and of Your people Israel, when they pray toward this place. Hear from heaven Your dwelling place, and when You hear, forgive.
—2 Chronicles 6:20-21

October 4

He Will Strengthen Your Heart

I would have lost heart, unless I had believed that I would see the goodness of the LORD in the land of the living. Wait on the LORD; be of good courage, and He shall strengthen your heart; wait, I say, on the LORD!
—Psalm 27:13-14

My Prayer for Today

Father, I thank You that You never give me cause to give up on my faith goals. I know that my belief is the springboard for my faith. It is You who causes my belief to form what I desire in the spirit world and through my words You bring those desires into the natural world. (Hebrews 12:2; Mark 11:23-24.) You are the power behind it all, Father. I joyfully acknowledge You and recognize that without You, I can do nothing. (John 15:5.) Strengthen my heart, and fill me with Your patience. (Galatians 5:22 NIV.) Teach me to submit to the processes of faith.

My Confession for Today

I remain steadfast and confident in the fact that I will see the goodness of God in my life. His power is working in me mightily. My faith is producing an abundance of good fruit. I am strong and take heart for I know that He is with me. His power is right now working and will soon be manifested in my circumstances.

The Holy Spirit's Friendship Will See You Through

My Prayer for Today

Father, You have my whole heart. I love You for who You are and not just because You are God. Your commandments are my delight. They are not burdensome, but make perfect sense. It is my joy to obey them. I further give You thanks for the Holy Spirit who right now is dwelling within me. He is my comforter, counselor, and strength. (John 14:26 KJV; Isaiah 9:6; Ephesians 3:16.) By His continual guidance, I remain steady on the path of Your will.

My Confession for Today

I love Jesus with all of my heart, and I obey His commandments. By His request of the Father, I now enjoy the indwelling presence of the Holy Spirit. He is the Spirit of Truth, whom the world cannot receive because it neither knows nor recognizes Him. I do know and recognize Him. He is literally and actually within me at this very moment. God, the Holy Spirit, dwells within my heart.

If you love Me, keep My commandments. And I will pray the Father, and He will give you another Helper, that He may abide with you forever— the Spirit of truth, whom the world cannot receive, because it neither sees Him nor knows Him; but you know Him, for He dwells with you and will be in you.
–John 14:15–17

October 6

Jesus Will Manifest Himself to You

I will not leave you orphans; I will come to you. A little while longer and the world will see Me no more, but you will see Me. Because I live, you will live also. At that day you will know that I am in My Father, and you in Me, and I in you. He who has My commandments and keeps them, it is he who loves Me. And he who loves Me will be loved by My Father, and I will love him and manifest Myself to him.
—John 14:18–21

My Prayer for Today

Father, I give You praise for the work that You have done in me. By Your power I have received the new birth and by Your love You have entered my heart. (1 Peter 1:3 NIV; Acts 16:13; Romans 10:9.) As Jesus is in You, I am in Him, and we three are now one. (John 17:21.) What a wonder that is. All that I do, I do with and through You. My faith is charged by Your power and my wisdom is under Your management. You are now my constant tutor and by Your instruction I am destined to succeed. (John 16:13.)

My Confession for Today

Jesus has not left me alone, desolate, or helpless. He has come to me, with passion and purpose, to see that I have victory in all that I do. (1 Corinthians 15:57.) Because He lives, I live also. As Jesus is in the Father, I am in Him and He is in me. I show my love for Him by holding fast to His commands and doing all that He has taught me to do. I am deeply loved and appreciated by my heavenly Father, and Jesus Himself loves me and manifests Himself to me.

The Hosts of Heaven Are Committed to Your Success

My Prayer for Today

Father, You alone are the ruler of all creation. You command the hosts of heaven and they obey. At this present moment, there are angels around me who are committed to do Your will. You surround me with Your favor like a shield and free me from every enslaving circumstance. (Psalm 5:12.) You have erased my sin and daily load me with Your benefits. (Psalm 103:12.) You alone are my God and my salvation. I rest content within the shadow of Your wings. (Psalm 36:7.)

My Confession for Today

The great angelic army of the living God has surrounded me. They have descended from His great mountain to shield me on every side and to see to it that I am kept safe from the onslaughts of the enemy. My heavenly Father takes up my every burden as His own. (Hebrews 4:15; 1 Peter 5:7.) He bears them daily so that I may dwell in His presence in peace and comfort. He gives me a copious supply of daily provisions to fill all of my needs. He is my salvation from every trouble and my escape from the snares of death.

The chariots of God are twenty thousand, even thousands of thousands; the Lord is among them as in Sinai, in the Holy Place. You have ascended on high, You have led captivity captive; You have received gifts among men, even from the rebellious, that the LORD God might dwell there. Blessed be the Lord, Who daily loads us with benefits, the God of our salvation! Selah
—Psalm 68:17–19

October 8

You Are Forgiven

And I said: "I pray, LORD God of heaven, O great and awesome God, You who keep Your covenant and mercy with those who love You and observe Your commandments, please let Your ear be attentive and Your eyes open, that You may hear the prayer of Your servant which I pray before You now, day and night, for the children of Israel Your servants, and confess the sins of the children of Israel which we have sinned against You. Both my father's house and I have sinned."
–Nehemiah 1:5-6

My Prayer for Today

Father, You are truly a great and awesome God. Your character and personality are Your best attributes. It is such a joy to be a part of what You are doing in the earth. To know that You have forgiven me and remember my sins no more (Jeremiah 31:34); to know that You have entrusted me with a mission and have chosen to be my partner throughout, these are the greatest of blessings. By Your mercy and grace I have my part in the covenant. Your ear is now always open to my prayers and Your eyes never leave me.

My Confession for Today

The Lord is a great and awesome God who keeps His covenant of love with me as a commitment commanding His utmost attention. He has removed all sin from me and causes me to stand by His grace. (Psalm 103:12; 1 Peter 5:12.) His ears are ever attentive to the sound of my voice and His eyes watch over me without fail. He is pleased to hear my prayers and is quick to respond to my faith. (1 John 5:14-15.)

Be Rooted and Grounded in Love

My Prayer for Today

Father, I freely and joyfully bow my knee to Your majesty. By Your power I am now called into Your family. You have renewed and strengthened my spirit so that I am truly and in every way Your own child. (Romans 8:16.) You give me such depth of understanding as to know the very love of Christ which passes knowledge. You cause me to be filled with Your fullness. In all that I do, I have Your power to see it through.

My Confession for Today

Being rooted and established in love, I have the ability to understand the intense love of Christ. I am now filled with the fullness of God. Right now, He is able to do exceedingly abundantly above all that I can ask or imagine. He does it according to His power that works in me. I find the answers to my prayers within me: The same power (God's) that spoke the universe into existence is poised within me at this very moment.

That He would grant you, according to the riches of His glory, to be strengthened with might through His Spirit in the inner man, that Christ may dwell in your hearts through faith; that you, being rooted and grounded in love, may be able to comprehend... what is the width and length and depth and height— to know the love of Christ which passes knowledge; that you may be filled with all the fullness of God. Now to Him who is able to do exceedingly abundantly above all that we ask or think, according to the power that works in us.
–Ephesians 3:16-20

October 10

Ask and Receive that Your Joy May Be Full

Therefore you now have sorrow; but I will see you again and your heart will rejoice, and your joy no one will take from you. And in that day you will ask Me nothing. Most assuredly, I say to you, whatever you ask the Father in My name He will give you. Until now you have asked nothing in My name. Ask, and you will receive, that your joy may be full.
—John 16:22-24

My Prayer for Today

Father, in this life I know that happiness can be fueled by others, but it should never depend upon others. Happiness is a choice. It is a state of being that is in my own power to enjoy. It is all a matter of focus. Do I choose to focus on the negative, or do I enjoy all of the wonderful blessings You have given. I choose to be happy, Father. You are a great and awesome God who grants my every desire. (Proverbs 10:24.) You are always with me to fill me with all joy as I receive all that You have for me. (Psalm 16:11.)

My Confession for Today

My heart rejoices in Jesus, and no one can take my joy from me. I am now a born again child of God—the very brother/sister of Jesus Himself. (Romans 8:17.) In His name, I have all that I desire from God. My heavenly Father freely grants me whatever I desire that is in accordance with His will and purpose as established in His Word—it is a done deal the moment I ask in Jesus' name. (John 14:14.) Therefore, I will continually ask, receiving all that I desire from God, so that my joy may be made complete.

God Has Given You His Glory

My Prayer for Today

Father, what a wonder it is that You make no distinction between Your love for Jesus and Your love for me. At any moment I just might hear Your voice from heaven saying, "This is my beloved son/daughter in whom I am well pleased." (Matthew 3:17.) You love me so much that You determined that we will never separate. (Romans 8:38-39.) By Your will and power You have made us one spirit together. I am in You and You are in me. Because of this, all that I do is done in You and with You.

My Confession for Today

The glory which You gave Me I have given them, that they may be one just as We are one: I in them, and You in Me; that they may be made perfect in one, and that the world may know that You have sent Me, and have loved them as You have loved Me.
—John 17:22-23

I have become a partaker of the glory and honor which the Father gave Jesus. In Jesus, I am now one with the Father. Jesus is in me, He is in the Father, and we three are one so that the world may know that Jesus came forth from the Father and that the Father loves me the same as He loves Jesus. What a wonder it is to know that, despite my shortcomings, I have become the target of God's love.

October 12

He Guides You with His Own Eye

You are my hiding place; You shall preserve me from trouble; You shall surround me with songs of deliverance.... I will instruct you and teach you in the way you should go; I will guide you with My eye. Do not be like the horse or mule, which have no understanding, which must be harnessed with bit and bridle, else they will not come near you.
—Psalm 32:7-9

My Prayer for Today

Father, You are so good to me. I trust in Your love and find refuge in Your embrace. You surround me with songs of deliverance, and Your instruction keeps me on the path of life. I do not need to see my victory in order to know that I have it. (1 Corinthians 15:57.) I have Your Word, and that's enough. Even when I fail You I remain confident, for Your mercy surrounds me and Your right hand upholds me. (Psalm 5:12; 63:8.) I relinquish personal ability and trust in You alone for my salvation. (Ephesians 2:5,8.)

My Confession for Today

God is my hiding place against all harmful attacks. He preserves me from trouble and surrounds me with songs of deliverance. The God of the universe, my own heavenly Father, counsels and watches over me with a relentless eye. He teaches me His ways and gives me His perfect instruction on all I need to do. I'm not like a horse or a mule that needs to be led about by bridle and bit. I totally understand God's will in my life. His unfailing love surrounds me and He sees to it that there's certainty in all I do. (Psalm 32:10.)

Nothing Shall by Any Means Harm You

My Prayer for Today

Father, I thank You that I have power over all the power of the enemy and that nothing shall by any means harm me. You are the greater One and You are living within my spirit. (1 Corinthians 3:16.) Therefore, there is nothing that Satan and his minions can do to make me afraid. I am Your born-again son/daughter with the authority and power of heaven within me. By Your power, Father, I flatten the enemy under my feet. (Psalm 91:13.)

My Confession for Today

All wicked spirits are subject to my authority in Jesus' name. I have all of the authority that I need to trample down serpents and scorpions and I have mental, physical, and spiritual strength over and above all that the enemy possesses. There is nothing that Satan can do to harm me in any way. Nevertheless, I do not find great joy in my ability to cast out demons, or the fact that they are subject to my authority, but I rejoice that my name has been written in heaven and that I am honored as a son/daughter of the living God.

Behold, I give you the authority to trample on serpents and scorpions, and over all the power of the enemy, and nothing shall by any means hurt you. Nevertheless do not rejoice in this, that the spirits are subject to you, but rather rejoice because your names are written in heaven.
–Luke 10:19-20

October 14

The Father and the Son Reside Within You

Jesus answered and said to him, "If anyone loves Me, he will keep My word; and My Father will love him, and We will come to him and make Our home with him."

–John 14:23

My Prayer for Today

Father, I truly love Your Word. Your commands are a delight to obey. They bring life and joy to all who receive them. (Proverbs 4:20-22.) They are not burdensome, but are a perfect guide to bring me in harmony with the intended design of Your creation. (Genesis 1:1.) My heart is open to receive them, Father. Teach me Your ways and lead me on the path of Your glorious will. (Psalm 25:4.)

My Confession for Today

I show my love for Jesus by making His Word the center of my life. I make it my purpose in life to know and obey His commands, and to live according to the precepts that He has taught me. God the Father and His Son, Jesus, love me so much, and are so pleased that I have become a part of the family, that they have taken up residence within me. (John 1:1,14; 1 Peter 4:17 NIV.) They are always here whenever I need them and are overjoyed in my conversation and fellowship.

God Gives You Pleasures Now and Forevermore

My Prayer for Today

Father, thank You for dwelling within my heart. In Your presence is fullness of joy and at Your right hand are pleasures forevermore. Your presence is here within me, and Your right hand is beside me. Show me the path of life, Father. Help me to enjoy all that You have promised. Teach me the ways of giving and receiving, and help me to walk in the ways of faith that You have established. (2 Corinthians 5:7.)

My Confession for Today

What a joy it is to be a child of God! (1 John 3:9-10 NIV.) My heart leaps within me and my tongue rejoices in His praise! (Acts 2:26 NIV.) I am raised with Jesus and shall never be abandoned to hell. He has made known to me the path of life and fills me with joy in His presence. At His right hand, I shall have abundant pleasures for all of eternity.

Therefore my heart is glad, and my glory rejoices; my flesh also will rest in hope. For You will not leave my soul in Sheol, nor will You allow Your Holy One to see corruption. You will show me the path of life; in Your presence is fullness of joy; at Your right hand are pleasures forevermore.
—Psalm 16:9–11

October 16

The Lord's Counsel Is Trustworthy

The counsel of the LORD stands forever, the plans of His heart to all generations.
—Psalm 33:11

My Prayer for Today

Father, You are the creator of all and You know what is best for me. (Isaiah 45:12,18.) Teach me how to live in harmony with the original intention of creation. (Genesis 1:28-30.) Strengthen me in the ways of faith and reveal to me the purpose of Your commands. Your counsel stands forever. It does not change, for it is perfect. The plans of Your heart extend to all generations. Open my eyes to it all, Father. (Psalm 119:18.) Help me to know my purpose and the reason for which I am placed in the earth for such a time as this. (Ephesians 1:11; Esther. 4:14.)

My Confession for Today

My Father's plans and purposes stand firm. They are settled in heaven for all of eternity. I am confident that every one of His promises is fulfilled in my life. He has placed within me unique gifts and talents, and He fills me with a passion to pursue my life's mission. By His guidance, I always do an excellent job. I am the best He has to fulfill the purpose to which I am called.

He Takes the Weight Off Your Shoulders

My Prayer for Today

Father, I rejoice that in Christ Jesus, You have established Your covenant with me. All that You are and all that You have are pledged to me, and all that I am and all that I have are pledged to You. Remember our covenant, Father. Remember the blood of Jesus that is its security and fulfill Your promises. (Hebrews 7:22; 8:6.) You are the Lord my God and You redeem me with an outstretched arm and with great judgments. Pour out Your blessing upon me according to Your Word and teach me the ways of faith by which I am required to walk.

My Confession for Today

The Lord has established His covenant with me. He has delivered me out of the hands of my enemies. He has lifted me out from the burdens of the oppressor and has freed me from the yoke of bondage. The Lord has rescued me with a mighty, outstretched arm. My heavenly Father springs to action at the call of my prayer and delivers me with powerful acts of judgment.

"I have also heard the groaning of the children of Israel whom the Egyptians keep in bondage, and I have remembered My covenant. Therefore say to the children of Israel: 'I am the LORD; I will bring you out from under the burdens of the Egyptians, I will rescue you from their bondage, and I will redeem you with an outstretched arm and with great judgments.'"
–Exodus 6:5-6

October 18

God Even Puts Your Troubles to Good Use

Blessed be the God and Father of our Lord Jesus Christ, the Father of mercies and God of all comfort, who comforts us in all our tribulation, that we may be able to comfort those who are in any trouble, with the comfort with which we ourselves are comforted by God.
—2 Corinthians 1:3-4

My Prayer for Today

Father, I praise You for Your grace and mercy. If it were not for these, I would have no hope. (Hebrews 4:16.) Help me to keep in mind all that You have done for me. Show me how to use Your healing power within me to help others with the same anointing You used to help me. May I always remember that Jesus' substitution abounds in me and the abundance of Your grace secures me. (2 Corinthians 5:21; Romans 5:25; 5:17.) I am what I am, and I can do what I can do, by Your power alone. (Zechariah 4:6; Philippians 4:13.)

My Confession for Today

My heavenly Father is the Father of mercies and the God of all comfort. His compassion towards me is boundless. He comforts, encourages, and assists me through all of life's troubles, so that I can comfort, encourage, and assist others who are going through the same things that I have gone through. Because of my oneness with Him, I carry the anointing to help others. For in the same way I am identified with Christ's sufferings, so also does His comfort, encouragement, and assistance flow through me in abundance. (1 Peter 4:13.)

Be Strong in the Lord and the Power of His Might

My Prayer for Today

Father, I declare that You are my strength and my shield. (Psalm 28:7.) You alone are the power by which I live and through which I am established. No matter what I face—demonic influence or the devil himself—I have all the power I need to stand. Nothing can cause me to shrink back or be afraid, for I do not stand by my own power, but by the very power that created the universe! (Hebrews 1:2 NIV.)

My Confession for Today

I am strong in the Lord and in the power of His might. I wear the full armor of God continually so that I can stand against the devil's evil schemes. As a soldier in God's army, I am well able to stand my ground as a conqueror when Satan's forces attack. (2 Timothy 2:3; Romans 8:37.) And having done all that I need to do to defeat them, in whatever the situation, I stand as the victor with the devil under my feet where he belongs. (Romans 16:20; Psalm 91:13.)

Be strong in the Lord and in the power of His might. Put on the whole armor of God, that you may be able to stand against the wiles of the devil. For we do not wrestle against flesh and blood, but against principalities... powers... rulers of the darkness of this age...spiritual hosts of wickedness in the heavenly places. [So] take up the...armor of God, that you may be able to withstand...and having done all, to stand.
—Ephesians 6:10–13

October 20

The One Within You Has No Limits

I will hope continually, and will praise You yet more and more. My mouth shall tell of Your righteousness and Your salvation all the day, for I do not know their limits. I will go in the strength of the Lord GOD; I will make mention of Your righteousness, of Yours only.
—Psalm 71:14-16

My Prayer for Today

Father, thank You for removing my righteousness and establishing me in Yours. I place all of my hope and trust in You alone. Instead of my strength, I move forward in Yours. Instead of my own will, may Yours be done. (Matthew 6:10.) You know things about me that I've never even considered. I'd be a fool to follow my own will when yours is available to me. By my will I have mistakes and misdirection, but by Your will I have joy unspeakable and perfect fulfillment. (1 Peter 1:8.) Again I say, Thy will be done, Father!

My Confession for Today

When hope seems lost and it seems that God has forsaken me, I will not lose faith. When my enemies take counsel for my destruction thinking that I am alone and without help, God rises in my defense. (Psalm 71:10; Proverbs 30:5 NLT.) When they persecute me and plot my ruin, God makes haste to rescue me. (Psalm 35:4; 18.) He confounds and consumes every adversary of my soul. (Psalm 35:12.) So my hope shall remain. I praise Him continually, even in the midst of terror and destruction. I speak forth His salvation in spite of the circumstances.

You Can Accomplish Anything You Desire

My Prayer for Today

Father, what a joy it is to know that I am Your child and that You hold me securely in Your almighty hand. (John 1:12; 10:27.) You are in me, and I am in you. (John 17:20-23.) No matter what I face in life, I have the anointing to see me through. Therefore, Father, this day I shall be bold and step forward in unwavering faith, for I know that in You my victory is made certain and I cannot fail. (1 Corinthians 15:57.)

My Confession for Today

I greatly rejoice in the Lord because of my Father's favor. (Psalm 5:12.) I am never in want. I know the secret of being content in any situation I'm in. I know what to do when I find myself in adverse circumstances and when I am living in God's abundance. I have learned, in any circumstance, the secret of facing every situation as a conqueror, whether well fed or hungry, whether having all sufficiency and enough to spare, or not having a dime to my name. The secret is this: I can do all things through the power of Christ that is within me. With His anointing, there isn't a single circumstance that can hold me down! I am sufficient in His sufficiency. (2 Corinthians 9:8.)

Not that I speak in regard to need, for I have learned in whatever state I am, to be content: I know how to be abased, and I know how to abound. Everywhere and in all things I have learned both to be full and to be hungry, both to abound and to suffer need. I can do all things through Christ who strengthens me.
–Philippians 4:11-13

October 22

You Have All Things that Pertain Unto Life and Godliness

Grace and peace be multiplied to you in the knowledge of God and of Jesus our Lord, as His divine power has given to us all things that pertain to life and godliness, through the knowledge of Him who called us by glory and virtue, by which have been given to us exceedingly great and precious promises, that through these you may be partakers of the divine nature, having escaped the corruption that is in the world through lust.
–2 Peter 1:2-4

My Prayer for Today

Father, I thank You that by Your divine power I now have all things that pertain unto life and godliness. Every provision is right now mine to receive by faith. Nothing is held back from me. In my Lord Jesus every promise is mine to receive. I have escaped the corruption that is in the world through lust and I have received sonship, righteousness, and every blessing that is bestowed on Your heirs. (1 Corinthians 1:30; Romans 8:16-17.)

My Confession for Today

Grace and peace are mine in abundance through the knowledge of God and of Jesus Christ my Lord. Through His divine power I have been given all things that pertain unto life and godliness. God Himself has called me into His own glory and goodness. In Jesus, all of God's great and precious promises are given to me personally. Through these promises, I have become a partaker of His divine nature and have escaped the corruption in the world caused by evil desires.

You Are a Reflection of God's Glory

My Prayer for Today

Father, I have turned to You and true to Your Word, You have taken away the veil. I now know that I am a reborn and recreated son/daughter in whom You have placed Your Spirit. (John 1:13.) I am not as I once was. I am Your child and heir. (Romans 8:10-11,14-17.) You have made me to be conformed to the very image of Your Son. As He is, so am I in this world. (1 John 4:17.) His faith is now my faith. His power is now my power. And His purpose is now my purpose.

My Confession for Today

When I became a born-again child of God, He removed the veil that kept me from understanding His Word. (John 3:7,15.) I now operate in the fullness of a God-given ability to understand every aspect of the Scriptures. (Luke 24:45.) The Lord Himself dwells within me, and where the Spirit of the Lord is, there is emancipation. I have been completely set free from anything that would hinder me from obtaining all that God has for me. Now that the veil has been removed, I am free through the Word to become the very mirror image of the Lord in all of His glory.

Nevertheless when one turns to the Lord, the veil is taken away. Now the Lord is the Spirit; and where the Spirit of the Lord is, there is liberty. But we all, with unveiled face, beholding as in a mirror the glory of the Lord, are being transformed into the same image from glory to glory, just as by the Spirit of the Lord.
—2 Corinthians 3:16-18

October 24

He Increases Your Greatness

You, who have shown me great and severe troubles, shall revive me again, and bring me up again from the depths of the earth. You shall increase my greatness [my honor and joy], and comfort me on every side.
—Psalm 71:20–21

My Prayer for Today

Father, I submit myself to Your training regimen. Work out all of my impurities that I may live my life reflecting Your character in every way. (2 Corinthians 3:18.) It is my own sin and disloyalty that have robbed me of my proper station. But You are kind and merciful to me. You show me favor beyond reason and are more than willing to turn me back to the ways of life. (Psalm 5:12; 30:5.) Buffet me as much as I can take, Father. Train me in the way that I should go so that You will be honored in all that I do. (Proverbs 22:6.)

My Confession for Today

When troubles overwhelm me and it seems the weight of the world is on my shoulders, God shall quicken me once again. (John 6:63 KJV.) Though many distresses and misfortunes have rained upon me, I shall rise with the strength and power of heaven in my wake. God takes His stand with me in every circumstance. He increases my greatness, restoring honor and joy to me, and comforts me on every side.

He Pours His Anointing on All of Your Work

My Prayer for Today

> He who tills his land will be satisfied with bread, but he who follows frivolity is devoid of understanding.
> —Proverbs 12:11

Father, though I am a happy and lighthearted person, I am not given to frivolity. There is a time for every purpose under heaven, and I am wise to know when to have fun and when to work. (Ecclesiates 3:1.) By Your wisdom, I know that true happiness cannot be attained through pleasure seeking. There is only one way to achieve absolute fulfillment in life and that is to be the person You created me to be. (Psalm 139:14-16.) When I move forward in Your will, You pour Your anointing on my gifts and talents. You gave them to me for a purpose, and I will use them in service to You and all of humanity. (Ephesians 1:11; Psalm 90:17.)

My Confession for Today

I do not chase after fantasies or get-rich-quick schemes that require no work on my behalf. It is the diligence of my hands that brings me abundant wealth. What I have, I have earned through industriousness and keeping the precepts of the Lord my God. I am a hard worker with a creative mind to solve problems and create provisions. My career brings me absolute happiness and fulfillment. I am a self-aware person and know what I am called to do in life.

October 26

The Lord Influences Things in Your Favor

"Now these are Your servants and Your people, whom You have redeemed by Your great power, and by Your strong hand. O Lord, I pray, please let Your ear be attentive to the prayer of Your servant, and to the prayer of Your servants who desire to fear Your name; and let Your servant prosper this day, I pray, and grant him mercy in the sight of this man." For I was the king's cupbearer.
–Nehemiah 1:10–11

My Prayer for Today

Father, I am Your child whom You have redeemed by Your great power and strong hand. By faith I have received the free gift of righteousness. (Romans 5:17.) Because of this great privilege, I claim my right to come boldly before Your throne. (Hebrews 4:16.) I claim You as the first love of my life. I claim Your friendship and partnership. (James 2:23.) Indeed, I claim every promise given to those You love. By Your Word, favor goes before me in all that I do. (Psalm 5:12.)

My Confession for Today

The Lord has redeemed me from destruction by His great strength and powerful right arm. His ear is attentive to my prayers, for I delight in revering His name. By Him, I have success today and find favor with those I come in contact with. I move forward in the full knowledge that God's influence is upon me. Therefore, I fully expect good things to come my way.

Heed Godly Counsel

My Prayer for Today

Father, teach me to harness the power of words so that I can bring forth good fruit to Your glory. Mentor me in the ways of commerce and cause Your favor to flow in all of my business dealings. Give me wisdom to know what to do and when to do it. (James 1:5.) Show me the barons with whom I should associate so that I may know the ways of prosperity. And in all things, Father, keep me within the boundaries of Your will.

A man will be satisfied with good by the fruit of his mouth, and the recompense of a man's hands will be rendered to him. The way of a fool is right in his own eyes, but he who heeds counsel is wise.
—Proverbs 12:14–15

My Confession for Today

I understand the laws of the Spirit regarding the power of the tongue. By the fruit of my lips, my life is filled to overflowing with good things, just as surely as the work of my hands rewards me. I listen to sound advice and find good, honorable role models to help guide me in my prosperity. I am a child of God; therefore, I am a child of increase. (John 1:12; 1 Corinthians 3:7.) In all that I do, I recognize God's power within me to be prosperous and successful.

October 28

You Shall Flourish Now and Forevermore

The mountains will bring peace to the people, and the little hills, by righteousness. He will bring justice to the poor of the people; He will save the children of the needy, and will break in pieces the oppressor. They shall fear You as long as the sun and moon endure, throughout all generations. He shall come down like rain upon the grass before mowing, like showers that water the earth. In His days the righteous shall flourish, and abundance of peace, until the moon is no more.
—Psalm 72:3-7

My Prayer for Today

Father, when others see me, may they see Your goodness in me. Cause Your abundant supply to flow into all that I set my hand to do. Make me an example to the world of what it is like to serve You. Shield me from the wicked who seek my downfall and make harmless every move made against me. Remove their ability to disrupt my life or cause any hindrance to my progress. According to Your Word, Father, fill my life with an abundance of peace.

My Confession for Today

I am well provisioned for kingdom living and God's justice reigns in my life. I am His own son/daughter and royal heir. (John 1:12; 1 Peter 2:9.) He has clothed me in His righteousness and exalted me to the position of highest honor. (Isaiah 61:10.) I am a defender of the afflicted and a hero to needy children. (Psalm 72:4 NIV.) I am like the rain that falls on a mown field, and like a fresh spring rain, I water the earth. I thrive at the heights of success and good health, and my prosperity will abound until the moon is no more.

God Rescues You From the Oppressor

My Prayer for Today

Father, You alone are the power by which I live. In You I live and move and have my being. (Acts 17:28.) You redeem my life from oppression and shield me from violent attacks. You take me by the hand and lead me on a path full of joy and prosperity. Daily I shall praise Your name, for You are a merciful and loving Father and Your compassion toward me endures forever.

My Confession for Today

I am an epistle to the wayward and strength for the weak. I am known as a deliverer of the needy and of those who cry out for help. I stand up for the afflicted one who has no one to turn to. In righteousness I am blessed with a long and satisfying life. Gold is continually given to me in abundance and people go out of their way to bless and pray for me every day. It is God who accomplishes these things in my life and I will render Him praise befitting of His marvelous deeds. May the whole earth be filled with His glory!

He will redeem their life from oppression and violence.... He shall live; and the gold of Sheba will be given to Him; prayer also will be made for Him continually, and daily He shall be praised. There will be an abundance of grain in the earth, on the top of the mountains...; and those of the city shall flourish like grass of the earth. His name shall endure forever.... And...all nations shall call Him blessed.
–Psalm 72:14-17

October 30

The Destroyer Cannot Get Near You

The LORD will pass through to strike the Egyptians; and when He sees the blood on the lintel and on the two doorposts, the LORD will pass over the door and not allow the destroyer to come into your houses to strike you.
—Exodus 12:23

My Prayer for Today

Father, I thank You that Jesus has become my Passover lamb. (1 Corinthians 5:7 NIV.) His blood cleanses me from my guilt and protects me from the destroyer. (1 John 1:7.) When judgment comes, I am not affected. I have passed from judgment to life. (John 5:24.) You have transformed me from being Your enemy to becoming Your son/daughter. (John 1:12.) Instead of destruction, You have made me an heir to Your kingdom. (Romans 8:17.) Instead of being struck with death, I am now filled with eternal life. (John 3:15.)

My Confession for Today

When the destroyer comes to put plagues on the world, the Lord will not allow him to come into my house. A hedge and a shield of protection have been built around my family and the destroyer cannot touch us. (Job 1:10.) The blood of the Lamb is upon my household. Therefore, I remain safe.

You Counter the Enemy's Attack like a Lioness Devouring Her Prey

My Prayer for Today

Father, I stand before You as Your divinely protected and divinely commissioned son/daughter. I have no fear of unholy power for I am covered by the blood of the Lamb! (Revelation 12:11.) Father, may it continually be said of me, "Look what the Lord has done!" You have made me to be different from the common man. I am a re-created son/daughter filled with Your power and might. (Ephesians 2:10; Acts 1:8.) When the enemy comes against me, I rise like a lioness and lift myself up as a lion. Satan may roar like a lion seeking whom he may devour, but I'm the one doing the devouring here. (1 Peter 5:8.)

My Confession for Today

For there is no sorcery against Jacob, nor any divination against Israel. It now must be said of Jacob and of Israel, 'Oh, what God has done!' Look, a people rises like a lioness, and lifts itself up like a lion; it shall not lie down until it devours the prey, and drinks the blood of the slain.
—Numbers 23:23-24

There is no spell that can work against me. No sorcery or divination can have any power over me. When the enemy attacks, I rise up as a lioness and lift myself up as a lion. Greater is He who is in me than he who is in the world. (1 John 4:4.) Right now, the very power that God wrought in Christ when He raised Him from the dead is within me. (Romans 8:11.) Therefore, I will not fear sorcery and witchcraft.

November 1

Keep Moving Forward

Moses said to the people, "Do not be afraid. Stand still, and see the salvation of the LORD, which He will accomplish for you today. For the Egyptians whom you see today, you shall see again no more forever. The LORD will fight for you, and you shall hold your peace." And the LORD said to Moses, "Why do you cry to Me? Tell the children of Israel to go forward."
—Exodus 14:13–15

My Prayer for Today

Father, I thank You for being my partner in life. Your desire is that I become a part of what You are doing. I will not be the fool who sits around expecting miracles when You have already given me the power to get the job done. I will move forward in faith and purpose with signs and wonders accompanying me as I go. (Romans 8:37; Mark 16:20.) I have Your unfailing promise that You will never leave me nor forsake me. (Hebrews 13:5.) You fight for me and ensure my victory no matter what the odds or the enemy.

My Confession for Today

I am fearless in the face of danger. I stand firm and confident under God's powerful hand. He works for me to produce a mighty salvation. I am still and at peace for I know that God, my heavenly Father, the Creator of the universe, loves me and fights on my behalf. (Psalm 46:10; Isaiah 40:28.) Therefore, I will not allow fear to hold me back, but will go forward and complete the task I am given.

Your Prosperity Comes from Sowing and Reaping

My Prayer for Today

Father, I thank You for the confidence You instill in me. (1 John 5:14.) Thank You for showing me that despite the circumstances, my faith prevails. You are always prospering what I set my hand to do. (Psalm 1:3; Deuteronomy 28:12.) Every moment I spend doing nothing increases my capacity to receive nothing, but every seed that I sow increases my harvest exponentially. Give me direction, Father. Show me the path to take, and I will move forward and fearlessly do what You call me to do. (Psalm 16:11.)

Then He said, "What is the kingdom of God like? And to what shall I compare it? It is like a mustard seed, which a man took and put in his garden; and it grew and became a large tree, and the birds of the air nested in its branches."

—Luke 13:18-19

My Confession for Today

I operate the principles of the kingdom in the spirit of faith that has been given to me. (Hebrews 12:2.) I understand that when I sow these principles into my life, they are like grains of mustard seed. Though they are small in comparison to all of the other seeds that have been sown in me, through faith and patience, I can water them until their roots have choked out everything else and all that is left is the God-kind of life. (Hebrews 6:12.) In this manner, I receive such an abundance of blessings that I have all that I need and plenty left over. (2 Chronicles 31:10.) I declare that my life is a refuge to everyone in my circle of influence.

November 3

You Are Born Again by the Will of God

But as many as received Him, to them He gave the right to become children of God, to those who believe in His name: who were born, not of blood, nor of the will of the flesh, nor of the will of man, but of God.
–John 1:12-13

My Prayer for Today

Father, I thank You that through Jesus, You gave me the right to become Your child. In Him, I am now Your heir. (Galatians 4:7; Romans 8:17.) I am Your very offspring, reborn and re-created through an act of Your perfect will. I now stand as a free man/woman, not of my own will and power, but by Your will and power. (Galatians 5:13.) All that I am is found in Jesus and all that I can accomplish is found in You.

My Confession for Today

I have received Jesus as my own Lord and personal Savior. I have put my complete trust and confidence in His name. I have welcomed Him into my heart and have given Him free reign over my life. He, in turn, has given me the right and the privilege to become an actual son/daughter of God. I have been born of God through spiritual regeneration. (John 3:5-6 NIV.) I was born, not in the womb, but of the spirit through the living Word. (John 1:1-4,14.) I am a genuine son/daughter of Almighty God!

Remember His Wonders of Old

My Prayer for Today

Father, You are faithful in all things. (1 Corinthians 1:9.)Your Word is true and Your promises never fail. (1 Kings 8:56; 2 Corinthians 1:20.) I recount all that You have done from generation to generation, and I remember all that You have accomplished in me. I meditate on all of Your work and talk of Your deeds. There is none greater than You. You have declared Your strength in me and make mighty wonders to be commonplace in my life.

My Confession for Today

When hope seems lost and I begin to feel that God is indifferent to my needs, I remember all that He has done in my life. When I am so troubled that I cannot even find the words to speak, I remember His intervention in days of old. I meditate upon His great works. I remember the great salvation that He wrought for me. My Father is the Lord Most High. There is none greater than He. He will not forget me or leave me comfortless. (Isaiah 49:15; John 14:18 KJV.) This day He will act on my behalf.

And I said, "This is my anguish; but I will remember the years of the right hand of the Most High." I will remember the works of the LORD; surely I will remember Your wonders of old. I will also meditate on all Your work, and talk of Your deeds. Your way, O God, is in the sanctuary; Who is so great a God as our God? You are the God who does wonders; You have declared Your strength among the peoples.
–Psalm 77:10-14

November 5

Believe What You Say and You Shall Have It

A man's stomach shall be satisfied from the fruit of his mouth; from the produce of his lips he shall be filled. Death and life are in the power of the tongue, and those who love it will eat its fruit.
—Proverbs 18:20–21

My Prayer for Today

Father, You have placed all of Your provision at the gates of my faith. It is my believing and speaking that satisfy my stomach and fill my life with an abundance of good things. The boundaries of my health are built with my tongue. (Proverbs 18:21.) Therefore, set a guard at my mouth, Father. (Psalm 141:3.) Train me to speak the right things every time. (Psalm 49:3 NIV.) Convict me if at any time my words violate Your ways of life. Show me how to speak in ways that please You and bring You glory in this earth.

My Confession for Today

My words produce the fruit that fills my stomach, and my lips produce the harvest by which I am satisfied. The elements of life and death yield themselves to the force of my faith. My words are seeds of life and prosperity to the kingdom of God, but death and destruction to the kingdom of the enemy. I sow my words wisely and reap a harvest that makes my Father proud.

God's Career Choice for You Is a Joy to Perform

My Prayer for Today

Father, help me to turn a deaf ear to those who turn You into a killjoy. Your Word declares that You rejoice in my prosperity and at Your right hand are pleasures forevermore. (Psalm 35:27; 16:11.) It is You who gives me power to get wealth and to enjoy the benefits. (Deuteronomy 8:18.) You keep me occupied with the joy of my heart. The thing that brings me the most fulfillment is the thing You have called me to do. It is easy for me to say, "Thy will be done," for Your will is the root of my happiness. (Matthew 6:10 KJV.)

My Confession for Today

As a child of God, it is my right to have tremendous satisfaction on the job, and to be able to thoroughly enjoy the fruit of my labor. God has given me great wealth and many possessions, and He enables me to enjoy them. I lay claim to my right to have a job that brings me happiness and fulfillment. This is God's gift to me and I receive it with thanksgiving.

Here is what I have seen: It is good and fitting for one to eat and drink, and to enjoy the good of all his labor in which he toils under the sun all the days of his life which God gives him; for it is his heritage. As for every man to whom God has given riches and wealth, and given him power to eat of it, to receive his heritage and rejoice in his labor—this is the gift of God. For he will not dwell unduly on the days of his life, because God keeps him busy with the joy of his heart.
—Ecclesiastes 5:18–20

November 7

He Not Only Teaches You, but He Gives You the Answers to the Test

The Helper, the Holy Spirit, whom the Father will send in My name, He will teach you all things, and bring to your remembrance all things that I said to you.
–John 14:26

My Prayer for Today

Father, thank You for not leaving me without help in this world. (John 14:16,26.) By the Holy Spirit, teach me all things and bring to my remembrance all that You have said to me. Help me to never forget the lessons I have learned and the progress I have made. Keep backsliding far from me. Improve my performance every day as I step forward in the path of Your will.

My Confession for Today

The Holy Spirit, who is my Comforter, Counselor, and Strengthener, whom the Father has sent to me in Jesus' name, teaches me all things. (John 14:16 AMP.) By Him I receive all of the wisdom that I need in any given situation. I have a keen understanding of the ways of faith and I know all that I need to do in order to build a happy and prosperous life. Through Him I have resources beyond measure and power beyond comprehension.

You Are a Branch of the Vine

My Prayer for Today

> Abide in Me, and
> I in you. As the
> branch cannot
> bear fruit of itself,
> unless it abides in
> the vine, neither
> can you, unless you
> abide in Me. I am
> the vine, you are
> the branches. He
> who abides in Me,
> and I in him, bears
> much fruit; for
> without Me you
> can do nothing.
> —John 15:4-5

Father, I trust in Your love. I know that You would never do anything to harm me. So, it is easy to place my life into Your hands. I am now one with Jesus, and one with You. (John 17:21.) Do whatever it takes to make me better, Father. Purge and prune me so that I can multiply and produce fruit in increased measure. (John 15:2.) Pour Your power into me and make me to be what You want me to be.

My Confession for Today

Jesus is the true vine and my Father is the master gardener. (John 15:1 NIV.) I am a branch of the true vine. My Father is constantly caring for me and training me to bear a harvest of maximum yield. He makes me what I am—joyfully molding and forming me, until I continually increase and bear richer and more excellent fruit. My life is totally dependent upon the true vine. Just as a branch cannot live, let alone bear fruit, if it is not in vital union with the vine, neither can I live and bear fruit unless I remain in vital union with Jesus. Apart from Him, I can do nothing.

November 9

Set Your Heart on a Pilgrimage to Do God's Will

Blessed are those who dwell in Your house; they will still be praising You. Selah. Blessed is the man whose strength is in You, whose heart is set on pilgrimage. As they pass through the Valley of Baca, they make it a spring; the rain also covers it with pools. They go from strength to strength; each one appears before God in Zion.
—Psalm 84:4-7

My Prayer for Today

Father, my heart is set on a pilgrimage to do Your will. The vision is before me and Your strength is within me. Though I pass through the valley of tears, it shall become a spring filled with joy. In You, I move from strength to strength, ever increasing in power and prosperity, and in the end I shall take my place in heaven as a son/daughter in the royal family of the King. (1 Peter 1:4; 1 John 5:11.)

My Confession for Today

I dwell in the very house of God, and I am blessed in every way. I make the valley of tears a spring filled with joy. I have remarkable ability to do the task that is set before me. My unique talent and gifting causes me to be a blessing to the world. I press on from endeavor to endeavor and increase from strength to strength. I am a self-actualized son/daughter of God who is a tremendous blessing just because I am who He created me to be.

You Only Are Righteous Through Faith

My Prayer for Today

Father, I stand before You in the righteousness that comes through faith in Jesus Christ. I do not bring any good deed, holy living, penance, or obedience to the commandments of the law as proof of my worthiness. My righteousness was achieved by the sacrifice of my Savior, and through Him alone do I claim my rights as Your child and heir to the kingdom. (Hebrews 9:26; 10:10 NIV; Hebrews 1:14 KJV.)

My Confession for Today

I am worthy to enter the throne room of God and claim my position as His son/daughter. (Hebrews 4:16.) I have every right to boldly approach the Father for communion and fellowship, or just to get a hug. Jesus Himself has become my righteousness, and through His sacrifice I can now stand in God's presence without any sense of guilt or inadequacy. (2 Corinthians 5:21.)

Therefore by the deeds of the law no flesh will be justified in His sight, for by the law is the knowledge of sin. But now the righteousness of God apart from the law is revealed, being witnessed by the Law and the Prophets, even the righteousness of God, through faith in Jesus Christ, to all and on all who believe. For there is no difference; for all have sinned and fall short of the glory of God.
—Romans 3:20–23

November 11

Jesus Is Your Passover Lamb

Being justified freely by His grace through the redemption that is in Christ Jesus, whom God set forth as a propitiation by His blood, through faith, to demonstrate His righteousness, because in His forbearance God had passed over the sins that were previously committed, to demonstrate at the present time His righteousness, that He might be just and the justifier of the one who has faith in Jesus.
—Romans 3:24–26

My Prayer for Today

Father, I thank You that I am justified freely by Your grace. Jesus alone is my justification, righteousness, and redemption. By His blood only, not by any works of goodness, do I stand before You as holy and just. I've proven myself to be a lawbreaker apart from His substitution. If I'm guilty of one point, I'm guilty of all. (James 2:10.) So I choose Your provision of righteousness. I'm justified by the law only so far as Jesus fulfilled it. My life is hidden in Him, and I identify with Him in all ways. (Colossians 3:3.)

My Confession for Today

I'm justified, regenerated, and in right standing with God. This wonderful gift is given to me freely by His grace through the redemption that Jesus provided for me. God presented Jesus in my place as a mercy seat and sacrifice of atonement. (Romans 3:25.) I'm identified with all that Jesus did. It's as if I was there suffering the penalty of my sentence. This displays God's righteousness on legal grounds. My price was paid, my redemption complete. (1 Corinthians 6:20.) So I receive the covenant promises legally by faith.

God Carves a Path of Favor for You to Follow

My Prayer for Today

Father, I thank You that the time of my favor has come. You are now pleased to bless me and cause me to prosper this very day. You build me up and establish me as one of Your own. (Acts. 20:32.) You give me the desires of my heart and never despise my prayers. (Psalm 37:4.) No matter what I face, I know I have the victory for You are now on my side and fully committed to my success. (1 Corinthians 15:57; Psalm 118:6.)

My Confession for Today

I am living in the time of God's favor. Justice has no right to condemn me for Jesus has paid my price. (Romans 8:1; 1 Corinthians 6:20.) I now take pleasure in all of the good things of God. (Matthew 7:11.) I revel in His goodness and mercy. The heathen shall see what God is doing in my life and they shall fear Him. Through me, the kings of the earth shall see the glory of His majesty. The Lord Himself is building me up and manifesting Himself through me in all of His splendor. (1 John 3:10; 2 Corinthians 4:11.)

You will arise and have mercy on Zion; for the time to favor her, yes, the set time, has come. For Your servants take pleasure in her stones, and show favor to her dust. So the nations shall fear the name of the LORD, and all the kings of the earth Your glory. For the LORD shall build up Zion; He shall appear in His glory.
—Psalm 102:13–16

November 13

Life Is Hard, so Give It to Jesus

We are hard-pressed on every side, yet not crushed... perplexed, but not in despair; persecuted, but not forsaken; struck down, but not destroyed—always carrying about in the body the dying of the Lord Jesus, that the life of Jesus also may be manifested in our body.
–2 Corinthians 4:8-10

My Prayer for Today

Father, though I go through many trials in this life, You never leave my side. You are the power by which I live and the strength that sees me through. (Ephesians 6:10.) No matter what I face, victory awaits me on the other side. (1 Corinthians 15:57.) Nothing can negate the fact that I am Your born-again son/daughter. My inheritance is secured for all of eternity and no trial or tribulation can overcome it. Nothing can reverse the anointing that is forever within me. Nothing can make me afraid or cause me to shrink back from the salvation that is right now mine in Christ Jesus my Lord. (Hebrews 13:6.)

My Confession for Today

At times I may be surrounded by oppressors, but I am never smothered or crushed by them. When I am confronted with many perplexing and complicated situations, I am never driven to despair. When I suffer persecution, God always takes His stand with me so I never have to bear it alone. I may even be struck down, but I am never destroyed. I always bounce right up and get back into the fight. My name resounds in the devil's mind as a stubborn, tenacious, hardheaded man/woman of God who never gives in or quits.

Fruit Abounds to Your Account

My Prayer for Today

Father, increase my receiving that I may increase my giving. As You are the God of increase, increase me more and more that I may experience You more and more in my life. (Psalm 71:14.) Help me to see and do things the way You see and do them. In You, I abound. You are my source of supply and there is nothing that You hold back from me. I am never without the necessities of life. You are not satisfied with the mediocrity of just getting by. Teach me Your ways and prosper me according to the laws of abundance.

My Confession for Today

I share in the process of giving and receiving that God has established in the earth. (Genesis 8:22.) I do all that I can to amply supply the ministries I support. My desire is to see God's ministers living like true ambassadors of heaven. This heart attitude causes my offerings go up before the Lord like a sweet fragrance and makes them acceptable for an abundant return. Because of my persistent and joy-filled generosity, I have God's Word that He will supply all of my needs according to His riches in glory through Christ Jesus.

For even in Thessalonica you sent aid once and again for my necessities. Not that I seek the gift, but...the fruit that abounds to your account. Indeed I have all and abound. I am full, having received from Epaphroditus the things sent from you, a sweet-smelling aroma, an acceptable sacrifice, well pleasing to God. And my God shall supply all your need according to His riches in glory by Christ Jesus.
–Philippians 4:16-19

November 15

He Is the Lord Who Heals You

So he cried out to the LORD, and the LORD showed him a tree. When he cast it into the waters, the waters were made sweet. There He made a statute and an ordinance for them, and there He tested them, and said, "If you diligently heed the voice of the LORD your God and do what is right in His sight, give ear to His commandments and keep all His statutes, I will put none of the diseases on you which I have brought on the Egyptians. For I am the LORD who heals you."
–Exodus 15:25–26

My Prayer for Today

Father, I have a greater thing than what You promised the Israelites of old. My covenant rights are not based on my obedience, but on the obedience of the One who gave His life for me. By His sacrifice, I claim this promise. (Hebrews 7:22.) You are the Lord who heals me, and You do not place any disease upon me. My life is hidden with Christ. (Colossians 3:3.) In Him I live and move and have my being. (Acts 17:28.) Anything placed upon me must be placed upon Him. So, I boldly claim that healing is mine, in Jesus' name.

My Confession for Today

I have a covenant with God. I diligently listen, giving my complete attention to His Word, and I do what is right in His sight. My ear is open to His voice, and I am prepared to follow His commands. I have His Word that no disease can come upon me that is brought upon the world; for my God is Jehovah Rapha, the God who heals me. (Exodus 15:26.) He is the Lord of my health.

You Are Not Saved by Works, but Works Are Good and Profitable to You

My Prayer for Today

Father, it is You who set in motion the salvation that I now enjoy. All-knowing, You saw what I'd be from the start to the finish of my life. You chose me, set me apart, and caused me to be a recipient of Your covenant. (Psalm 139:16.) I'm Your child and heir. I stand in Your mercy and grace. Teach me to use them as a springboard, not a crutch. I am not saved by works of righteousness, but help me to produce them in abundance.

My Confession for Today

When the kindness and love of God appeared, He saved me, not because of any righteous works that I had done, but because He loves me so much that all He could think about was how to grant me His mercy. I have been born into the family of God. I am not what I once was, but an entirely new creation. (2 Corinthians 5:17.) So having been justified by God's grace, I have become an heir with the assurance of eternal life. He is now my partner in all things and through Him I produce an abundance of good and profitable fruit.

Not by works of righteousness which we have done, but according to [God our Savior's love and] mercy He saved us, through the washing of regeneration and renewing of the Holy Spirit, whom He poured out on us abundantly through Jesus Christ our Savior, that having been justified by His grace we should become heirs according to the hope of eternal life...these things I want you to affirm constantly, that those who have believed in God should be careful to maintain good works.
–Titus 3:5-8

Jesus Is Your Substitute and Great High Priest

Christ came as High Priest of the good things to come, with the greater and more perfect tabernacle not made with hands, that is, not of this creation. Not with the blood of goats and calves, but with His own blood He entered the Most Holy Place once for all, having obtained eternal redemption.

—Hebrews 9:11–12

My Prayer for Today

Father, I acknowledge that my salvation and redemption are eternal. Jesus entered the Most Holy Place once and for all on my behalf. He does not have to do it again and again. My sin has been eradicated by His blood, and I am now secure for all of eternity. His holiness is now my holiness and His works are now my works. All that He is and all that He has are now mine to claim. (Galatians 3:29.) I thank You for this wonderful truth, Father. Help me to live my life honoring such mercy and grace.

My Confession for Today

Jesus is my faithful and loving high priest. He went through the better and more perfect tabernacle in heaven on my behalf, carrying His own blood to secure my eternal redemption. This satisfied the claim that justice had on me. I am now completely acquitted of all charges. I am free! (Galatians 5:1.) Through Jesus' wonderful deed of love, He sealed for all time my rights and position as a child of God. (Ephesians 1:13; 4:30.)

You Can Claim Unlimited Benefits

My Prayer for Today

Father, I thank You for being who You are. You are not the god of man-made religion. You do not think like men or require what they require. (Isaiah 55:9.) When they twist Your Word to meet their own ends, I have Your Spirit within me to keep me on track. (Ezekiel 36:27.) You are the God who blesses His children. You satisfy my mouth with good things so that my youth is renewed like the eagle's. You forgive all my sins. You heal all of my diseases and redeem my life from destruction. You are so good to me, Father. Help me to live like You, be like You, love like You, and bless like You.

My Confession for Today

I praise the name of the Lord out of the depths of my soul. With all that is in me I bless His holy name. (Psalm 103:1.) I call to mind all that God has done for me, all that He has for me, and all that He is doing in my life. He has forgiven my sins and healed me of every possible disease. He has redeemed my life from destruction and has crowned me with His love and compassion. He satisfies my every desire with good things so that my youth is renewed within me, that I may soar into this life like an eagle on the wing.

> *Bless the LORD, O my soul, and forget not all His benefits: Who forgives all your iniquities, Who heals all your diseases, Who redeems your life from destruction, Who crowns you with lovingkindness and tender mercies, Who satisfies your mouth with good things, so that your youth is renewed like the eagle's.*
> *–Psalm 103:2-5*

November 19

God Is Never Mad or Disappointed in You

The LORD is merciful and gracious, slow to anger, and abounding in mercy. He will not always strive with us, nor will He keep His anger forever. He has not dealt with us according to our sins, nor punished us according to our iniquities. For as the heavens are high above the earth, so great is His mercy toward those who fear Him; as far as the east is from the west, so far has He removed our transgressions from us.
–Psalm 103:8-12

My Prayer for Today

Father, thank You for never failing to look past my faults and teach me Your ways. Your anger was completely appeased at the cross. All that there is for me now is Your blessing. As the heavens are high above the earth, so great is Your mercy toward me. As far as the east is from the west, so far have You removed my sins from me. I cling to You in love, Father, and call on You to be my mentor and guide, teaching me the ways of faith, and leading me on a miracle-filled path that takes me straight into Your arms.

My Confession for Today

My Father makes all of His ways known to me. (Psalm 25:4.) In any given moment, whatever the circumstance may be, I can expect His boundless favor and unconditional flood of compassion. He does not punish me like my sins deserve or repay me according to the evil things that I have done. For as high as the heavens are above the earth, so great is His love for me. As far as the east is from the west, so far has He removed all of my sins from me. They will never be brought up again.

God Knows You Thoroughly and Loves You Dearly

My Prayer for Today

Father, this life is but a grain of sand on eternity's beach. I know that my mission here has a time limit. Therefore, teach me to number my days. (Psalm 90:12.) Teach me to set high goals and prepare efficient plans, and to never forget that You are always with me. (Hebrews 13:5.) Make me a self-aware and self-actualizing individual who does the very thing I am created to do.

My Confession for Today

Watch a loving father enjoying and delighting in his child is a shining example of the way my heavenly Father enjoys and delights in me. His compassion for me is beyond definition. I have His Word that His love will never be taken from me, for He knows how I am formed. (Jeremiah 31:3.) He knows my shortcomings and my limitations. He knows everything about me, and yet His love for me remains. (Psalm 139:1-4.) My life is caught in the swell of His love. He extends His favor and His righteousness to my children and my grandchildren, as He does with all who have found their security in Christ Jesus our Lord.

As a father pities his children, so the LORD pities those who fear Him. For He knows our frame; He remembers that we are dust. As for man, his days are like grass; as a flower of the field, so he flourishes. For the wind passes over it, and it is gone, and its place remembers it no more. But the mercy of the LORD is from everlasting to everlasting on those who fear Him, and His righteousness to children's children.
–Psalm 103:13-17

November 21

Have a Place to Pray and Go There Every Day

Now in the morning, having risen a long while before daylight, He went out and departed to a solitary place; and there He prayed.

—Mark 1:35

My Prayer for Today

Father, my friendship and partnership with You is my first and most vital necessity. It is at the forefront of all of my priorities. Nothing can remotely compare to the need I have for Your fellowship. Fill me with Your love as I draw near to You in faith. Converse with me as one converses with his best friend. Reveal to me Your secrets and cause me to understand Your precepts. (Psalm 119:27.) Warn me of impending dangers and lay bare the traps that are set to ensnare me. (Psalm 141:9.) For You are my strength and my shield, and the Comforter in whom I have placed my trust. (Psalm 28:7; John 14:26.)

My Confession for Today

I imitate my Lord Jesus and find a specific time of day, when all is quiet and free of distraction, to spend time in prayer and fellowship with my heavenly Father. I place His fellowship as my most important priority. I set Him high above the needs of my body and soul. It is by my spirit that I worship my Father and control the issues of life. (John 4:23-24.)

Plunder the Strong Man!

My Prayer for Today

> *No one can enter a strong man's house and plunder his goods, unless he first binds the strong man. And then he will plunder his house.*
> *—Mark 3:27*

Father, I am in the world, but because of Jesus I am not of the world. (John 17:16,18.) This world may be ruled by Satan and his minions, but in Christ I have authority over them. (Ephesians 6:12 KJV; Luke 10:19.) Teach me how to use my authority, Father. Show me what I need to do to chase Satan from the land and establish Your kingdom. Use me to plunder his house and take back what he has stolen.

My Confession for Today

I have power and authority over and above all of the power and authority of the enemy. I am keenly aware of Satan's strategies and know exactly what to do to expel him from my life. He may be referred to as "the strong man," but his strength is impotent when facing the Greater One who is within me. (1 John 4:4.) When the strong man (the devil) comes, I have authority to bind him, commanding him to cease all operations. (Matthew 16:19.) In the name of Jesus, I can render him paralyzed and plunder his household, taking back all that he has stolen.

Always Remember Where the Power Comes From

Beware that you do not forget the LORD your God by not keeping His commandments… judgments, and… statutes which I command you today, lest—when you have eaten and are full, and have built beautiful houses and dwell in them; and when your herds and your flocks multiply, and your silver and your gold are multiplied, and all that you have is multiplied; when your heart is lifted up, and you forget the LORD your God who brought you out of the land of Egypt, from the house of bondage.
—Deuteronomy 8:11-14

My Prayer for Today

Father, I confess Your Word that I'm blessed. You've given me beautiful houses to dwell in. My silver and gold and all that I have greatly increases and I live in the abundance that You desire for me. Help me never to forget the power by which it came. (Deuteronomy 8:18.) May my heart never be lifted up to think that it was by my own power. You alone are the strength by which I live and the source of all my supply. (2 Samuel 22:33; Philippians 4:19.) I will praise You and give You rightful credit for all that You've done.

My Confession for Today

I am careful to keep my Father in my mind at all times. I am resolved to be God-inside minded. When I build magnificent dwellings to live in, I remember Him. As my silver and gold multiplies, I recognize Him. As all that I have increases, I give Him credit. As I dwell in the realm of abundance that He has provided for me, I give Him the praise and honor that are due Him.

God's Purpose Is to Do You Good

My Prayer for Today

Father, I thank You that You are my faithful guide. This world has so many obstacles and hindrances. The greed of men blocks me at every turn. Yet You are above them. There are none who can stand against You, Father. Therefore, lead me on a plain path for Your name's sake. (Psalm 27:11.) Teach me the ways of faith and show me the direction You want me to take. Prosper me in the midst of the wilderness and cause my enemies to be as nothing in my presence.

My Confession for Today

I always take notice of my Provider and recognize that it is He who has brought me out of bondage. He has led me through the wilderness, trampling down the fiery serpents and scorpions along the way. He has brought me water from the rock and fed me with the manna of heaven. (Nehemiah 9:15.) All that He does for me, is for good. (Romans 8:28.) He is good to His children. He is good to me.

Who led you through that great and terrible wilderness, in which were fiery serpents and scorpions and thirsty land where there was no water; who brought water for you out of the flinty rock; who fed you in the wilderness with manna, which your fathers did not know, that He might humble you and that He might test you, to do you good in the end.

—Deuteronomy 8:15-16

November 25

You Have Divinely Ordered Power to Get Wealth

Then you say in your heart, "My power and the might of my hand have gained me this wealth." And you shall remember the LORD your God, for it is He who gives you power to get wealth, that He may establish His covenant which He swore to your fathers, as it is this day.
—Deuteronomy 8:17–18

My Prayer for Today

Father, I never think that my own power can get me anything. I fully recognize that all things are held together by the word of Your power. (Hebrews 1:3.) Without You, I can do nothing. (John 15:5.) But I am not without You, Father. You are my mentor and guide who leads me on the path to constant victory. You fill me with the anointing for increase and cause me to understand the ways of faith. (1 John 2:20; Psalm 115:14.) Keep it coming, Lord. Increase me daily in wisdom, strength, and every form of prosperity.

My Confession for Today

I know that it is not my own power that has brought me into the land of abundance. It is God who has given me power and supernatural ability to create wealth in order that He may establish His covenant with me. I am a wealth creator. Day and night, I am given unfailing ideas for the production of wealth in my life. God expects me to take part in His gracious provision. He wants me to have material things. It is the way I'm supposed to live. I will never forget Him or take Him for granted. I will never fail to recognize how my wealth has been achieved. To God be the glory!

God's Righteousness Is a Free Gift

My Prayer for Today

Father, as in Adam's sin I died, in Jesus' sacrifice I am made alive. I am now the recipient of Your grace and righteousness. Your wrath has been appeased. All that's left is Your blessing. By grace and the free gift of righteousness, I now reign in this life. By faith I have the right to receive all that I desire within the boundaries of Your will. (Proverbs 10:24.) I'm so grateful for these truths. Praise Your holy name.

My Confession for Today

God has joyfully given me the free gift of grace, justification, and righteousness. His gift to me has no strings attached, but He gives it to me freely so that I may have continuous fellowship with Him in a legitimate Father and son/daughter relationship. Though Adam's sin condemned me, God's free gift has brought me justification; for as Adam's sin brought me death, God's abundant provision of grace and free gift of righteousness has made it so that I can reign in this life as a king. (Revelation 1:6.)

The free gift is not like the offense. For if by the one man's offense many died, much more the grace of God and the gift by the grace of the one Man, Jesus Christ, abounded to many...the judgment which came from one offense resulted in condemnation... the free gift which came from many offenses resulted in justification. For if by the one man's offense death reigned through the one, much more those who receive abundance of grace and...the gift of righteousness... reign in life through the One, Jesus.
—Romans 5:15–17

His Power Works in You Mightily

To them God willed to make known what are the riches of the glory of this mystery among the Gentiles: which is Christ in you, the hope of glory. Him we preach, warning every man and teaching every man in all wisdom, that we may present every man perfect in Christ Jesus. To this end I also labor, striving according to His working which works in me mightily.
—Colossians 1:27-29

My Prayer for Today

Father, thank You for revealing to me the power by which I can live a godly life. There is but one source of true riches and that is Christ in me. He is my strength and my salvation. In Him I live and move and have my being. (Acts 17:28.) He is my everlasting security and the very entrance to the provision of heaven. As He is in You, I am in Him, and we three are one. (John 17:21.) In all of my labor I strive according to His working which works in me mightily.

My Confession for Today

I proclaim the mystery that was hidden throughout the ages, but has now been made known to me. The riches of the glory of God are within me in Christ Jesus. All that I need to produce the life of my dreams is within me at this very moment. I take hold of that image within me, believe it with all of my heart, and speak it forth with power and purpose. To this end I labor, striving with all of His power and ability that so effectively works within me.

God Opens His Hand and Fills You with Good Things of Every Kind

My Prayer for Today

Father, others may toil for their provision in life, but my provision comes from You. Your hand is always open to me, and I am filled with good. Everlasting stores of provision are mine this very day. Whether it is seed for sowing or fruit to be harvested, I have all that I need and more. (Isaiah 55:10; Zechariah 8:12.) What a joy it is to be Your child, Father. All praise be to Your holy name.

These all wait for You, that You may give them their food in due season. What You give them they gather in; You open Your hand, they are filled with good.
—Psalm 104:27-28

My Confession for Today

I am calm and patient when waiting upon the Lord. I know that He answers my every prayer and will grant my petition in due season. His hand is open to me and my harvest overflows with good things. I receive miraculous healing, abundant provision, resourceful ideas, and an open door of favor. (Psalm 107:20; Philippians 4:19; Proverbs 8:12 KJV; Psalm 5:12.) Power flows through me freely and easily. (Luke 10:19 KJV.) Fulfilling my mission is less like work and more like play. I'm living a happy and prosperous life. (Joshua 1:7-8.)

November 29

Be Unmovable in Every Circumstance

He who observes the wind will not sow, and he who regards the clouds will not reap. As you do not know what is the way of the wind, or how the bones grow in the womb of her who is with child, so you do not know the works of God who makes everything. In the morning sow your seed... in the evening do not withhold your hand; for you do not know which will prosper...or whether both alike will be good.
—Ecclesiastes 11:4–6

My Prayer for Today

Father, You are my Lord and my God. You are far above all pomp and circumstance. Your power is far above the power of the world's economic woes. (Ephesians 1:19-22.) When men guide us into destruction, You are there to prosper Your children. (Psalm 37:19.) Therefore, take notice of the seed that I have sown, and cause it to increase in a shower of Your abundance. (Ezekiel 34:26.) I sow it regardless of life's circumstances for I know You are faithful to Your promise. (1 Corinthians 1:9.)

My Confession for Today

Circumstances do not control my giving. I plant my seed regardless of life's storms and reap my harvest in the midst of adversity. (Genesis 8:22.) God alone is my provider, and I am focused on the precepts of His Word. (Philippians 4:19.) I sow my seed in the morning and work with my hands until evening, for I have His Word that He will prosper what I set my hand to do and that I will reap an abundant harvest from what I have sown. (Deuteronomy 28:8; Psalm 1:3.)

He Is Clearing the Path Before You

My Prayer for Today

Father, You are my strength and my shield. (Psalm 28:7.) In You I have certain victory, and by Your guidance I have inevitable success. (1 Corinthians 15:57.) You have prepared my objective and clear the way so that I can easily achieve it. (Isaiah 42:16.) I have no fear of any enemy or circumstance because I have Your divine protection. (Psalm 32:7 NIV.) Though I may face troubles of every kind, by Your anointing I will persevere to the end and win my prize. (Hebrews 10:36 NIV; Philippians 3:14.)

My Confession for Today

The Angel of the Lord goes before me to protect and guard me on my way and to bring me to the place that He has prepared for me. I am truly an unstoppable force in this earth. The Lord shows Himself to be an enemy to my enemies, making them powerless to cause me harm. His very Angel has gone before me this day to clear my path and ensure my success.

> *I send an Angel before you to keep you in the way and to bring you into the place which I have prepared... if you indeed obey His voice and do all that I speak, then I will be an enemy to your enemies and an adversary to your adversaries. For My Angel will go before you and bring you in to the Amorites and the Hittites and the Perizzites and the Canaanites and the Hivites and the Jebusites; and I will cut them off.*
> *–Exodus 23:20 –23*

December 1

You Are the Sower Who Sows the Word

The farmer sows the word. Some people are like seed along the path, where the word is sown. As soon as they hear it, Satan comes and takes [it] away.... Others, like seed sown on rocky places, hear the word and...receive it with joy...since they have no root, they last only a short time. When trouble or persecution comes because of the word, they quickly fall away. Still others, like seed sown among thorns, hear the word; but worries of...life... deceitfulness of wealth...desires for other things...choke the word, making it unfruitful. Others, like seed sown on good soil, hear the word, accept it, and produce a crop— thirty, sixty or... a hundred times what was sown.

—Mark 4:14–20 NIV

My Prayer for Today

Father, teach me to be a master planter of the Word. Till me as soil being prepared for precious seed. (Psalm 126:12.) Make me to be good ground for Your Word that I may speak it with power and authority. Make me deeply rooted and well watered; my roots spread to the edge of the stream that I may bear a hundredfold fruit in my life. (Jeremiah 17:8.)

My Confession for Today

The Word has taken root deep within me and when the winds of trouble and persecution arise, I remain secure and steadfast. All of the cares and worries in the world cannot cause the seed of the Word within me to perish. My life constantly produces an abundance of good fruit. I am good ground that regularly produces a hundredfold return harvest.

Your Belief Gives You Limitless Possibilities

My Prayer for Today

> *Jesus said to him,*
> *"If you can believe,*
> *all things are*
> *possible to him*
> *who believes."*
> *—Mark 9:23*

Father, You have taught me that belief is the launching pad for my faith. If I can believe, all things are possible for me. Therefore, teach me to program my mind for unwavering belief. Show me how to believe like You believe. Look to the things that are hindering me and remove them from my life. Make me to see things as they truly are, and not as the circumstances are showing. (2 Corinthians 5:7.) Clarify my mind's eye and help me not to trust in my physical eye. Help me to make Your Word my final authority, Father. Help me to be ever-increasingly productive in this walk of faith to which I am called.

My Confession for Today

I believe in God's power and ability within me. Therefore, all things are possible for me. I am strong and of good courage. (Joshua 1:7-8.) All of my goals are realized and none of my words fall to the ground. (1 Samuel 3:19.) Every word that I speak in faith attaches itself to spirit substance and brings forth into this life the intentions of my heart. (John 6:63; Hebrews 11:1.) This is a good day for me. It is the day that the Lord has made and I will rejoice and be glad in it. (Psalm 118:24.)

December 3

God's Mercy and Grace Toward You Are Everlasting

Nevertheless in Your great mercy You did not utterly consume them nor forsake them; for You are God, gracious and merciful.

—Nehemiah 9:31

My Prayer for Today

Father, if it were not for Your mercy, I would be destined for destruction. Only by Your grace can I live according to Your calling. So, I boldly declare that I am set free. I am covered by the blood of Jesus and there is no reason left for You to hold back Your blessings from me. (1 Peter 1:2.) As Your Word says, if I can believe, all things are possible for me. (Mark 9:23.) I believe in Your grace and mercy, Father. This is my foundation. I believe that every single promise You have given is now mine to receive. (2 Corinthians1:20.) This is my journey into Your will for my life.

My Confession for Today

God has been patient with me my whole life. He has always been with me to do me good. I cannot count the times when His hand has been evident in my life. He admonishes me by His Spirit through His prophets, (Amos 3:7; Luke 1:70; 1 Thessalonians 5:20) but His mercy for me never fails. He is always there for me regardless of the circumstances or the things that I do wrong. (Hebrews 13:5.) He is a great and awesome God and is my covenant partner in this life. (Deuteronomy 7:21; Genesis 17:2-5; Romans 9:6-8.) Nothing that I ask of Him is trifling in His eyes.

God Gives You Good and Perfect Gifts

My Prayer for Today

> *Every good gift and every perfect gift is from above, and comes down from the Father of lights, with whom there is no variation or shadow of turning.*
> *–James 1:17*

Father, You have given me gifts beyond number. You bless me with a perfect career, a fine home, a loving family, and an endless supply of provisions. You grant me every desire of my heart to receive by faith. (Psalm 37:4.) Every promise of health and provision are mine to receive. I also thank You, Father, that Your gifts are good and perfect. You never give me anything that I ask based on my lust, but only those things that are conducive to a godly life. Thank You for being such a wonderful and wise provider, Father. (Genesis 22:14.) All praise be to Your holy name.

My Confession for Today

I am the recipient of God's favor and blessings. He has chosen me as one to whom every good promise belongs. He has set me apart as His own and causes me to prosper supernaturally. (Psalm 4:3 NIV; 1:3.) I am blessed when I come in and blessed when I go out. (Deuteronomy 38:6.) All of my needs are perpetually met. (Philippians 4:19.) I stand in His presence without guilt. He heals all of my diseases and redeems my life from destruction. (Psalm 103:3-4.) He is the Lord my God who showers me with every good and perfect gift.

December 5

Give Your Spirit the Dominion

The hour is coming, and now is, when the true worshipers will worship the Father in spirit and truth; for the Father is seeking such to worship Him. God is Spirit, and those who worship Him must worship in spirit and truth.
—John 4:23-24

My Prayer for Today

Father, hold me by my hand and help me to understand my purpose and place in Your kingdom. (Ephesians 1:11.) Help me to see how things are done and to do them with the expertise of a master. Open my eyes to spiritual understanding so that I can live according to Your precepts. You are Spirit and all that I can see had its beginning in You. You are before all things and in You all things exist. Make me perceptive of these realities, Father, so that I may worship and serve You in spirit and in truth.

My Confession for Today

I am a genuine worshipper of my heavenly Father. He sought me out and has called me to fellowship with Him in an actual Father and son/daughter relationship. I make my contact with Him through my spirit. I clearly hear His voice and He hears mine. As spiritual beings, we fellowship with each other in spirit and truth.

Be Bold and Intercede

My Prayer for Today

Father, train me to have character like that of Phinehas. Make me one who stands up and intervenes on behalf of the people. Purge from me any selfish ambitions and give me eyes that can see the needs of those whom You love. Make me a hero of faith who displays unyielding courage and confidence in everything that I do. (Hebrews 11.)

My Confession for Today

I have the power to stand in the gap for the wicked. (Ezekiel 22:30.) When the devil comes in with his flood of turmoil and plagues, I take my stand against him. (Isaiah 59:19; Ephesians 6:11.) When I intervene, his plan is checked and can go no further. I hold a position of rank and authority in the spirit realm. I am seated together with Jesus in heavenly places. (Ephesians 2:6.) Therefore, every dark force must obey my commands in Jesus' name. (Luke 10:19.)

Thus they provoked Him to anger with their deeds, and the plague broke out among them. Then Phinehas stood up and intervened, and the plague was stopped. And that was accounted to him for righteousness to all generations forevermore.
–Psalm 106:29–31

December 7

There Is No Condemnation Left for You

There is therefore now no condemnation to those who are in Christ Jesus, who do not walk according to the flesh, but according to the Spirit. For the law of the Spirit of life in Christ Jesus has made me free from the law of sin and death.
—Romans 8:1-2

My Prayer for Today

Father, I thank You that I now can stand before You free of guilt and condemnation. I now am ruled by the law of the Spirit of life in Christ Jesus. My sins are erased never to be brought up again. (Isaiah 43:25.) Draw close to me now as I seek Your fellowship. (James 4:8.) Make me as one who pleases You in every way. Fulfill the righteous requirement of the law through me, Father. Cause me to be the very person You have created me to be.

My Confession for Today

There is therefore now no condemnation (pronouncement of guilt) for me, for I am in Christ Jesus. I have become one with Him. The law of the Spirit of life in Christ Jesus has set me free from the law of sin and death. I can now move forward this day in full confidence that God will find no reason to retract His blessings from me. His favor covers me constantly and His anointing ensures my prosperity and success. (Psalm 5:12; 2 Corinthians 1:21.)

Be a Volunteer in the Lord's Army

My Prayer for Today

Father, I freely offer myself in service to You. I volunteer all that I am and all that I have. Show me what You want me to do and I will do it with all of my might. Let Your power flow through me as I move forward to do Your will. Help me to navigate through the obstacles and trying circumstances. Raise me up above my enemies, that they may not hinder my prosperity. (Psalm 27:6.)

Your people shall be volunteers in the day of Your power; in the beauties of holiness, from the womb of the morning, You have the dew of Your youth.
—Psalm 110:3

My Confession for Today

I am a warrior in the army of Almighty God. (Joshua 5:14; 2 Timothy 2:3.) I am willing to fight and destroy the enemy on any battlefield. I have a fiercely confident demeanor and my belief never fails. I move forward in a spirit of faith and power that causes the forces of darkness to cringe. I spring forth as a conqueror clad in royal garments. (Psalm 110:3 NLT.) The enemy shall see me as God sees me—"arrayed in holy majesty" (v. 3 NIV)—born again as "from the womb of the dawn" (v. 3 NASB)!

December 9

He Sent His Word to Heal You

He sent His word and healed them, and delivered them from their destructions. Oh, that men would give thanks to the LORD for His goodness, and for His wonderful works to the children of men!
—Psalm 107:20-21

My Prayer for Today

Father, as You have spoken, so it shall be. (Psalm 36:9.) You sent Your Word to provide power for me whenever I would need it. Therefore, I claim the promises as my own. I declare before You that I am saved and healed. You have delivered me from my destructions and placed me on a path of prosperity. Your goodness forever surrounds me and Your favor paves the way before me. (Psalm 5:12.) With Your Word as my guiding light, I am destined to do well. (Psalm 119:105.)

My Confession for Today

God has sent His Word into this earth to heal me and rescue me from death. His love for me never fails. (1 Corinthians 13:8.) He is always working to bring good things into my life and perform mighty deeds on my behalf. (Deuteronomy 3:24 NLT.) Oh, that others would recognize how good my Father is. In Him I have peace, prosperity, health, and good things of every kind. At His right hand I enjoy pleasures in abundance. (Psalm 16:11.) It is a privilege and a joy to serve Him.

God Teaches You to Do Things the Way He Does Them

My Prayer for Today

Father, I know by Your Word that You operate in faith. The very worlds were created by the word of Your mouth and all things are held together in the same way. (Hebrews 11:3.) I can do nothing of myself. Make my ways Your ways, Father. Open the eyes of my understanding that I may see clearly how to work Your precepts. (Ephesians 1:18.) With You as my faithful guide, all things are possible for me. (Mark 10:27.)

My Confession for Today

I can do no divine work in and of myself. Without God, I am nothing. Yet, with Him, nothing is impossible for me. (Luke 1:37.) He has left me His Word and His example, and has instructed me to do all things in the exact same way that He does. My heavenly Father dearly loves me and regularly shows me what I must do in this earth. Even now He is doing things through me that fill the heart with wonder and astonishment. With Him as my guide and master instructor, I am destined to do great things.

Then Jesus answered and said to them, "Most assuredly, I say to you, the Son can do nothing of Himself, but what He sees the Father do; for whatever He does, the Son also does in like manner. For the Father loves the Son, and shows Him all things that He Himself does; and He will show Him greater works than these, that you may marvel."
–John 5:19-20

December 11

You Shall Not Face Indictment, but Have Passed from Death into Life

As the Father raises the dead and gives life to them, even so the Son gives life to whom He will. For the Father judges no one, but has committed all judgment to the Son, that all should honor the Son just as they honor the Father. He who does not honor the Son does not honor the Father who sent Him. Most assuredly, I say to you, he who hears My word and believes in Him who sent Me has everlasting life, and shall not come into judgment, but has passed from death into life.
–John 5:21–24

My Prayer for Today

Father, I thank You that in Christ Jesus I have passed from death into life. I no longer have to concern myself with my eternal destiny, for You have sealed me into Your family forever. (Ephesians 1:3.) Jesus took all of the judgment that was mine. He took my sentence upon Himself and now I am free to serve You, not by the letter of the law, but by the Spirit. (2 Corinthians 5:21; Romans 8:2; 2 Corinthians 3:6.)

My Confession for Today

By the blood and will of Jesus, I have eternal life. I have taken my stand with Him as a covenant partner. (Hebrews 13:20.) Through me, He still can raise the spiritually dead and give them life. (Romans 8:10; Ephesians 2:4-6.) I am entirely in the hands of Jesus and I shall never be condemned or experience the wrath of God. My ears have been opened to receive the Word of God with understanding and I have put my total trust and reliance on the power of my heavenly Father to fulfill it in my life. (Isaiah 50:4-5.)

In Christ, You Have Done the Will of God

My Prayer for Today

Father, You know me better than I know myself. (Psalm 139:1-4.) Help me to understand my purpose and to follow Your lead in all that I do. (Ephesians 1:11.) I enlist Your assistance in every decision I make today. Be my shield against ungodly influence. (Psalm 3:3.) Of myself I can do nothing, but with You I can do all things. (Philippians 4:13.)

My Confession for Today

I know for sure that I possess eternal life. The sentence of my judgment was placed upon Jesus. I shall never come into condemnation, for I have already passed over from death into life. (John 5:24.) He is my Lord and Redeemer, and I am identified with Him in every way. Like Jesus, I have been raised to a new life. All that I do for the kingdom is wrought in and through God. I don't make a single decision apart from His counsel. All of my judgments are just and right, because I don't seek my own will and purpose, but the will and purpose of my Father in heaven.

As the Father has life in himself, so he has granted the Son to have life in himself. And he has given him authority to judge because he is the Son of Man. Do not be amazed at this, for a time is coming when all who are in their graves will hear his voice and come out—those who have done good will rise to live, and those who have done evil will rise to be condemned. By myself I can do nothing; I judge only as I hear, and my judgment is just, for I seek not to please myself but him who sent me.
–John 5:26–30 NIV

December 13

All by Grace Through Faith

If by grace, then it is no longer of works; otherwise grace is no longer grace. But if it is of works, it is no longer grace; otherwise work is no longer work.
—Romans 11:6

My Prayer for Today

Father, guard me against religious deception and from those who would shackle me with a yoke of bondage. Maintain within me the knowledge that holiness comes by grace through faith and not of works. May I never dishonor You or trample the blood of Jesus underfoot by trying to earn my place in the kingdom. (Romans 4:14; Galatians 3:17.) I declare before You that Jesus alone is my salvation and faith alone is the path to holiness. (2 Timothy 3:15; Ephesians 2:8.)

My Confession for Today

I am a child of God by grace (unmerited, undeserved favor). Works do not earn me any merit points with God to bring me into a closer relationship with Him. That would nullify His grace towards me. My relationship with God cannot be earned in any way. There is not a single work of righteousness that can bring me any closer to Him than I am right now. (Titus 3:5.)

You Are Identified With Christ in Every Way

My Prayer for Today

Father, I stand before You as one who is crucified with Christ. (Galatians 2:20.) I am flawless in every way, for I'm not my own, nor do I stand by my power, but I stand in the perfection of my Lord. I've put off the body of the sins of the flesh, not by my own will and power, but by the sacrifice of Christ. Not a single charge can be laid against me. I'm clean and pure with all the rights and privileges of an heir to the kingdom. (James 2:5.)

My Confession for Today

I was once dead in the uncircumcision of my sinful nature, but God brought me to life with Christ. He forgave all of my sins at that time, first to last, having cancelled the written code, with its regulations that proved my guilt. He took it all away and nailed it to the cross. When I made Jesus the Lord of my life, He lifted the burden of the Law from my shoulders; for Jesus has fulfilled the Law and set it aside, and all that He did has been credited to my account. In Him, I'm not under the rule of the Law, but under grace!

Buried with Him in baptism, in which you also were raised with Him through faith in the working of God, who raised Him from the dead. And you, being dead in… trespasses and the uncircumcision of your flesh, He… made alive together with Him, having forgiven you all trespasses, having wiped out the handwriting of requirements that was against us… having nailed it to the cross. Having disarmed principalities and powers, He made a public spectacle of them, triumphing over them in it.
—Colossians 2:12-15

December 15

Greatly Delight in His Commandments

Blessed is the man who fears the LORD, who delights greatly in His commandments.... Wealth and riches will be in his house, and his righteousness endures forever. Unto the upright there arises light in the darkness; he is gracious, and full of compassion.... A good man deals graciously and lends; he will guide his affairs with discretion...he will not be afraid of evil tidings; his heart is steadfast, trusting in the LORD.... He has...given to the poor...his horn will be exalted with honor.
—Psalm 112:1–9

My Prayer for Today

Father, I greatly delight in Your commandments. They are life to me in abundance and keep me on the path of Your will. By the precepts of Your Word, my household is blessed forever. As I walk this walk of faith, You cause wealth and riches to pour into my life. When the hearts of others fail for fear, I remain steadfast. You never fail to make me wise so that I can face any situation with confidence.

My Confession for Today

I give proper reverence to God and find great delight in His precepts. I am blessed in all that I do. Wealth and abundance of riches are in my house and my righteousness has no end. I am gracious and compassionate, just like my Father. Good things rain down upon me continually, for I have learned the blessings of generosity and give freely to advance God's kingdom. When fear comes against me, I face it with a grin. I know the One in whom my trust is set and my victory in the end is absolutely certain.

Place No Other Love Before the Lord

My Prayer for Today

Father, You are the first love of my life. If it ever comes down to a choice of following You or any other way, I choose You. It doesn't matter who it is or what they offer. You come first. All other loyalties are subservient to my commitment to You.

My Confession for Today

All that I have given, or given up, for the Lord's sake and the Gospel, will come back to me one hundred fold in this life. I reap homes, mothers, fathers, brothers, sisters, lands, and more, now in this life, and in the age to come—eternal life. I also know that persecution will come to me when I receive God's blessings, but that makes no difference to me. The devil can gripe and moan all he wants. I still have the blessings!

Then Peter began to say to Him, "See, we have left all and followed You." So Jesus answered and said, "Assuredly, I say to you, there is no one who has left house or brothers or sisters or father or mother or wife or children or lands, for My sake and the gospel's, who shall not receive a hundredfold now in this time—houses and brothers and sisters and mothers and children and lands, with persecutions—and in the age to come, eternal life.
–Mark 10:28-30

December 17

Walk in the Spirit

The fruit of the Spirit is love, joy, peace, longsuffering, kindness, goodness, faithfulness, gentleness, self-control. Against such there is no law. And those who are Christ's have crucified the flesh with its passions and desires. If we live in the Spirit, let us also walk in the Spirit.
—Galatians 5:22-25

My Prayer for Today

Father, teach me to reflect Your character in all that I do. (2 Corinthians 3:18.) Everything that You do is good. You are always generous and never in want. You surround Yourself with the faithful and turn away evil. (Matthew 5:21; 1 Corinthians 1:29.) Your very nature is love. (1 John 4:16.) No one to whom You have given life ever has need to fear. You comfort them and extend them eternal mercy. (Psalm 71:21.) Help me to have the same attitude, Father. Make me like You in every way.

My Confession for Today

I am a true branch of the Vine. (John 15:5.) Because of this, the fruit produced by the spirit – love, joy, peace, patience, kindness, goodness, gentleness, faithfulness, and self-control is found in me. As a born-again child of God, I have been crucified with Christ. My old sinful nature, with its passions and desires, died with Him on the cross and I now live by my re-created spirit, as led by the Holy Spirit. (Romans 8:3 NLT; Galatians 2:20.) So as I live by my spirit, my conduct will reflect what my spirit desires.

The Lord Is Mindful of You

My Prayer for Today

Father, thank You for the blessing You have given me. You are ever-mindful of me and never fail to keep company with me. You never consider me a burden, but receive me with utter delight. Though I have failed a thousand times, You accept me as one who is faultless in every way. (Hebrews 8:12.) Every time I draw near to You, You pour forth more blessing. Again and again, You cause me to increase. Yours is character so precious and perfect that it defies logic or even description. I am humbled by Your unquenchable mercy and elated by Your favor and love. (Psalm 106:1; Proverbs 3:3-4; Jeremiah 31:3.)

My Confession for Today

The LORD has been mindful of us; He will bless us; He will bless the house of Israel; He will bless the house of Aaron. He will bless those who fear the LORD, both small and great. May the LORD give you increase more and more, you and your children. May you be blessed by the LORD, who made heaven and earth.
—Psalm 115:12-15

I am always on God's mind. He is continually finding ways to bless me. My joy knows no bounds as He showers me with His wonderful gifts. He makes both me and my children to increase so that we have an abundance of all good things. He has placed all of His creation into my hands so that I will never lack the things that I need. Everything that my Father has created in this earth is put here for my provision. There is more than enough for all of us to draw upon so that we can live a life of wealth and abundance.

December 19

Regard No One According to the Flesh

The love of Christ compels us, because we judge thus: that if One died for all, then all died; and He died for all, that those who live should live no longer for themselves, but for Him who died for them and rose again. Therefore, from now on, we regard no one according to the flesh...if anyone is in Christ, he is a new creation; old things have passed away; behold, all things have become new.
—2 Corinthians 5:14–17

My Prayer for Today

Father, I thank You for identifying me with Jesus. He is my substitute who brings me into perfect fellowship with You. I'm saved by His sacrifice only, not by any personal power I have to do Your will. I died, was buried, and rose again with Him. In Him I live, move, and have my being. (Acts 17:28.) In Him, I am Your child and stand totally secure in the covenant. (Hebrews 7:22.) In Him, I have the right to receive all of my desires by faith.

My Confession for Today

I do not regard myself, or any others in Christ, from a worldly perspective; for I was reborn together with Christ in His resurrection and, in Him, I have become a new creation (a new species of man)—a part of a new and godly race. My old man who was a member of Satan's family with Satan's own nature, was crucified with Jesus. (1 John 3:8 AMP; 3:10 NLT; Romans 6:6.) Now my spirit has been recreated with the very nature of God and I have become an actual child in His royal family. I no longer live for myself, but for Him who died for me. (Galatians 2:20.) His ways are now my ways and His will is my will.

You Are the Ambassador of Heaven

My Prayer for Today

Father, all things are of You. This salvation that was purchased for me is of You. (Acts 20:28.) My blessings are of You. My ability to stand in Your presence without guilt or inadequacy is of You. (Hebrews 4:16.) You are my all in all. (1 Corinthians 15:28.) I claim nothing apart from You, but I claim everything in You. Teach me to share these truths with others. Show me how to reach them so that they can enjoy what I have as well.

My Confession for Today

God has honored me with the ministry of reconciliation. I am an ambassador for Christ, as though God were making His appeal to mankind through me. God made Jesus, who was sinless, to become sin for me. In Him, I've been made the very righteousness of God. So I invite all, as Jesus' chosen representative, to be reconciled to God... His righteousness and justification are now made available to anyone who calls on His name.

All things are of God, who has reconciled us to Himself through Jesus... and has given us the ministry of reconciliation...that God was in Christ reconciling the world to Himself, not imputing their trespasses to them, and has committed to us the word of reconciliation. Now...we are ambassadors for Christ, as though God were pleading through us: we implore you on Christ's behalf, be reconciled to God. For He made Him who knew no sin to be sin for us, that we might become the righteousness of God in Him.
–2 Corinthians 5:18–21

December 21

The Word Will Steer You in the Right Direction

With my whole heart I have sought You; oh, let me not wander from Your commandments! Your word I have hidden in my heart, that I might not sin against You. Blessed are You, O LORD! Teach me Your statutes. With my lips I have declared all the judgments of Your mouth. I have rejoiced in the way of Your testimonies, as much as in all riches. I will meditate on Your precepts, and contemplate Your ways. I will delight myself in Your statutes; I will not forget Your word.
–Psalm 119:10–16

My Prayer for Today

Father, Your Word is a sure guide in all circumstances. Even when it doesn't specifically address an issue, the power of its spirit provides wisdom for sound judgment. Teach me how to walk within its pages. Bring to my remembrance all that You have taught me so that I may increase and prosper according to Your will. (John 14:26.)

My Confession for Today

I keep my way pure before the Lord and do those things that the Word commands. The Lord teaches me all of the inner workings and practical relevancy of His Word. My lips recount all of His laws as I meditate on them continually. I rejoice in following His statutes as one rejoices in discovering great treasure. I daily give of my time to the Word, being careful not to neglect it. As I do, God gives me revelation knowledge to expand my horizons and obtain an even greater reward. I know that only good things are prepared for me and, through obedience to the Word, I will live a long, full, and satisfying life.

The Lord Opens Your Eyes to the Wondrous Things from His Word

My Prayer for Today

Father, Your love is beyond human understanding. You gave Your Son so that You could adopt me, re-create me, and father me as Your very own. You don't hold back a thing from me, but pour forth such bountiful blessings that there's not enough room to receive them. You don't give as the world gives. Your gifts are eternal, incorruptible, and ideal to the receiver. You pronounce me faultless, guiltless, and free. You guard me from the threats of my enemies and cover me with the right hand of Your righteousness.

My Confession for Today

Every minute of the day, God's Word goes before me. I am totally consumed with desire for it, for in it, I live free of rebuke, scorn, contempt, and the curse. Let the mockers and slanderers say what they may, I will not turn from meditating on and living by the precepts that God has established for me. They are my delight and sure counsel, and in them I am blessed in all that I do.

Deal bountifully with Your servant, that I may live and keep Your word. Open my eyes, that I may see wondrous things from Your law... do not hide Your commandments from me. My soul breaks with longing for Your judgments at all times. You rebuke the proud...who stray from Your commandments. Remove from me reproach... for I have kept Your testimonies. Princes...sit and speak against me, but Your servant meditates on Your statutes. Your testimonies...are my delight and... counselors.
—Psalm 119:17–24

December 23

Joyfully Follow God's Lead in Your Giving

In a great trial of affliction the abundance of their joy and their deep poverty abounded in the riches of their liberality. For ...according to their ability... and beyond their ability, they were freely willing, imploring us with much urgency that we would receive the gift and... fellowship of the ministering to the saints...not only as we had hoped, but they first gave themselves to the Lord, and then to us by the will of God.
–2 Corinthians 8:2-5

My Prayer for Today

Father, thank You for the example of the Macedonians. Per their example, I give myself to You in all of my financial decisions. I am a lender and not a borrower. (Deuteronomy 28:12.) I keep a careful accounting and am willing to give even in the midst of trials and suffering. Teach me to be a good steward of the money You have given me, Father. Make me wise in the ways of prosperity. (John 16:13.)

My Confession for Today

No matter what my situation is, it brings me abounding joy and pleasure to give as much as I am able, and even beyond my ability, to the work of the Lord. I am always looking for an opportunity to share in God's ministry through my financial blessings. I never give out of compulsion, but give willingly and cheerfully. If I feel compelled, I will withhold my gift until I am certain of God's counsel. He is my ever-present mentor and guide who supervises my faith. (Hebrews 12:2.) So there is no telling what I might do, because when God and I get together in this, blessings can flow from any direction.

You Are One of God's Highly Favored Children

My Prayer for Today

Father, I thank You that like Mary, I have found favor with You. (Psalm 5:12.) I have every cause to rejoice, for You are now my God and Father. Because of the sacrifice of Jesus, I am now a joint heir with Him. (Romans 8:17.) He is my Brother, You are my Father, and the three of us are now one. (John 17:20-23.) I never have reason to fear again. All blessing has been bestowed upon me and I now have Your favor guiding me into the realization of my dreams.

My Confession for Today

Like Mary, God has set me apart as one who is unique and special. (Psalm 4:3.) He makes His declaration to all that I am one of His favored ones and that He is with me in all that I do. (Psalm 87:5; Hebrews 13:5.) I have no reason to fear, for I have found favor with God and He is faithful to take good care of me. (Psalm 30:5; 1 Corinthians 10:13.)

Having come in, the angel said to her, "Rejoice, highly favored one, the Lord is with you; blessed are you among women!" But when she saw him, she was troubled at his saying, and considered what manner of greeting this was. Then the angel said to her, "Do not be afraid, Mary, for you have found favor with God."
–Luke 1:28-30

December 25

All of the Good Things of the Earth Are Yours

Of Benjamin he said: "The beloved of the LORD shall dwell in safety by Him, who shelters him all the day long; and he shall dwell between His shoulders." And of Joseph he said: "Blessed of the LORD is his land, with the precious things of heaven, with the dew, and the deep lying beneath...with the precious produce of the months...the best things of the ancient mountains, with the precious things of the everlasting hills, with the precious things of the earth and its fullness."
–Deuteronomy 33:12-16

My Prayer for Today

Father, I have found my dwelling place between Your shoulders. Thank You for loving me so much. No matter what I've done, You always accept me. You hold me close to Your heart and fill me with confidence each day. (Isaiah 40:11 NIV; Proverbs 3:26). The very provision of heaven is mine to enjoy. Teach me to receive it all and to make my beliefs steadfast and unwavering. Be my ever-present guide every day, now and forevermore.

My Confession for Today

My Father loves me. He lifts me up in His tender embrace all day long, and I find my dwelling place between His shoulders. I am kept in perfect safety in Him. He blesses me with precious gifts from heaven and from the deep that couches beneath. He gives me all the precious gifts that are under the sun and the finest that the months can yield. He gives me the best that the earth has to offer and grants me abundant favor in His presence. (Exodus 3:21.)

Be Strengthened According to the Word

My Prayer for Today

Father, Your Word is the lamp that lights my way through the dark paths of this world. (Psalm 119:105.) Open the eyes of my understanding so that I may know Your Word thoroughly. (Ephesians 3:20.) Reveal to me the hidden treasures within it, and show me how to work its precepts to meet all of my needs. (Proverbs 2:1-4.) Give me wisdom and revelation, Father. Help me to clearly see Your purposes and where I fit into Your master plan. (Ephesians 1:11.)

Make me understand the way of Your precepts; so shall I meditate on Your wonderful works. My soul melts from heaviness; strengthen me according to Your word.
—Psalm 119:27-28

My Confession for Today

I am blessed with an intimate understanding of God's precepts. As I meditate on the Word, revelation knowledge is engrafted into my soul. When I am weary and sorrow fills my heart, I turn to the Word, for in it I find strength and a zeal for persistence that spurs me on to victory. By the promise of God, I live a happy, healthy, and abundantly prosperous life.

December 27

Sow Bountifully, Reap Bountifully

I thought it necessary to exhort the brethren to go to you ahead of time, and prepare your generous gift beforehand, which you had previously promised, that it may be ready as a matter of generosity and not as a grudging obligation. But this I say: he who sows sparingly will also reap sparingly, and he who sows bountifully will also reap bountifully.
–2 Corinthians 9:5-6

My Prayer for Today

Father, I've learned from You that You sow bountifully. The billions of galaxies in Your creation are evidence that You are no small thinker. (Psalm 8:3.) Extravagance is part of the perfection of Your character. So as Your child, I will think the same way. I set my goals so high as to be a worthy son/daughter in whom You dwell. I sow bountifully and reap bountifully. And in all things, I give glory to the One to whom I owe all things.

My Confession for Today

I always give generously with great joy in what I am doing for the advancement of the Gospel. I never give grudgingly or regretfully. I fully understand that seedtime and harvest is at work in my giving, as it is in everything else that I do. (Genesis 8:22.) If I sow sparingly, I will reap a sparing harvest. But if I sow generously, I will reap a generous harvest. Each time I have opportunity, I pray to determine what I should give so that I will have no regrets. I will never give reluctantly or under compulsion, but only with a willing and joy-filled heart, for God loves and blesses the cheerful giver. (2 Corinthians 9:7.)

Partner with God in Your Giving

My Prayer for Today

Father, all that I have is from the stores of Your provision. So, all that I can give comes from You. Help me to see the abundance You have provided. Cause me to reap a harvest from all of my giving. Make all grace abound toward me so that I have all sufficiency in all things and can abound to every good work. You are the supplier of seed and the Lord of the harvest. Make my harvest flow with Your everlasting abundance.

My Confession for Today

Once I have given from my heart (with all joy), God is able to make every favor and earthly blessing abound toward me so that I have all sufficiency in every circumstance and can abound in every good work. God has made my harvest synonymous with righteousness. Therefore, I expect His abundant return on my giving. He who supplies me with seed to sow and bread to eat has also supplied and increased my store of seed and has enlarged and multiplied the harvest of my righteousness.

Let each one give as he purposes in his heart, not grudgingly or of necessity; for God loves a cheerful giver. And God is able to make all grace abound toward you, that you, always having all sufficiency in all things, may have an abundance for every good work.... Now may He who supplies seed to the sower, and bread for food, supply and multiply the seed you have sown and increase the fruits of your righteousness, while you are enriched in everything for all liberality.
–2 Corinthians 9:7-11

December 29

Your Giving Multiplies in Every Direction

The administration of this service not only supplies the needs of the saints, but also is abounding through many thanksgivings to God, while, through the proof of this ministry, they glorify God for the obedience of your confession to the gospel of Christ, and for your liberal sharing with them and all men, and by their prayer for you, who long for you because of the exceeding grace of God in you. Thanks be to God for His indescribable gift!
—2 Corinthians 9:12-15

My Prayer for Today

Father, You are my one true provider. I have no blessing except what You have given. All of my ability to give comes from You alone. So, Lord, increase my abundance. Fill my storehouses more and more so that I may give in increased measure. Bless me Father, so that I may be a blessing to others and supply the needs of Your ministry.

My Confession for Today

Through my giving, I am made rich in every way so that I can be generous in every way. My giving not only supplies the needs of the Church, but overflows in every direction causing many to thank God for what is being done. The fruit produced by my generosity touches the hearts of many and draws them to God. Furthermore, because of my generous giving, God inspires the hearts of others to add their faith to mine, thereby increasing my harvest. I thank God for this remarkable system of giving that He has established. What a wonder it is!

God Has Put Unique Wisdom in Your Heart that No One Else Has

My Prayer for Today

Father, thank You for making me unique among all of Your creation. I am fearfully and wonderfully made. (Psalm 139:14.) There is none like me in all the earth. Before the beginning of time, You made Your plan and gave me a purpose. (Ephesians 1:4,11.) No one can fulfill that purpose like I can. Therefore, Father, make me wise to understand who I am and what I am created to do. Show me the joy of living in Your perfect will. (Romans 12:2.)

Then Moses called Bezalel and Aholiab, and every gifted artisan in whose heart the LORD had put wisdom, everyone whose heart was stirred, to come and do the work.
—Exodus 36:2

My Confession for Today

As God's child, I am very wise and well able to do what He has called me to do. (Numbers 13:30.) God has placed in me a mind of wisdom and supernatural ability. (1 Corinthians 2:16.) Therefore, I stir up my spirit to this end and fulfill my calling in this earth. (2 Timothy 1:6.) I am a self-actualized child of the living God. My unique gifts are a blessing to the kingdom. When I put them to work, I solve problems and make life easier to live.

December 31

Associate with Those Who Love the Lord

You are my portion, O LORD; I have said that I would keep Your words. I entreated Your favor with my whole heart; be merciful to me according to Your word. I thought about my ways, and turned my feet to Your testimonies. I made haste, and did not delay to keep Your commandments.... I am a companion of all who fear You, and of those who keep Your precepts. The earth, O LORD, is full of Your mercy.
—Psalm 119:57-64

My Prayer for Today

Father, all year I've purposed in my heart to keep Your Word. I've entreated Your favor and You have responded with a flood of Your abundance. I am filled with Your mercy. As I enter a new year, I carry Your grace, power, and companionship. New beginnings await me as I move from faith to faith, increasing more and more, always with Your hand in mine. (2 Corinthians 3:18; Psalm 115:14; Isaiah 42:6.) You are my first love, friend, Savior, Redeemer, and the One to whom I owe all things. I am Yours forever.

My Confession for Today

My covenant with Almighty God has been sealed and ratified. (Hebrews 7:22.) I obey His every command. I seek His face with all of my heart, for He alone can provide what I need to fulfill my destiny. His favor rests upon me and my path is made clear and certain. (Psalm 5:12; 61:11.) All of my ways are in keeping with His statutes. I give God glory for His Word, for in it I have my victory. I am the friend and partner of all who hold fast to the Word with unwavering confidence.

About the Author

James R. Riddle is an educator, author, and public speaker who has spent over twenty-five years of his life studying faith from both a scriptural and scientific perspective. He believes that success is a self-actualizing journey of service and that to serve God is to be the person you are created to be. His friendly and honest approach, coupled with his sincere compassion for the Lord and humanity has won him an interdenominational audience.

"My chief calling in life," James says, "is to show people how to walk in harmony with the Father. He loves us all more than any of us realize, and He wants us to live happy and fulfilling lives. His love is the foundation of all of my teaching. From that premise I can show why we are valued above all of creation, what it is that makes our thoughts and words so powerful, and what it means to find our **P**assion, take **A**ction, and discover a life-changing **T**ransformation that results in true and enduring **H**appiness."

This P.A.T.H. concept has become the keystone of James' life and ministry. He spreads his message of love and individualized purpose from the pulpit, to the classroom, boardroom, into the living room, and beyond.

James is a man who practices what he preaches. In February of 2008 he was told by his doctor that he would never run again. Today he is a masters track and field athlete who runs three to five miles a day and at the age of fifty can run a hundred meters in less than thirteen seconds. Ask him how he did it and you will hear the Word, "If you can believe, all things are possible to him that believes!"

James holds an honors degree in Creative Writing from the University of Texas at El Paso. He, his wife Jinny, and his four sons (Caleb, Jermaine, Jerome, and Chris) reside in El Paso, Texas. His *Complete Personalized Promise Bible* series has sold well over 100,000 copies.

PRAYER OF SALVATION

God loves you—no matter who you are, no matter what your past. God loves you so much that He gave His one and only begotten Son for you. The Bible tells us that "...whoever believes in him shall not perish but have eternal life" (John 3:16 NIV). Jesus laid down His life and rose again so that we could spend eternity with Him in heaven and experience His absolute best on earth. If you would like to receive Jesus into your life, say the following prayer out loud and mean it from your heart.

Heavenly Father, I come to You admitting that I am a sinner. Right now, I choose to turn away from sin, and I ask You to cleanse me of all unrighteousness. I believe that Your Son, Jesus, died on the cross to take away my sins. I also believe that He rose again from the dead so that I might be forgiven of my sins and made righteous through faith in Him. I call upon the name of Jesus Christ to be the Savior and Lord of my life. Jesus, I choose to follow You and ask that You fill me with the power of the Holy Spirit. I declare that right now I am a child of God. I am free from sin and full of the righteousness of God. I am saved in Jesus' name. Amen.

If you prayed this prayer to receive Jesus Christ as your Savior for the first time, please contact us on the Web at **www.harrisonhouse.com** to receive a free book.

Or you may write to us at

Harrison House • P.O. Box 35035 • Tulsa, Oklahoma 74153

The Harrison House Vision

Proclaiming the truth and the power

Of the Gospel of Jesus Christ

With excellence;

Challenging Christians to

Live victoriously,

Grow spiritually,

Know God intimately.

Fast. Easy.
Convenient.

For the latest Harrison House product information and author news, look no further than your computer. All the details on our powerful, life-changing products are just a click away. New releases, E-mail subscriptions, testimonies, monthly specials—find it all in one place. Visit harrisonhouse.com today!

harrisonhouse